What has been said ab

"I found this book to be eye-opening. It is my profound hope that it will contribute to the end of domestic violence."

—Jack Canfield, Co-author of *Chicken Soup for the Woman's Soul*

"Having witnessed an abusive relationship culminating in the death of my mother at the hands of my father, I found this peak behind the door of another victim's hell on earth filled with many similar warning signs. I wish this book had been around as a resource for those around me when I was growing up."

—David N. Kitler international award-winning wildlife artist

"Jacquie Brown's book, *Off the Map* is a brilliant, poignant, powerful portrayal of the physical, emotional, relational and spiritual consequences of domestic violence. Her courageous story and deep insights into the many layers of abuse provide a pathway to truth, grace and most profoundly, hope."

—Ian T. Dr. Min

"*Off the Map* is a nightmarish account of a brave and exceptional woman who struggled through the darkness of domestic abuse, bulimia, depression, alcoholism and more into the light of forgiveness and redemption. Jacquie Brown cleverly weaves her candid and painful story with numerous practical tools and resources to help others navigate the daunting and seemingly hopeless road out of domestic violence. This is an extremely important and timely book—a must read and encouragement to us all, especially those longing for hope and freedom from the prison of abuse."

—Jerry Orthner, author of *ANGELS: Friends in High Places*

"As a by stander, not knowing how to help a person in an abusive relationship, this book helped me to understand what they were going through, from their perspective not mine. We all think we know what we would do in a situation and can give all kinds of advice but until you walk a mile in someone else shoes you can't really know. This book can help you learn how you can best help an abused person and to know if you are a victim yourself."

—Marg P., loved one of a victim

"I found this book extremely informative... Loved it! ... Read it!"

—Kim B.

"This book is an enlightening read for a person who knows someone in a domestic violence situation. I would definitely recommend this book to friends and colleagues."

—Diane P.

"The story needs to be told. The information needs to be shared. Who should read this book?

• I think every young woman should read this book to empower herself before committing to a long term relationship and to support her friends and female relatives.

• I think every psychology student in post-secondary school should read this book, especially those who aspire to counseling careers.

• I think law enforcement officers and workers should read this book to better understand what's happening when they are called to domestic violence scenes."

—Crystal K.

"Oh my gosh, Jacquie, you will help literally thousands of vulnerable women with your information, courage, and support!"

—Colleen S.

"Through a veil of tears and with great heartache I read Jacquie's book, for I realized that many of the circumstances she described mirrored my own life.
I was struck to the core with the knowledge that another woman was experiencing the same pain as I was at the same time. I also realized how the courage and insight of one person transfers to others and can inspire them to step beyond their circumstances and find courage and strength to take steps necessary to protect themselves and their loved ones.
May all who read Jacquie's forthright and compelling work be inspired to become all they are meant to be in this life.
Knowing that we are not alone in our plight can go a long way to helping us make the necessary changes."

—Loretta J., domestic violence victor

"Thank you, thank you, for writing in a honest open way that allows me (and many others, I am sure) to enter into and gain an understanding of what is a reality for many, many women. This book will have a huge impact.

—Daryl G.

"'WOW' is all I can say! You have voiced what for me has only been a silent and secret knowledge for many years."

—Grace B.

"What you've written is amazing. Just amazing!"

—Julie Ann S.

"Jacquie shares from her own life with us in this book and unveils the inner workings of her courage, reveals the keys to her personal victories and yet expands her book to instruct others with steps how to escape safely. *Off The Map: Follow Me Out of Domestic Violence* offers practical, insightful teaching, steps of action and a way to escape from the destructive cycle and a way to make a divine shift from being a victim to a victor. Jacquie has written a book that flows from her heart and her life and provides light on demystifying domestic violence, gives a cutting edge road map that offers hope and a way to find freedom.

With my experience of working in and managing a women's domestic violence shelter for over 12 years and currently managing health and wellness for the homeless population, it is my honor to recommend this book to anyone who may be in or has been in an abusive relationship or for people who choose to assist victims and make a difference. It is a must read for anyone who requires increased awareness of domestic violence and abuse. Great job Jacquie!!"

—Lenora W., RSW, Past Director of a women's domestic violence shelter, currently Health & Wellness Coordinator for the homeless.

"*I found this book to be eye-opening. It is my profound hope that it will contribute to the end of domestic violence*"
~ **Jack Canfield, Co-author of *Chicken Soup for the Woman's Soul***

Follow Me Out
of Domestic Violence

Jacquie Brown

ISBN:978-1-77069-457-6

Printed in Canada

Word Alive Press
131 Cordite Road, Winnipeg, MB R3W 1S1
www.wordalivepress.ca

WORD ALIVE PRESS
Just Write!

MIX
Paper from
responsible sources
FSC
www.fsc.org   FSC® C016245

Library and Archives Canada Cataloguing in Publication

Brown, Jacquie
        Off the map : follow me out of domestic violence / Jacquie Brown.

Includes bibliographical references and index.
ISBN 978-1-77069-457-6

        1. Abused women. 2. Family violence. I. Title.

HV6626.B765 2012   362.82'92   C2012-901455-9

TABLE OF CONTENTS

ACKNOWLEDGEMENTS   xi
INTRODUCTION   xiii
   How to Use This Book   xiii

one: I WONDER HOW IT ALL BEGAN   1
two: REALMS OF ILLUSION   17
   Statistics   17

Something to Keep in Mind   18
The Mists of Illusion   22
His Illusions and Facade   23
Our Illusions and Facade   26
Enlightenment   30
What If?   34

three: LIVE AND LET DIE   35
four: AND THE THUNDER ROLLED   49
Statistics   49
Something to Keep in Mind   50
Abuse: The Action of the Ideology   50
Explosive Emotions   53
Battered and Beleaguered: The Abuse Cycle   54
The Tyranny: The Types of Abuse   55
The Tyrant: Types of Abusers   64
Extreme Identity Theft   64
Enlightenment   65
What If?   67

five: YOU CAN CHECK OUT ANY TIME
       BUT YOU CAN NEVER LEAVE   69
six: WE ARE PRISONERS OF OUR OWN DEVICE   85
Statistics   86
Something to Keep in Mind-   86
The Dance of the Abused-   86
Why We Stay   87
How We Adapt   90
How We Are Affected   93
The Damage Done   95
Other Damage   98
How We Respond   98
Fundamental Human Necessities   104
Could We Choose Differently?   105

seven: THE DARKEST HOUR IS JUST BEFORE DAWN   107
eight: FREE YOUR MIND AND THE REST WILL FOLLOW   121
     Statistics   121
     Something to Keep in Mind   122
     Drawing Back the Dusty Drapes   124
     Swinging the Windows Open   127
     Soaring   133

nine: GOT THAT GET AWAY FEELIN'   135
ten: IT IS STILL UNWRITTEN   153
     Statistics   154
     Something to Keep in Mind   154
     Prepare the Path: The 5 Ws and How   154
     Why Prepare?   155
     Who Can Help   158
     What Will You Need? What Do You Have?   161
     Where Do I Go?   175
     When Do I Leave?   176
     How Do I Go?   177
     A Lot to Think About   179

eleven: I'M ON MY WAY FROM MISERY TO HAPPINESS   181
twelve: FROM THIS MOMENT ON   203
     Statistics   203
     Something to Keep in Mind   204
     A Hedge to Heal   204
     Self-Nurturing Supplants Self-Destruction   205
     Reclaim Your Mind, Regain Your Soul   208
     Reclaiming Our Lives   209
     Dancers Who Dance on Injustice   211

thirteen: AT LAST   213

APPENDIX A   232
     Precautions While Still With the Abuser   231

Your Children's Safety   232
Safety at Home   232
Safety at Work   234
Health   234
Emergency Bag   235

APPENDIX B   237
Precautions After Leaving the Abuser   237
Protecting the Children   237
Other Safety Steps   238
Data Safety   239
Physical Safety   240
Legal   241

ENDNOTES   245
ADDITIONAL RESOURCES   249
INDEX   251

Acknowledgements

THIS BOOK WOULD NOT HAVE BECOME A REALITY WITHOUT THE faith, encouragement and support of many amazing people. I can't begin to convey my deep and humble gratitude. How do I thank someone who has shared who they are in order to help me give myself away, in order to give others their lives back?

But these are some of the people I wish to thank. First and foremost, my new husband, whose support and encouragement enabled me to dedicate myself full time to completing the book. His encouragement kept me persevering when fear or procrastination blocked my way. He held me through the hard parts and rejoiced at each milestone.

All my children: The ones born to me and the ones blest to me. I wish I could name them, but since I have changed the names and places in my story to protect people, I cannot name them here.

All of my siblings, my mom, and, even though he is not here in body, my dad. Again, I wish I could name them, but they know who they are.

I am very grateful for all the wonderful people at the emergency shelter and the second stage housing, especially Lenora. My experience with them not only gave me back my life, but also provided food for this book. The prayers and encouragement of my pastors, Carla, Ian, James and Jerry, gave me light and strength.

Many people graciously edited and supplied me with feedback on various parts of the book. Friends and family: Daryl, Grace, Jeff, Julie Ann, Jutta, Paul. A wonderful ladies' book club who were a delight to meet and insightful in their help, including Alice, Audrey, Crystal, Diane, Donna Mae, Elaine, Elise, Kim, Raylene, Sylvia, Terri and Terrie.

I am also immensely grateful for my coaches, Steve Harrison, Jack Canfield, Teri Hawkins and Rachael Jayne Groover, who shared their wealth of knowledge and vision of possibilities with me and transformed my vision of a dark tunnel with one little speck of light at the end into a glorious, beautiful garden vista.

I'd also like to thank my lawyers, Timothy O'Hara and Wayne Logan, for their wise counsel. Of course I am grateful for my editor, Lori Mackay, who polished and perfected my words, and Jen Jandavs-Hedlin, who expertly and patiently guided me through the self-publishing process.

Thank you, one and all. I am eternally grateful.

INTRODUCTION

HOW TO USE THIS BOOK

OFF THE MAP DEMYSTIFIES DOMESTIC VIOLENCE. IT BRINGS TO light how we are ensnared and why we stay trapped. It also reveals our self-destructive coping mechanisms and ultimately the way out of the dungeon to discover the treasure of life.

The book begins with the illusions and perceptions of both parties that draw us into the relationship. It then moves through the long litany of what domestic violence entails. Most people think of domestic abuse as beatings, but throwing insults and dishes at us is abuse; isolating us from friends, family and finances is abuse; denying spiritual pursuits is abuse; coercing us into sex is abuse.

This book deals with the baffling phenomena of why we stay in the relationships and our self-destructive coping mechanisms, such as eating disorders and addictions. As we begin to grasp the extent and consequences of our conditions and relationships, we move closer to accepting the possibility of escape. The task of planning and preparing, in secret, to start our life over is daunting, but the abundant life that awaits us on the other side is our rich reward.

The unique format of *Off the Map* incorporates a chapter containing a piece of my story followed by a chapter that reveals and then explains the underlying dynamics or aspects of domestic violence. It covers the progressive stages of the abusive relationship and the destruction that follows in the wake of each stage until we find freedom.

The book brings a deeper understanding to the victims of domestic violence of the deadly dance that holds them captive. This insight will also guide the agencies and people assisting the victims: front-line police officers; the medical, education and legal systems; nonprofit organizations; and friends and family as they reach out to help save lives.

The blend of stories, theories, facts, tips and explanations moves along a continuum from the entrapment through the escape and out into the land of the living. The enlightenment the book provides will empower victims to leave the violence and inspire them to reach for the victory on the other side.

As you picked up this book to scan, you may have had someone else in mind who you believe needs help, but if you read the survey questions with an open mind you may discover they apply to you. Often women do not recognize the abuse they are enduring. They become so used to the treatment that they believe it is normal, whereas if they thought of a loved one suffering such treatment, they would be heartbroken and want them free.

For additional information and resources please visit my website at www.jacquiebrown.com.

Abuse Survey[1]

SIGNS THAT YOU'RE IN AN ABUSIVE RELATIONSHIP

Your Inner Thoughts and Feelings

Do you:

- feel afraid of your partner much of the time?
- avoid certain topics out of fear of angering your partner?
- feel that you can't do anything right for your partner?
- believe that you deserve to be hurt or mistreated?
- wonder if you're the one who is crazy?
- feel emotionally numb or helpless?

Your Partner's Belittling Behavior

Does your partner:

- humiliate or yell at you?
- criticize you and put you down?
- treat you so badly that you're embarrassed for your friends or family to see?
- ignore or put down your opinions or accomplishments?
- blame you for his own abusive behavior?
- see you as property or a sex object, rather than as a person?

Your Partner's Violent Behavior or Threats

Does your partner:

- have a bad and unpredictable temper?
- hurt you, or threaten to hurt or kill you?
- threaten to take your children away or harm them?
- threaten to commit suicide if you leave?
- force you to have sex?
- destroy your belongings?

Your Partner's Controlling Behavior

Does your partner:

- act excessively jealous and possessive?
- control where you go or what you do?
- keep you from seeing your friends or family?
- limit your access to money, the phone, or the car?
- constantly check up on you?

I Wonder How It All Began

THE PREVIOUS EVENING I HAD WATCHED AS ROB TURNED INTO
our driveway. A sense of foreboding weighed down my spirit
like lead. Rob was Ed's cousin. What trouble would follow in
his wake? Rob hadn't worked in two years, and I wondered where his
money came from. There was trouble for me after anyone came to our
house, but Rob meant more trouble than usual.

It was unusual to have someone stop at our farm. Very few people came to visit. Ed was not the sociable type. However, Rob did stop by occasionally; they lived on farms close to one other growing up.

Ed asked him in for a beer. We sat at the kitchen table, and one beer led to another and another. I remained the quiet servant at Ed's elbow, listening to the conversation.

I ran through my training in my mind. There were no safe options, but I had to decide which behaviors would minimize potential trouble. I knew Ed's requirements of me when other men were around: no talking unless they swore, and then I was to confront them; no eye contact; only serve Ed, no one else; no leaning on the table; keep as much distance as possible from them, but still stay close to Ed.

This list grew after every time someone visited our house because there was always something I did that Ed did not like. I knew I wouldn't be able to do everything right, but what was more frightening was how helpless I was to control the actions of others for which I would pay the price. Most people eventually ignored me when I wouldn't respond. Not Rob. He would continue to try to include me in the conversation in spite of my silence.

Throughout the evening, I looked down at the table or at Ed, never at Rob. If it was too hard to keep silent when Rob asked me a question, I would look at Ed to briefly answer as if Ed had asked the question instead of Rob. I poured Ed's drinks but never Rob's, and I sat with Ed between us.

Fear and apprehension built up in me over the course of the evening. I wanted to hide, but where? If I went into the living room, I couldn't turn on the television—Ed decided when the TV was turned on, and I sensed he would consider it an insult to him. He disapproved of me reading, so that was not an option. Since it was dark out, going outside would draw attention and questions. I didn't dare go to bed when another man was in the house or before Ed decided it was okay. There was no safe choice, so I withdrew into myself, hoping his anger wouldn't come.

I thought I was doing all right until that breath of a laugh escaped me at Rob's humorous comment. Ed's eyes darted towards me, flashing anger. I knew the look, and I knew I would pay for it later.

If it had been something humorous on television, I would only have heard the familiar, condescending "What's the matter with you?" But since I had laughed at another man's comments, I knew I was in trouble. I was not allowed to laugh without Ed's initial laugh giving me permission, and never at another man's joke, even if Ed found it funny.

Since laughing is almost instinctive, training myself to stifle my humor was hard. I also felt it was an insult to the person making the humorous comment if I did not at least smile. However, in Ed's mind, I belonged to him and therefore was only to laugh at his humor. Laughing at someone else's was like being unfaithful.

In desperation to distract Ed from his angry chain of thoughts, I fixed him another drink and prepared a plate of cheese and crackers. The rest of Rob's visit I spent sitting beside Ed in silent, submissive subservience. Enduring the night was agony as I sat in fear of the angry storm I knew was brewing in Ed.

They drank until early morning, when his cousin finally left. Ed was so drunk by that point he was close to passing out. He slumped in his chair with his chin on his chest; greasy and disheveled hair hid his face. Slurred expletives occasionally boiled out of him. He knew I was there, but he was too drunk to engage in the rage I had expected.

Yet he still held me bound. If I went to bed and left him in the kitchen, when he sobered enough to realize he was alone he would come looking for me—yelling insults, banging doors or throwing things.

I tried to help him out of his chair. We both tumbled to the floor as he lost his balance. I decided to drag him to bed, so I hooked my hands under his arms and across his chest and pulled him backwards to the bedroom. I rolled him onto the bed and covered him up. I gently lay on the bed as well and hoped that he was withdrawn enough into his drunken stupor that he would not notice me.

There was snoring for a few minutes. Then it stopped. I froze and held my breath. I heard the covers move and felt his foot slam into my back.

I was on the floor. My mom and dad had always said that in all the years of their marriage neither had slept on the couch. They always slept together whenever Dad was home from his weeks on the oil rigs.

Because of their example, I thought to be a good wife I should never sleep in the living room. So I spent the night on the floor by the bed and awoke to his flinty silence.

Ed maintained his punishing silence throughout the morning. I was bewildered and frightened by his anger. What was he going to do? How could I make things better?

I dutifully followed Ed out to the corral. As I watched Ed pour oats in the trough for the horses, I agonized over the past night. The horses crowded around the trough, eager for their treat. I waited for Ed to put the bucket back in the grain bin, knowing that if I started back to the house before him my perceived independence would be cause for criticism.

He passed in front of me without a glance in my direction, and I fell in step behind him. Suddenly, he stopped, turned, grabbed me by the back of the neck and shoved me down, face first, towards some horse manure.

"That's where you belong. In the horseshit, you piece of filth, you stupid bitch," he said. He turned his back on me and stormed to the house.

Shame and pain filled my heart, and tears filled my eyes. I believed him. I believed I was the incompetent, immoral, stupid picture he always painted of me. I tried so hard to be the perfect person he wanted me to be, thinking "If I just do this or don't do that, then his rage will stop." But it was always there—sometimes exploding and sometimes simmering.

I stumbled back to my horse and buried my face in her neck. Her warmth and earthy aroma soothed my sorrow somewhat. I believed that at least she loved me.

What Ed did and said played over and over in my mind. He always found something I had done wrong whenever someone was at our house, no matter how diligently I tried to adhere to his rules.

According to him, I would have been a whore if he had not come into my life. I was appalled the first time he declared this. How could he even consider it, let alone voice such an unbelievable accusation?

My heart ached and I felt helpless, and I wondered how it all

4

began. How had I become trapped in this nightmare instead of living the dream of my young girl's heart, the dream of finding my prince, my true love?

My early years were happy ones for the most part. I have five brothers and sisters, and we had a lot of fun together. But my dad was away from home a lot because he worked on oil rigs.

He was my friend. We often sat in quiet contemplation together. We shared a love of sports, and I occasionally went fishing with him. I remember so clearly walking beside him through the long green grass between the railroad tracks and the trees one summer day.

I was maybe eight years old. We had been fishing at a quiet little fishing hole. As we walked, I heard a murmur behind us. Then it grew into a rumble. As the noise increased, my fear and confusion also increased.

Suddenly, the roar was deafening and the ground was shaking. I turned and saw the huge engine of a train coming around the bend. It blocked the trees and filled the sky. I was terrified and didn't know which way to run. Then I felt my father's strong protective arms around me as the train rushed by. Even though I was in the presence of danger, I was safe in his arms and in his love.

I enjoyed my childhood, but fear would never leave me. I hid from visitors; I hid from noise; I hid from the beasts under my bed. I believed I was not worthy of anyone's time, not worthy of having desires, not worthy of anyone's love. I was afraid of rejection and abandonment. I think it stemmed from a time when I was four. I remember my parents took me to a lady's house, and I watched from her window as my parents and my brothers and sister drove away. I was left behind with a lady I did not know.

She put me in a huge bed with a pink satin comforter on it. Later, I woke up crying from a nightmare in which I had again watched in agony as my family drove away and abandoned me. In my dream I made myself long and skinny and slipped inside the bumper of our family car so I wouldn't be left behind. I was with them, but not part of them. Of course, the lady was just caring for me for the evening, but I had no understanding of this concept. This became a recurring nightmare and the foundation of my fear of rejection and abandonment.

Even though I was well liked and well loved, especially by my parents, the belief was planted in my heart from my early childhood that I had to struggle to be perfect and useful in order to avoid being left behind. I had to be good in order to deserve love, and when I was good, my fears of rejection and abandonment receded into the shadows. Performing well in my responsibilities, schoolwork and sports was rewarded with praise that gave me a sense of belonging and significance. But my fears never went away. They haunted and taunted me, telling me I was a fraud, that I was not the person I appeared to be, that in reality I was insignificant, incompetent and unlovable.

My mom and dad had a very loving relationship. As children we often saw them kissing in the kitchen. I thought all marriages were like my mom and dad's, and, since I was a romantic, I longed to find my prince, my soul mate. All my life I worked to win people's acceptance, and occasionally admiration, but I longed for someone to love me for just me, not the facade.

When I was eighteen, Ed came into my life. My dad was transferred to another city, and I chose to stay behind at a friend's to finish grade 12. One weekend my friend and I went to visit her parents in a town a few hours' drive away and decided to go to a dance at the local legion hall. At the dance, she was off being the social butterfly while I remained the wallflower. Several guys asked me to dance, but they were part of a rowdy group of workers, and I didn't feel comfortable accepting. That was until one person joined the group who was actually dressed for a dance and who seemed more self-controlled. As he approached me, I debated whether or not to refuse him too, but he appeared harmless, and I decided one dance wouldn't hurt.

After one tentative dance, Ed sat with me, and we tried to talk over the loud music. Even though he was smaller than most men, he had a quiet, serious, superior way about him that held a sense of power. His dark hair and dark eyes matched his seriousness. He was intriguing.

Past his shoulder, I saw my friend weaving her way through the dancers back to our table. She leaned around Ed, trying to say something to me, but the music was too loud and I couldn't hear her.

I looked at Ed. "What did she say?"

"She's leaving soon," he spoke into my ear.

So I nodded at her, and she made her way back through the crowd. Soon after, the last dance was announced, and I went in search of my friend to go home. She was nowhere to be found, and I learned later the question she asked me was if I had a ride to her parents' place. Ed said he would drive me, and when he walked me to the door, he asked me for my address to write to me. Write to me? This seemed like an unusual thing for a young man to do. It intrigued me, so I gave him my address.

He wrote and called and took me out when he came to the city on the weekends. This was the beginning of my relationship with Ed.

When he was away during the week, he was very concerned about what I did. When we were together on the weekends, he did not let me out of his sight. He wanted me all to himself. He wanted me beside him, my attention on him and my conversations solely with him. He let me know what clothes looked good on me, how my hair looked the best. He saw things I had never considered before about the attitudes and actions of my friends. I echoed his belief that he was the only friend I needed.

I never had anyone pay so much attention to me or let me know how much he loved me. Could this be my Prince Charming? I felt like a princess. Yet I felt a murmuring that something wasn't quite right.

Throughout the spring and summer, my devotion grew. Cords that connected me to my past were severed one by one, and the cords that bound me to Ed increased and strengthened.

By the fall, our dreams turned to a home of our own and children to fill it. Then one bright, crisp winter day, we were married in the little church where Ed was once an altar boy. It was supposed to be the happiest day of my life, but I remember thinking, *I'm not sure this is right. What if I'm making a mistake?*

Ed and I began our new life on his family's farm, living with his parents. As soon as we were married, he subtly began to disempower me. If I talked to anyone, his judgment and sarcasm would follow…so I stopped talking to people. I had no driver's license then…so I stayed on the farm. He didn't want me to work…so I had no income. His hurtful comments eroded what little self-esteem and self-confidence I had.

Little did I know that worse was yet to come.

As soon as we moved into our own little house not far from his parents, Ed's brooding silence turned to explosive rage. I constantly struggled to please or pacify him. My vigilance to avoid or minimize his violence was endless. I tried so hard to be good, but everything I did was wrong, and everything that went wrong was my fault. I felt like my husband loathed me. I was full of shame and sorrow. I was lost and confused.

———————

My horse shifted her weight and nuzzled my hair. As I stood with my back against the rail of the corral, I was still lost and confused. I cried and dreamed of a day when I no longer did things wrong and Ed's anger would finally stop. At the time, I felt fortunate he loved me enough to teach me how to be his perfect wife. I believed I would eventually learn everything required to avoid his anger. However, the previous night told me I had a long way to go, because I did not even understand why my behavior was wrong. I gave him no reason to be jealous, and I did not know how to make half the population of the world disappear in order to avoid any interaction with males.

I slowly made my way back to the house.

As I walked, I wondered to myself, *What should I do? Should I say I'm sorry for whatever I did to upset him? Do I reason and try to explain? How angry is he? How long will it last? Maybe I shouldn't say anything and wait this out?*

My hand was on the doorknob of the door into the house. I hesitated. I knew he expected me to follow him, so if I stayed outside it would anger him more. I opened the door.

I took my jean jacket off and hung it on a hook in the entry. Leaning against the door, I pulled my boots off while I strained to hear which room he was in. The refrigerator door slammed in the kitchen next to me. The bottle opener clattered, and I heard the pop of a beer cap.

I did a mental estimate of how much liquor was left in the house. If there was little alcohol in the house, he would be angry with me for not buying enough, and he'd go to town to the bar. Then I would at least have a few hours of peace but potentially big problems to deal with later: Would he cause trouble in the bar? Would he have someone drive him home? The last person who did that was scary, and he and Ed stayed up for hours drinking more after they got here. I could receive a call from the RCMP telling me he was in jail for drinking and driving or for fighting.

I estimated there was about a bottle of whiskey and a few beers left. He would probably stay home, which meant no reprieve from the fear and tension.

I stayed in the porch, hoping he would move into the living room. Our house was so small, avoiding him was difficult. The house was a square, twenty-five feet by twenty-five feet. The kitchen and living rooms were in the front, with doors off each into two small bedrooms. Between the bedrooms, there was a small washroom, which opened to both bedrooms. Therefore, it was possible to walk in a circle through all the rooms.

I heard him go into the living room, so I started to walk quietly—toes first, then lowering my heels, like a ballerina—partly to conceal where I was and partly from training. (After several disdainful comments about sounding like an elephant, even though I am small, I learned to glide silently when I walked.)

I moved through the kitchen to the first bedroom and continued through the washroom to the back bedroom, which was ours. The bed fit wall-to-wall under the narrow window. The black heavy corduroy curtains, always closed, produced a gloom in the room that matched my soul.

I sat on the bed in the corner next to the dresser so that it was between the door to the living room and me. I worried and listened and waited. I wished I could read while I waited; I missed it. I used to love to read before I was married, but Ed disapproved of it. Now the only book in the house was the Bible I received as a child from Sunday school. However, even if I had been allowed to read, that was not the time. I needed to stay alert.

Hours went by as I sat on the bed and waited. My nerves were taut. I was sure he knew I was in there. I heard him in the kitchen getting drinks, but I couldn't tell if he stayed there or went back into the living room. I debated if I should try to go around to the kitchen to make supper or stay in our room. I weighed the possible scenarios and remained indecisive.

Suddenly the door crashed open.

My heart started pounding; fear sent pins-and-needles sensations down my arms to the back of my hands. I stopped breathing and remained silent and motionless. His abrupt aggressive stride into the room, his pursed lips and his angry harsh eyes staring down on me filled me with panic.

"Get out here. Now," he ordered.

His head jerked towards the other room. His icy level tone was more frightening than if he had yelled. He turned and walked out of the room. Reluctantly, I moved off the bed and followed him through the living room. He wouldn't talk to me in the living room. It was too comfortable.

He went to the kitchen and stood with his back to the sink. One hand held his drink; the other was partially in his jean pocket.

I slipped into the chair at the end of the table by the living room door and waited for the questioning to begin. Several minutes went by.

I stared at one square in the green brick pattern of the linoleum and kept him in my peripheral vision. Was I supposed to say something? If I assumed he was angry about his cousin talking to me and tried to explain, I might needlessly open up a dangerous subject. His jealousy made him the most volatile. If I told him I didn't know what he was angry about but that I was sorry for whatever part I had in upsetting him, it could give him the opportunity to forgive me as a way to move out of this anger stage.

On the other hand, if I didn't even know what I had done wrong, he could blow up about how stupid I was. If I said nothing when he expected me to talk, his anger would turn to rage, intensified by the drinking. I waited in silence and furtively watched him and wondered what he would do.

Ed was not a big man, 5 feet 7 inches and 150 pounds, but he had told me stories of what he had done to bigger people and the fear he generated in them. I saw this when he got into fights at the bar. Men did not expect someone Ed's size to move past words into actually throwing punches, so he would catch them off guard. He was tenacious, quick and ruthless—he always finished in domination. So he was very practiced at generating fear, and in my case it was a simple task. I could not remember any time in my life when fear was not lurking below the surface.

Suddenly Ed's glass shattered against the wall by my head. Broken glass shards sprayed across the table and me. The whiskey and cola left dark trails as it ran down the wall. He breathed hard and fast through his nostrils; his lips were tight and his fists were clenched.

Fear pounded through me. I was too afraid to move. I stayed frozen in my chair and watched his eyes, narrowed in hatred and disgust.

"Something's going on between you two, and I want to know what it is," he demanded.

My intuition told me he was beyond any point of reason. As absurd as his accusation was, I knew from past experience that words of denial or defense would push him deeper into his rage. I was quiet as I heard him shout degrading, demeaning, unjust curses.

If I stayed silent, he could take it as acquiescence, which sometimes starved the storm until it ran out of fuel, but not this time. He fired questions at me that didn't make sense.

"I heard you two talking when you thought I was asleep. Has he been here when I've been at work?" he yelled.

I was shocked and confused. I recalled the previous night and tried to make sense of Ed's accusations. Ed was awake the entire time his cousin was here. He did not pass out until after Rob left. There was never a conversation between Rob and me.

I retreated in fear from any conversation with any man, except my father, and even with him Ed made sure I suffered because of it. I never answered the door if Ed was not home. I did everything I could to avoid situations that would ignite Ed's wrath. The less contact I had with all people, the better for me.

I would never want his cousin here. I did not even want Ed to be with him; Rob was trouble.

I didn't understand. I did not even look at his cousin. I had learned the hard way to look at the table or Ed. Even when we went out for the evening, I was not allowed to look up or watch the band or dancers, because no men were permitted in my field of vision.

I wanted to deny the assertions, but in the past when I denied something too strongly, he accused me of hiding something, so my brain scrambled to find the best way to answer. "I don't want anything to do with anyone but you," I answered, hoping my devotion would soften his heart.

"Shut up, you stupid bitch," he hissed.

My confusion was replaced with pain as my tears started to flow.

"You're pathetic. Why don't you run home to Mommy, you Smith?"

He used my maiden name of Smith the same way he used other swear words to describe me.

"If you'd had stricter parents, you wouldn't have become a slut. Your mother's a bitch."

Anguish ripped my heart. Suddenly, I jumped to my feet and ran out the door, not realizing I had no shoes on. I wanted to escape, to hide. I headed for the trees across the road.

I climbed through the barbed-wire fence and disappeared into the woods. I ran recklessly until I tripped over a deadfall tree. I stopped crying, held my breath, lay there in the leaves and listened, afraid he might have followed me. Even though it was summer, last year's leaves were still crunchy, so I would hear him coming.

Nothing.

I curled up in a ball and sobbed softly for what felt like forever. Eventually, my sorrow was satiated, and the strange calm came that often followed the tears. I turned on my back. I looked up. The emerald leaves shimmered in the breeze against the sapphire sky. Beauty, oblivious to the ugliness of humanity, surrounded me. I imagined the leaves whispered words of love. Maybe they would care for me like J. R. R. Tolkien's Ents.

I lay there and listened and thought and tried to make sense of Ed's increasing anger towards me. What had I done by choosing this man to marry? How could someone who supposedly loved me as much as he said he did be so malevolent?

He wanted me to be as ashamed of my family and of who I was, as he was. It broke my heart. I wished I could "run home to Mommy," but my ego was afraid to admit I had made a mistake. And now I was an adult; I was not supposed to go back home.

I thought back to the time before our marriage. Ed was often in fights in the bar because someone had used foul language in front of me. I felt special as he defended me. I never dreamt that soon after our wedding I would hear worse language than that coming from him, not just as expressions of speech, but directed at me: my new names.

They started when I was helping him build a gate. I misunderstood his instructions and did not hold a board the way he wanted. Angry, degrading words poured out of his mouth. What I heard shocked and terrified me. I tried to explain the reasoning behind my actions, sure that when he understood he would be sorry for what he had said, but the more I tried to explain, the angrier he got.

I was about twenty feet away from him, and I watched in horror as his hand that held the axe drew back high over his head. Confusion rooted me to the spot. The axe circled through the air and hit the ground a couple of feet away from me.

I chose to believe that he intended to miss me, but what did his change in behavior tell me? This new method of expressing his anger was added to the silence that had been his previous pattern.

As I lay among the trees and thought about these things, I believed that there must be a way of explaining myself to him. I had to, somehow, convey the message that it was never my intention to act or speak in a way that would upset him. If only I were wise enough to discover the right words. One day I would be. One day he would understand me, and the anger would stop.

Boom.

A gun blast froze my thoughts for an instant before they started to race. *It's not hunting season, so why a gunshot? It came from the direction of our house…Oh no!*

I bolted to my feet and raced through the bush back to the house, terror pounded through me at the horror of what he could have done to himself. Then I stopped in my tracks. Was he after me?

I refused to believe that. I started to run again. I was across the road, across the grass. I hesitated for a moment at the open door, as the possibility of what I could find inside sent shafts of fear through me. But I jumped through the door and raced through the rooms and found nothing.

Where was he? I ran out the door and around the house and stopped.

The shotgun was in his hands, the stock end on the ground, the barrel pointed skyward. He sat on the cement circle that used to hold a rain barrel. His head was slumped forward, and he was not moving. I touched his shoulder. He didn't move. He didn't speak, but I knew he was alive.

Relief was quickly replaced with apprehension. But then, I reasoned, his shotgun only held one shell at a time, and I sensed he had been sitting in that position since he fired the gun, so it was probably not reloaded.

"Would you have come back?" he asked the ground.

"Yes. I love you," I responded. By that time in our relationship, I no longer felt love, but I chose to love, just as you choose to love your children or parents when their actions or characters are unlovable.

"I'm sorry. But if you would have told him where to go instead of laughing at his jokes, none of this would have happened." He spoke firmly, but not in anger. "Your parents didn't teach you anything. I wish I could have kept you in my pocket when you were growing up."

When a wolf in a pack submits to the alpha male leader, it lies on its back with its paws in the air, exposing its vulnerable throat and belly. This is how I felt as I said, "I'm sorry. I wish my parents had been like you." I said it to please him, not because it was how I felt. I loved my parents and my childhood.

He got up and walked past me into the house. I followed him and realized I was in my stocking feet. I must have stepped on something, because one foot hurt.

I watched him as he opened the gun and removed the empty cartridge before hanging it back on the wall in the porch. He went into

14

the kitchen, opened the cupboard and reached for another glass. My heart sank as he poured another drink.

Back in his favorite position, leaning against the sink, he began to talk about what he was like when he was younger, about how he stood up to people, showing no fear. His focus had shifted from me to himself, so I felt safer and encouraged his new direction as I sat down at the table.

It was in my best interest to be a good listener, so I asked questions and made observations that supported his views. He talked on about his past for an hour or more until he was ready to show signs of forgiving me. He asked if I wanted to go for a drive. The thought that he'd had too much to drink to be driving crossed my mind, but I thought he probably knew it as well and would stay on the empty country roads. Any attempt by me in the past to convince him not to drive because of his drinking led to anger, defiance and recklessness.

I agreed to go, and he poured another drink in a travel mug, got the keys and went outside. I got my backpack, put on my shoes and followed him out to the truck.

two

REALMS OF ILLUSIONS

"Injustice anywhere is a threat to justice everywhere."
Martin Luther King Jr.

STATISTICS

Reports of women ever physically assaulted by an intimate partner (this does not include other types of abuse) ranged from a low of 10 percent in the Philippines to a high of 69 percent in parts of

Nicaragua. For Canada it was 29 percent, and for the United States it was 22 percent.[1]

Only approximately one-quarter of all physical assaults, one-fifth of all rapes, and one-half of all stalking perpetuated against females by intimate partners are reported to the police.[2]

SOMETHING TO KEEP IN MIND
Five Red Flags

Is your Prince Charming disguising a beast? Here are five red flags that mark the beast.

1. How well does he play in your yard?

- Your Places
  — When you bring him into an environment that is familiar, comfortable or enjoyable to you but is new to him, is he receptive and open, or is he sullen and withdrawn?
- Your Things
  — When you let him know that certain things are important to you, do you trust that they will be respected and safe in his presence, or do you fear he may trivialize and damage them?
- Your People
  — When he meets your family, friends and co-workers, does he appreciate their value in your life, or does he find fault with them and then with you for your relationship with them?
- Your Activities
  — When there are events and activities that are meaningful and enjoyable for you, does he encourage and accommodate your participation, or does he transform it into something unpleasant and unwelcome?

Your places, things, and people are areas where he will be at a disadvantage and you will be at an advantage. He will want to gain the upper hand.

For example, if you are invited to Thanksgiving dinner at your parents' with siblings, cousins, aunts and uncles coming, how does your partner react? It is understandable if he is nervous, uncomfortable and even reluctant, but red flags would be:

- if he makes critical or insulting comments about your family, their home or the upcoming event. He is hoping to make you feel guilty or ashamed about the people or occasion. This is the tip of the wedge that causes you to reduce your connection with them.

- if he demeans you or fights before the event. He is hoping that this will cause you to be especially attentive and compliant with him while you are there as you work to try to please him. Lowering your self-esteem inhibits your interactions with your family.

- if he refuses to go and belittles you for wanting to. He is escalating it to a loyalty issue, forcing you to choose between him and them. He is hoping you will choose him, which establishes his power. If you choose them, he believes he is then justified in making you feel guilty for not being loyal. This is another wedge.

- if he goes but becomes sullen and withdrawn. He is hoping to make you and your family feel so uncomfortable that you will be reluctant to attend gatherings in the future.

- if he initiates circumstances that make it impossible to attend. He is letting you know he is against gatherings with your family, and yet, to avoid blame, he shifts the blame off of himself onto the circumstances he created.

2. What's in it for him?

- Does he insist on knowing and adjusting:
—Who you associate with?
—What you have, like or do?
—Where you are going or have been?
—When you leave and return?
—Why you do things (demands explanations)?
—How you think, feel, act, look?
- When he gets upset:
— Is it focused on him or is it focused on you? Does he use "I" statements or "you" statements? Is it because he wants to go out

with the guys or because he doesn't want you to go out with the girls? If it's focused on you, it is related to his desire to control you.

— Is his treatment of you effective in shutting you up or changing your behavior? If he says one of your friends is self-centered, how do you feel when he sees you with her?

— Is there a double standard? Is it okay for him to talk to girls but not for you to talk to guys?

— Is he stuck in your head? At break are you wondering, "Why did he get upset?" At lunch are you thinking, "Next time I won't say anything"? At home-time are you wondering, "Is he still mad?" What if your focus on him causes you to make mistakes at work or school? Will he care? What if enough mistakes cause you to be fired or to fail your course? Will it elevate his control over you?

Knowledge is power, so the more knowledge he has about you the more power is available to him. He'll use the knowledge to justify his anger. It is a red flag if he seems overly interested in your business and he uses anger to adjust you.

3. Where's the pattern?

• When he's upset:

— Is he sorry after mistreating you but then gradually reverts to the same treatment until his anger once again erupts?

— Is it unreasonable or unfair? Is there a legitimate reason for him to be upset, or do you shake your head in disbelief?

— Is it becoming more intense and more frequent? Does his anger reach an unreasonable level for the circumstances?

— Is it getting broader in scope? Is the list of things that upset him growing?

— Can you sense when a "full moon" is approaching? Can you tell the time is getting close to another flare-up because intuitively you are becoming familiar with the pattern?

When you are in a relationship, there are going to be differences of opinion. However, it is a red flag if you recognize a pattern to the disagreements.

4. Where do the chips fall?

- Who starts the fights, who are they focused on, who is blamed, who benefits and who pays?
- When you go out for the evening, does he insist on paying for everything? Does he never seem to have any money and you always end up paying? It is a red flag if either of these extremes is the case.
- When you want to pay down debt and he wants to buy a new car, where does the money go? When you want a new stove and he wants a ski trip, where does the money go?
- Who dominates money decisions? Since money, in itself, holds so much power, if his agenda is power and control he will try to control the money.

Finances are a big challenge for many couples. However, if he is fair and flexible about who pays and where it goes, then he is not using money to manage you. However, if he is not, you need to look at his attitude. Selfishness might not be a red flag, but entitlement would be.

5. What's his hook?

- Does he get you to buy into his strength? Are you entranced by
—his age?
—his athleticism?
—his car?
—his career?
—his competence?
—his education?
—his high standards?
—his looks?
—his money?
—his rebellion?
—his status?

—his self-confidence?

—his sophistication?

—his suffering?

- Does he entice you with "candy"?

- Could his hook have been part of the process he used in choosing you as a partner? Maybe the college graduate purposely chooses the high school store clerk. Maybe the life of the party purposely chooses the wallflower.

There is always something special about him that he subtlety or blatantly emphasizes that he and you believe is disproportionate to what you deserve. What he chooses to demean about you will, by extension, magnify his hook. "You're a slob" magnifies his sense of style; "You're stupid" magnifies his intelligence.

All of these red flag pertain to power and control. To control you, he constantly adjusts the balance of power to tip the scales in his favor.

THE MISTS OF ILLUSION

Illusions slowly rise and swirl around and within both our abusive partner and us until we are so enshrouded in the mist that light no longer penetrates and gloom settles into our souls. These illusions have internal and external dimensions interwoven and dependent on each other.

His illusions are rooted in the perception of his ideal world and his sense of entitlement to it. His ideal world has two realms: the realm within his fortress, which is hidden from the outside world, and the realm of his territory beyond the fortress walls.

Our illusion or facade often has its genesis in the belief of our inadequacy and unworthiness. Our perceived inadequacy and unworthiness lead to an unconscious, or sometimes conscious, fear of rejection and abandonment. Because of this fear, we create illusions to hide our perceived failings. We build a facade as we become the compliant, subservient overachiever, hoping others will not see our unworthiness.

We sense that our self-preservation is dependent on maintaining these illusions. Because of our low self-esteem and lack of self-confidence, we believe we need to hide who we are in order for others to accept and love us. We watch and listen and then try to become what we believe people want us to be.

This desire to please others at our own expense attracts the abuser. He senses he will be able to mold us into his ideal. Our past conditioning and belief systems, as well as those of our partner, create illusions about life and ourselves that work as attractions for each other. They have prepared us to be codependents in a relationship that will feed off each other, intensifying the dysfunction.

Over time, the illusions get more complex, illogical, chaotic and destructive. Operating in this environment has physically, emotionally, psychologically and socially damaging effects on both parties. The damage is dynamic, and it permeates every area of our lives and progresses into an endlessly escalating horror show.

HIS ILLUSIONS AND FACADE

In the abuser's ideal world, he is "The King of His Castle." The abuser draws us into his world, and the nightmare slowly takes form. We are within his castle, his fortress. As master of his fortress, the abuser is convinced of his entitlement to his ideal world. He invents his own reality. Idealists

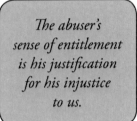

The abuser's sense of entitlement is his justification for his injustice to us.

set up structures and rules to achieve their ideals; they create an ideology. Ideologies generate specific beliefs, rhetoric (language, such as repeated words, comments and sayings) and enforcement systems (rules and punishment). The creation of this ideology is subtle and progressive; his focus is self-centered, self-serving and relentless.

He starts the relationship believing that we have the potential to be his perfect partner, the potential to be his ideal. To transform this ideal into reality he uses the components of the ideology: beliefs, language, and enforcement systems.

The "belief" component of the ideology is his belief in his entitlement. The arrogance, the certainty of his superiority, sets up a pattern of thinking that looks for the negative in us and the positive in himself. This establishes, in his mind, his right to power, control and domination. This belief is evident in every expectation, conversation and decision.

When the abuser has negative experiences, the fault will lie with us, with someone else or with his environment, never with himself. This belief is most often a result of early conditioning. A role model in the abuser's life, usually his father, has established a pattern of behavior to ensure that his own wants are satisfied. As the abuser sees his role model's aggressive, self-centered behavior rewarded rather than punished, the message is received. Our patriarchal achievement-oriented society reinforces the message and the abuser's sense of entitlement.

The rhetoric component of the ideology uses criticisms, insults, derogatory comments and disrespect to justify his abuse and to establish and reinforce our inferiority and his superiority.

The demeaning language is intentionally illogical and untrue, and it achieves its purpose of modifying our behavior and beliefs through our perceptions. Perceptions become the reality—his and ours. For his part, it is irrelevant whether or not his rhetoric is based in truth and logic. He will manipulate truth and logic as he sees fit to maximize his power, his control and the illusion he is creating. This leads to the common frustration of the abused that "He twists everything around to make it look like my fault." How do you use logic to argue against illogic?

The purpose of the illusion is to devalue us and elevate himself, disempowering us and empowering himself. The illusion is that we are inferior human beings that he owns and, as such, he is entitled to power and control over us. The frightening part is that he believes the illusion he creates.

Since logic is irrelevant to the abuser, the opportunities to degrade us are ever-present. For each positive belief he has about himself he has a corresponding negative belief about us (see table 1.1). He also convinces us to believe the lies. This accomplishes more than one of his objectives: it keeps us striving to become his ideal, and it creates a smoke screen, a hall of mirrors, distorting reality, which fosters confusion and doubt in our minds and increases our vulnerability.

TABLE 1.1 BELIEFS

ABUSER	ABUSED
Powerful	Weak
In Control	Helpless
Superior	Inferior (possession/object)
Intelligent	Stupid
Entitled	Subservient
Justified (double standard)	Intolerable
Capable	Incompetent
Self-sufficient	Inadequate
Protector	Vulnerable
Worthy of Respect	Pathetic
Demanding	Compliant
Dismissive	Insignificant
Important	Worthless
Virtuous	Immoral
Invincible	Invisible

A common pattern used by abusers is to reinforce the lie that we were worthless, immoral people in the past. He wants us to believe it is his high expectations of us that have saved us from ourselves.

We are a work-in-progress for him. We are his possession as he continues to mold us into his ideal: to look attractive, cater to his every whim and build his ego. We are never to disagree or have an opinion, and we are to keep our emotions in compliance with his desires.

His perceived entitlement, by extension, nullifies our rights and freedoms. He expects us to defer to his opinions and decisions; he believes we are to be "seen and not heard." We are to meet his emotional, psychological and physical needs. This is why our compliant nature and low self-esteem attract him. According to Cloud and Townsend in *Boundaries in Marriage*, "[Viewing us] only in terms of how [we] affect [him]…is self-centeredness…[which reduces us] to objects of [his] own needs…[not seeing us] as real people."[3] If we do not act according to his wishes, he uses his enforcement systems to achieve our compliance. Subsequent chapters cover this aspect of abuse in more detail.

> *He projects an illusion of himself for others that defies the reality of his treatment of us.*

The facade the abuser portrays outside the castle walls disguises the beast within. Yet on some level, since he hides the abuse from most people, he may know that the outside world, society in general, may not accept his beliefs. He projects an illusion of himself to others that defies the reality of his treatment of us.

By portraying what he believes is an admirable character relevant to the people in his life, he positions himself as a superior member of the group, whether the group is his sports and outdoor buddies or fellow executives. When the abuser promotes a positive image, it generates the positive feedback on which the abuser thrives.

Self-promotion is also high on his agenda for several other reasons. First, when others see him in a positive light, it causes us to doubt the inappropriateness and severity of his treatment of us. Second, it reinforces our belief in his superiority and our inferiority. Third, it isolates us from potential sources of help, because others will doubt he is capable of abuse since it is inconsistent with his facade.

The people he likes to associate with will not be people who place us in a positive light. If they do, they will likely receive the same negative language (from table 1.1) that we receive. Our family and friends are subject to this treatment. This is to discourage our association with them by making life difficult or dangerous for them and us. By isolating us from people who build us up and support us, the abuser leaves no one to interfere with his agenda to demoralize us. It also leaves no one for us to turn to for help when his abuse escalates.

Our Illusions and Facade

We have spent most of our lives hiding in fear. For me, fear was part of my identity from as early as I can remember. I hid from visitors, hid from noise, hid my feelings, hid my thoughts, hid the truth, hid from the monsters under my bed. I have found this to be true for other women as well. So we hide our thoughts, fearing ridicule; we hide our actions, fearing reproach; and we hide our desires, fearing disappointment. Our fears stem from our illusions of insufficiency and unworthiness. We believe we are not worth anyone's time, not worthy of having opinions or desires. We are afraid of imposing on others. We believe we are inferior, in some or many ways, compared to others—less competent, desirable and intelligent. Fear of failure and inadequacy lead to fear of rejection and abandonment.

Often our fears start in childhood. Unmet needs—especially emotional needs, such as for affection, nurturing or support—cause us to develop protective mechanisms. We develop these to try to prevent the illusions we believe from turning our fears of abandonment into reality. One method of protection is suppressing our needs to avoid the pain of having them denied—"I don't need hugs; I don't need conversations; I don't need playmates." Our illusions of unworthiness also cause us to feel guilty about asking from others. "If I ask, they'll probably say no and think I'm selfish."

One method of protection is suppressing our needs to avoid the pain of having them denied.

Another mechanism to avoid rejection is to recognize the needs and desires of others and do what we can to satisfy those. As is the case for many women who end up in abusive relationships, even from childhood we have been compelled to take on responsibilities beyond what is normally acceptable or fair. From housework and caring for our family members to counseling and serving our friends, we seem to be the self-sacrificing people others go to when they want something, knowing they won't be refused.

In our effort to be mature and responsible, we deny ourselves our childhood and the discovery of who we are as people. We hope to create value in ourselves, to have significance, by pleasing others. We pattern our identities on the opinions and desires of others since we perceive our own as flawed and unimportant. We are afraid of judgment, believing others will reject us if we show our true selves.

In order to achieve acceptance from others we monitor and adjust our behavior and thoughts to match theirs until our own dreams, desires, opinions and hopes disappear. Nathaniel Hawthorne states, "No [woman], for any considerable length of time, can wear one face to [her] self and another to the multitude without finally getting bewildered as to which may be the truth."[4] We take on the persona of who we believe the person in front of us wants us to be.

Abdicating decision-making is another means of protection. Avoiding opinions and decisions avoids accountability, responsibility and judgment from others. These protective mechanisms also help us to avoid confrontations, which avoids rejection. The less we ask for, the lower the likelihood of rejection; the more we give, the more acceptable we are. We have an illusion of control when we deny ourselves and decide to meet the needs of others. The choice is then ours, whereas we feel helpless and vulnerable if we rely on others to meet our needs, since the choice is then theirs.

Since we believe in illusions about our worth, we create illusions about who we are and hide within them.

> *We have an illusion of control when we deny ourselves and decide to meet the needs of others.*

Our perceived inadequacies generate paralyzing fear when we consider making our way in the world alone. We marvel at the competence of others, especially women, and believe we could never achieve what they do. Our underlying belief is that we are incapable of taking care of ourselves. We do not see our value or potential, so our search for a partner has an unconscious element of desperation. We feel we need someone else to take care of us.

We have no boundaries—no picket fence of protection around our yards. We do not communicate, with our words or actions, what is unacceptable to us. We have difficulty even determining what is unacceptable to us and that we have a right to communicate it.

Abusers see that we have no boundaries. Our self-doubt and our selfless serving of others fit in perfectly with the abusers' self-centeredness and sense of entitlement. However, abusers reveal very little of their true selves at the start. When the romance begins, they believe we are the ideal partners of their imagination. Their affection and attention are their way of sweeping us off our feet. They intentionally take us to new heights to cement our bond to them.

We interpret all the attention they pay to us and the concern they have for our actions and thoughts as love of who we are, but it is really a love for who they expect us to be. As is stated in *Why Does He Do That?* "The abusive man doesn't expose these self-focused fantasies to his new partner. In fact, he is largely unaware of them himself."[5]

We assume the reason for their actions is affection for us, not the desire to control us. Yet there are clues in their attention. Expressions such as "I'd like to hide you behind the stars" or "I wish I could have hid you in my pocket as you grew up" sound romantic on the surface, but they hint at the desire to isolate us from the rest of the world, which is one of the tactics of the abuser.

His obsession with us masquerades as love. Then, as we spend time together, he discovers that who we are does not coincide with his expectations of us. He begins to modify our beliefs and behavior through his language and enforcement system. This is usually subtle at first, but ever-increasing aggression enters his words and actions.

Since we were so infatuated with the image of who he appeared to be in the beginning, it is difficult for us to make a transition in our judgment of him when small isolated incidents of mistreatment happen. His change in behavior baffles us when it begins.

We struggle with confusion. What have we done to cause him to hurt us? We try various means to prevent his displeasure without success. What he tells us he wants one day will be the source of his anger another day; what looks good on us one day will bring stinging criticism the next. The rules and patterns are constantly shifting so that we are always walking on eggshells, on shaky ground, on shifting sand.

We are compliant out of our fear of confrontation, even if we sense something is not right. Assertiveness has never been part of our character. Peace and harmony are so important to us that we avoid confrontation almost at all costs.

When we buy into the rhetoric of his ideology that constantly belittles us and reinforces our illusions of inadequacy and unworthiness, we spiral downwards. Then our perceptions of ourselves become our reality; we become the stories we are told.

> We need to keep our safety uppermost in our minds as we search for the truth.

As he begins to implement his enforcement system, we soon learn to speak his language, the rhetoric of his ideology. Yet, in spite of our growing unhappiness, we want desperately to hold on to the illusion of him as the adoring suitor who swept us off our feet in the beginning.

To the outside world, we keep up the facade of a loving relationship, partly because of the expectations of our partner and partly because of our own desire not to appear a failure to friends and family, as well as to ourselves. Our focus remains on him and the relationship while we work to project to the outside world a picture of the perfect marriage and mate.

Our hiding in fear takes on dimensions we never dreamed of. Now, to maintain the illusion, we are sacrificing not only our needs and desires, but also our dignity and identity. The more we indulge our fear, the more it escalates, and with the fear comes the decay of our identity.

Enlightenment

A situation + what we think about it = how we feel

A situation (he manufactures or manipulates it)
What we think about it (he plays mind games with our thoughts)
How we feel (he generates the emotion in us that suits his purpose)

He harnesses our emotions and then takes the reins to control our actions.

Our illusions have paradoxical aspects. Our perceived worthlessness—the belief in the illusion that we are incapable of taking care of ourselves, unable to achieve accomplishments, and unwanted—contrasts with the reality of our capabilities, intelligence and past friendships. In addition, we believe the facade of usefulness and consideration that we portray is an illusion. It is a facade we ironically create by striving for excellence and by serving others. We are in darkness, blind to the evidence that our illusion of worthlessness is actually a lie and that our perceived facade of usefulness and consideration is actually true.

Hidden in this darkness is fear, whose foundation is lies. Lies are behind our low self-esteem and lack of self-confidence. Lies keep us captive, and fears bring decay. Whatever is not nurtured withers. Any hopes we had of being a capable, desirable person

Hidden in this darkness is fear, whose foundation is lies.

withered under the barrage of lies, the lies we told ourselves and the lies told to us by the abuser (see table 1.1). When we heard the lies and repeated them continually in our minds, they grew and became who we now believe we are.

The darkness of our fear creates tunnel vision. Our seeming self-preservation depends on our focus. We focus on the bad that could happen, and we are constantly worried about how to prevent, mitigate or reverse any damage. Surviving takes all our energy. There is no energy left for our dreams or identity, and they slowly disappear.

But the lies are still lies. Just because we believe something does not make it true. The reality we perceive is something we learned or created, but it is not necessarily what is true. When we change our perception to see positive aspects of ourselves, we empower ourselves to change our lives in amazing ways.

Challenging our illusions of insignificance and incompetence is a process, and it is difficult. If we start with one of the lies on his list (or ours) and look at it in various ways, we can begin to change our perception of it.

Ask yourself if others, besides your partner, see you this way. Ask if this is how you saw yourself before you met your partner or if there are inconsistencies with this view. Did this lie start in childhood? How does it affect your behavior, your choices? If this really were true, would your partner still want you around? Would he have chosen you? What does this say about him? Is it to his advantage to have you believe the lie rather than the truth?

There may also be some unconscious reasons that you do not want to let go of the lie. You may feel safer believing the lie; you may embrace your unworthiness because you fear what would be required to change your mindset. You should ask yourself how this lie serves you

Once we know the magician's tricks, he can no longer deceive us.

and what will be the cost of letting it go. Are expectations others have of you lower if you portray the lie? Can you use it as an excuse to avoid something difficult or explain something that has not turned out well? Can you hide in it?

Then you should ask what the cost has been of believing the lie. Have you given up the pursuit of higher education? Have you given up your spiritual beliefs, thinking you are unworthy? Have you given up looking after your appearance and health? Have you given up associating with other people?

It does not matter whether you start the process with the lie that is easiest to challenge or the one that hurts the most. Any one will be a good beginning. As you take each one and examine it, question its truth, search hard for evidence to the contrary, you can create a crack to let the light in. The more truth you discover, the more light there is to expose the lies. Remember, believing that good things about you are untrue is just as much a lie as believing that bad things are true.

Another important part of dissolving the illusions is to remember to question the abuser's illusions (to protect yourself, do this within yourself, as he will resist your challenging his entitlement). The fact that lies are still lies also applies to the abuser's beliefs and language. Just because he believes or says something does not make it true. Does he really have the right to demand that you live up to the illusion he desires you to become? Are his expectations of you stemming from love for you or himself? Is trying to transform yourself into his dream destroying you or preventing you from discovering who you really are? Is his concept of who you are now just an illusion?

Once we know the magician's tricks, he can no longer deceive us. As we gain understanding of the illusionist, the abuser, we gain a measure of freedom in our hearts, even if we keep it to ourselves. The damage from his destructive words diminishes when we refuse to believe them. We understand their purpose, and the abuser may not even believe them himself. He uses them for their desired effect on us: to tame us, train us and transform us into his impossible ideal.

He constantly raises the standard for the ideal partner he expects us to become in order to maintain his justification for his mistreatment of us. But the truth is, there is no justification.

What if good things about you are true? Consider what wonderful things await you if you embrace the truth. "Since I am capable of learning and it's all right for me to have good things in my life, I can take a course in something to develop my skills; I can pursue spiritual growth; I can learn to drive; I can improve my health and my appearance for myself; or I can pursue an activity I enjoy."

A word of caution about how much growth you reveal to the abuser: if he learns about your growth, he may increase the abuse to discourage it. You may need to be creative in how you acquire or disguise your self-improvement.

To establish the truth within, practice positive feedback where you repeat in your mind the truth. "I'm smart because I _____ _____." Do not say the lie is false, since our subconscious has difficulty recognizing negatives. For example, if you say, "I'm not stupid because I_____ _____," the subconscious mind will only hear "stupid" and then that will stay in your mind. As you go through your day, purposefully look for only things you do or think that support the positive truth. Refuse to look at anything that supports the negative. You can always reframe something as positive. Soon you will gain strength in believing good things about yourself. The more you practice, the better you get, and the more darkness and fear diminish.

Even as you are nurturing this truth in your mind and heart, you need to assess where, when, whether and to whom to express it. The abuser will not embrace this new line of thinking. It challenges his domination and control, so revealing the truth and your growth to him or someone who may tell him could be detrimental to your well-being as well as your continued growth. You need to keep your safety uppermost in your mind as you search for the truth.

As dark and lonely as the situation seems, you are not on this journey alone. Other women, including myself, have been in that dungeon and are now free to live in the light. Many of us are holding out our hands to help you escape as well.

Public awareness and outrage at the atrocities and injustice we suffer are also strengthening. Even though the abuser may be adept at hiding his true character, friends and family often have the feeling that something is not right. When we share with someone we trust, we gain their support and wisdom. We are often surprised at how deeply others care and how willing they are to help. There are also numerous public agencies that will guide us and support us even while we remain in the abusive relationship. (A later chapter will cover some of this.) This will allow others to love us and help us discover the truth to begin to love ourselves.

WHAT IF?

What if his professed love is actually obsession and oppression? The definitions that follow may cause us to reconsider his love.

Obsession: "the uncontrollable persistence of an idea or emotion in the mind."[6]

Oppression: to subject a person or a people to a harsh or cruel form of domination; "the exercise of authority or power in a burdensome, cruel, or unjust manner."[7]

Love: St. Paul's definition is *"Love is patient, love is kind. It does not envy, it does not boast, it is not proud. It is not rude, it is not self-seeking, it is not easily angered, it keeps no record of wrongs. Love does not delight in evil but rejoices with the truth. It always protects, always trusts, always hopes, always perseveres."*[8]

What if?
- Truth sets you free; lies chain you in bondage.
- Truth brings light, life and love; lies bring darkness, decay and despair.
- Truth brings peace; lies bring discord.
- Truth brings trust; lies bring fear.
- Truth brings the enlightenment needed to lift the veil and empower you to walk out of the mist and into the sunshine.

Live and Let Die

I WATCHED ED DRIVE DOWN THE DRIVEWAY AND TURN ONTO THE gravel road. I stood on the stones with Ashley, our daughter, in my arms and dutifully lifted my hand to wave goodbye. Connor, our son, was then three, and I encouraged him to wave bye as well as our green truck with the ATV in the back disappeared past the trees.

Ed would be gone on a hunting trip for at least five days. It was a relief to see him go.

Six years had gone by since we were married, and my husband's treatment of me had grown worse despite how hard I struggled to do what pleased him. My every word was guarded, and endless scenarios ran through my mind before I took a step, but nothing stopped the oppression.

After I tucked the kids into bed that night, I decided to indulge myself in the luxury of watching a romantic movie. It was called *Ice Castles*. I watched as the young man jumped over the boards of the ice arena to pick roses up from the ice, thrown by admiring spectators. The roses threatened to trip his blind sweetheart, who had just skated the performance of her life. She had gone blind during training, and her boyfriend had helped her believe she could still achieve her dream. Because I was alone, I was safe to immerse myself in the show, and a whisper of forgotten feelings of love brought an ache to my heart. As I watched with sad longing, a slow chill crept over me.

It had been so long since I watched or read a romance that I had forgotten what loving tenderness looked like. As I watched their tender love and admiration for each other, tears started to flow at the thought of my relationship with Ed. I realized I would never have that tender love; I would never have Ed's admiration. There would never be a Prince Charming for me.

Illusions wisped away, and the nightmare of my reality was revealed. I thought to myself, *The beast I'm married to is never going to turn into my prince. I have been trying to fix me for years, but the problem is not with me. It is with him. His love is an illusion; his abuse is reality.*

I was married for better or for worse, and I would have "worse"... for life.

I believed in my heart there was no escape.

That night, through my despair and misery, I sought comfort in food. But afterward through my panic and fear of the extra pounds, I discovered a solution. Bulimia became my friend.

It appeared to me that my battle to maintain the weight Ed required of me had just gained a powerful ally, a magical friend to help me cope with my struggles. I could now hide from the pain of my reality in the comfort of food without paying the consequences, the demeaning remarks from Ed every time I gained a couple pounds.

I delighted in it; I could eat all I wanted and never gain weight. I was elated, free at last in my secret life.

But it became much more than just a means to control weight. It became a lifeline. It seemed to anesthetize the pain and displace the agony of my thoughts. I felt like a child who had discovered a secret garden. I went there to cope, to escape, to self-soothe, to be free to choose, a respite from commands and consequences. It numbed my emotions, and I progressively withdrew from life into my secret garden. It was an ephemeral fog, a protective cocoon, a soft nothingness, an escape from the beast of abuse.

Years went by. Bulimia was still with me. It was a reprieve from Ed's oppression, but the beast was ever-present.

Ashley and Connor were four and seven. We outgrew our little house. We bought and moved into Ed's parents' farm home. They had semi-retired to their cottage on the lake.

Late one night I lay awake and listened. I could hear Ed and his brother, Mark, discussing the pipeline project on which Mark was the inspector. Ed was in the oil industry too, so their jargon was hard for me to follow. I mostly monitored the tone of the conversation. They were in the kitchen, but I could still hear them as I lay on the couch in the living room. It was 2:00 a.m., and I wished it were safe to go to sleep, but there were often fireworks between the two brothers.

We gave our bedroom to Mark and his new wife, Linda, who had come from the city to visit for the weekend. She had gone to bed. Her children, Shanna, sixteen, and Michael, twelve, were sleeping downstairs, and our children went to bed hours earlier.

The tone of the conversation in the kitchen changed. I stopped breathing and strained to listen. I heard Ed say, "So are you dating Linda's daughter too?"

An emotional mixture of shock and dread seeped into me as I thought, *Please don't let him have said what I think he said.*

It seemed like Ed was accusing Mark of having intentions towards the mother and the daughter. Mark had the same suspicion about Ed's comment.

"What are you implying?" Mark snapped. "Are you implying I'm sleeping with both of them? How sick are you to even think a thought like that!"

Ed threatened, "You better never have any thoughts of dating my daughter, or I'll kill you."

Ed was talking about Mark's stepdaughter and niece. Mark was justifiably enraged. It sounded like a fist connected with a jaw.

I was in the kitchen in an instant and saw Ed and Mark wrestling and yelling. I tried to stop Ed, but he shoved me aside. Then Mark was mad at Ed for how he was treating me. "You don't shove women around."

Ed's anger now turned to rage. "You don't tell me how to treat my wife."

Ed deliberately shoved me hard into the wall. Linda came into the kitchen at that point and took me in her arms and shielded me from Ed.

Ed yelled at me, "What the hell do you think you're doing? Get away from her."

"What am I supposed to do? Treat her the same way you treat your brother?" I said through my tears.

Mark tried to keep Ed away from me, and the wrestling started again. They fell down the stairs and put a hole in the wall. The wrestling abruptly stopped. Then they were just yelling at each other, and that gradually reduced to silent rage.

None of the children got up. They probably heard the noise but were too afraid to see what was happening. Ed stormed back through the kitchen, sending things flying as he made his way to the living room. He lay on the couch muttering curses.

Mark and Linda went down the hall to bed after a questioning look at me to see if I was all right. I nodded silently. I stood quietly in the dark kitchen until I heard Ed's deep, steady breathing. Hoping it was safe, I tiptoed in and lay down on the love seat. I dozed off and on, but I was too afraid to sleep.

The next morning Mark and Linda were up early. No one was speaking to Ed, and they hardly said anything to me as they knew it would only give Ed fuel for his anger.

I didn't offer them breakfast. I knew that it would anger Ed if I cooked for them. They quickly got ready and left with the two kids to go back to the city.

That morning after Ed went out, I explained to Ashley and Connor that their dad had said something that hurt Uncle Mark, that they had fought and that because I tried to stop the fight, Dad was mad at me.

I always explained to them why their dad was angry so that they didn't have to agonize over the unknown or mistakenly think that they had done something wrong. The Japanese have a saying, "Love the criminal; hate the crime." I often used this to help my children keep their dad's hurtful ways in a helpful perspective. Even though their dad did and said things that he shouldn't have, we could hate the things he did and still care about him as a person.

It was Friday, six days since Mark and Linda had left. I was expecting Ed's usual drunken state that happened every weekend, but I was more anxious than normal. He had not spoken to me since the previous weekend.

He had different types of silences. Sometimes he would not talk to me but would still tolerate my presence. This silence was the worst type. If I went into a room that he was in, he banged, broke, slammed or threw something. His expression was a mixture of loathing and anger. He purposely avoided eye contact; he looked past me or turned his back on me and stomped into another room. I got the message and avoided any room he was in. However, from experience, I knew that he expected me to periodically try to talk to him in case his anger had subsided and he wanted to say something to me.

I was busy cooking when I heard the dogs barking as the school bus stopped at our drive. Ashley was waiting for Connor as he came in the door.

Connor asked in a quiet voice, "Is Dad still mad at you?"

"I think so," I replied. The sadness and fear in their eyes as they looked up at me made me wish I had a different answer.

Ashley and Connor would use the information to monitor their behavior. They would stay out of Ed's way and be quiet to avoid antagonizing him further.

I was making stew and dumplings, one of Ed's favorite meals, and I was hoping he would eat with us tonight. As usual, all week I had supper ready when he got home from work, but all week he went straight into the living room to watch television. Each night, after I debated within myself a while, I would assume my most submissive demeanor and ask if he would like me to fix him a plate, but he would shove past me to go and stand looking out the dining room window until I left the living room. Then he would return to the couch.

I would fix him a plate anyway. Sometimes he left it untouched and sometimes it would end up on the floor. Maybe he ate in town after work. The kids ate alone. I would have a few bites as I put supper away but felt too vulnerable to eat with them. The safest action on my part was to do nothing, as anything I did was subject to insults and criticism later when he started speaking to me again.

Dinner was ready, and I went to check in the mirror to make sure there was nothing to draw criticism. My long brown hair was partially up in the style I finally found that drew the least insults. I had touched up my makeup a little earlier, and there were no pieces of lint on me. I am a small person and have never been overweight, but I had to wear shirts or sweaters that came past my waist and make sure they were pulled down in the back or I would hear the familiar "Fat ass." I thought I looked okay. I took a deep breath and went in the living room with Ashley and Connor.

I sat in the chair that allowed me to see down the road so I could watch for Ed's truck coming. In the distance, I saw the dust cloud from the gravel on the road move closer. Then the vehicle the dust was following came into view. My heart started pounding with fear. I moved to the top of the stairs to position myself to say "Hi" when he came in.

This was met with an icy stare. Then he said, "Why the hell didn't you water the horses? What the f—have you been doing all day?" I glanced out the window and saw the horses standing at the trough. My mind was so focused on Ed that I forgot to check the water trough. I saw them out in the field when I was preparing dinner, but now when I needed things to go right they had come for water as if to prove Ed's point of my incompetence.

I stumbled to get my jacket. "I'll go do it right now."

As I shrank past him, I heard him mumble "Stupid bitch" under his breath.

When I came back in the house, I found Ed at the kitchen window with a plate of stew. I took this as a good sign, even though I was uncomfortable knowing he had been watching me.

The fact that he ate supper this evening, as well as the few disdainful insults, indicated that his stage of punishing silence was over. It implied that I was now to stay in whichever room he was in instead of leaving it, so that I was present when he chose to lash out. His change in tactics could mean either he was ready to "forgive" me if I showed the proper contriteness for my "misbehavior" or he was preparing for confrontation to expound his justification, elevate himself and debase everyone else involved, for which I would be the scapegoat.

By eight o'clock, the kids were in bed. As I tucked each of them in and kissed them good night I tried to reassure them that their dad would probably be in a better mood tomorrow.

Other than the few comments when he came home, he had not spoken to me. The crack of the ice cube tray assaulted my senses as shards of ice scattered on the counter. He chose several cubes and dropped them into the whiskey and cola he just poured. This made seven since he got home from work. The empty tray clattered into the sink. Like a whipped dog, I watched him yet avoided eye contact.

"So did you and Mark have fun together talking about his new girlfriends?"

The accusation came out harsh and sarcastic. His eyes were narrowed and so were his lips. His look made me feel exposed and vulnerable, like a rabbit must feel when the shadow of the hawk passes over it. My tension and fear increased as I sensed that the direction he had chosen would escalate to a fight, not a transition to forgiveness.

How would I answer? My instinct was to deny the implied lies and defend my actions, yet I knew this could be turned around and used against me. He was intolerant of challenges to his words or behavior. I knew I could not keep silent or he would pretend he had struck on the truth.

I tested the waters and said, "I never spoke to him except to say bye to all of them. I think he misunderstood what you meant about Shanna."

"Shut up, you stupid bitch. You 'think'? You don't know how to think. They're f— all living in the same house. You're so f— stupid. Why don't you go and join them?"

I wanted to shrivel up and disappear. Now I knew his question was a setup. I also knew that I already gave him the ammunition he hoped for to launch into an attack on me. There was nothing I could say, at that point, that would diffuse the situation. I dropped my eyes; I dropped my head and sat silent, motionless—I burrowed deeper and deeper inside my dark internal tunnel. The constriction around my heart hurt; the lump in my throat hurt; the force of the waves of ugly words that crashed over me hurt.

The fight-or-flight response had another element in my case: freezing. I couldn't fly; escape was impossible. Fighting was not in me and would only enflame his fury. So I froze.

He put his boots and coat on, came back and poured another drink. He made the silent statement "I'm going to the bar…Go ahead and say something about drinking and driving and see what happens."

He grabbed the truck keys off the counter and turned towards the door. I put my hand on his arm and pleaded with him not to drink and drive. I tried to reason with him, but he shoved me aside and headed for the stairs. I ran past and stood in front of him, trying to get him to stay. He shoved me into the wall, yelled and called me disgusting names, criticized everything about me, searched for the words that would hurt me the most.

Fear gripped my being. My stomach tensed, and I huddled into myself, trying to disappear as tears flowed and I thought, *Am I really those foul degrading words I hear him calling me? He's right about my stupidity; I never learn. I'm always the catalyst for these explosions of torment. How do I solve it? How do I stop it? The agony and desolation is relentless. How do I escape?*

Time seemed to stand still as a thought seeped into my mind. *I know a way to escape.* I turned and raced up the stairs to the washroom, locking the door behind me. *I shouldn't have run. Now he knows something is unusual.* I hurried and swallowed several pills before he reached the door.

He yelled, "Open the door or I'll kick it in."

What do I do? I looked at the pill package. I looked in the mirror and saw terror and despair staring back at me. Tears streamed down my face. I felt the pain in my chest from the ache of my heart. Sobs came from the depth of my soul. A separate part of me saw my face through his eyes; my eyes were red from crying. The tears trailed mascara down my cheeks, and my hair had come loose, but it was mostly my expression of anguish that made me look ugly. He hated me looking ugly. The worse I looked, the worse he treated me. He was not going to like what he saw if I opened the door. *I'm scared. What do I do?*

He banged on the door, and I jumped with fear. I opened the door. He stood there looking at me, anger, disgust and disdain etched around his mouth, piercing from his eyes. He turned to the bedroom door behind him and told our daughter, Ashley, then age four, to get up; he went to our son's room and woke him. Connor was seven.

With the children standing beside him, he said, "This is what happens if you try and kill yourself."

I saw his rage and his hand coming at me. I felt the blow to my head, and I fell backwards. The blows kept coming, and I seemed to be in another world, unable to comprehend that I was being beaten instead of comforted. I did not understand. I saw Ashley's feet run back to her room. I felt blow after blow.

I could not get up because of the barrage of blows, but I saw Connor pushing on Ed's leg as he repeated "Daddy, don't hurt Mommy. Daddy, don't hurt Mommy." I was amazed at the courage in his little heart, but Ed was oblivious to him.

Ed finally stopped and left me there. I lay there stunned for a while. Then I went into each of the children's rooms to let them know I was okay. Then I went in our room and curled in a ball on the bed. I was beyond tears or fear. I was drained and numb. I closed my eyes and rocked myself. Shame filled me as I thought of my children left with Ed to raise them without me. How could I have been so selfish? What was I going to do?

I was startled from my cocoon as my wrist was yanked and I was dragged off the bed onto the floor and down the hall to the kitchen. Ed did not say anything as he left me there on the floor and went to stand by the window on the other side of the table. I got to my feet and stood by the sink, thankful that the counter and table were between us. His silence was oppressive. I stood and waited as questions went through my mind. *Am I supposed to do something? Am I suppose to apologize, explain? Why did he drag me out here?*

I had no strength for any more confrontation, so I stayed quiet and still. My head hurt from the blows. I heard the clock above my head tick the seconds by. It was dark outside, and I saw the reflection of his face in the window. I saw his eyes looking at me, so I quickly stared at the floor. I was so tired that I sank to the floor and lay on the rug. Footsteps stomped closer, and, as I looked up, he grabbed my wrist again and dragged me around the floor until I stumbled to my feet. He let go and resumed his position by the window.

I understood what was happening. He was not going to let me go to sleep, because he did not know how many pills I took. As long as I was awake, he knew I was alive. I dreaded the sleepless hours still to endure before the night was over.

My mind could not fathom why he chose to beat me instead of being moved with compassion for me trying to commit suicide. Then I realized I was not allowed to escape his dungeon. The beating was a lesson to never try it again. My life did not belong to me. I was his possession, and he decided if I was to live or die.

A couple of hours went by. Ed had not talked or moved from looking out the window. I was still by the sink, but standing there was agony. To rest my feet, I decided to chance sitting up on the counter and leaning against the cupboards.

I saw his reflection look back at me from the window. The anger was gone from his face. "You can go lie on the couch. It's been long enough, so you're probably okay."

The fear seeped away as I sensed the change in his mood, and with relief I slid off the counter and moved to the couch in the living room. Ed brought the blanket my mom had made me from off our bed and covered me up. He sat in the chair beside me and said, "I don't want to lose you. Why did you do that?"

Since he was showing concern for me, I chanced an explanation. "Your drinking scares me, and the way you treat me hurts so much. I try hard to do things right, and when I do something wrong, it's a mistake. It's not intentional. You never see any good in me. You are always looking for the bad. I feel worthless and hopeless."

He took my hand and said, "Give me some time. Be patient with me. It's never too late to start all over again."

We eventually went to bed, and the next morning he brought me coffee in bed and asked how I felt. Since I was fine, he suggested we take the kids to the provincial park at the lake and take the dogs for a walk. The kids were happy with this, but I knew that it was the fact that their father was no longer angry that pleased them more than the outing.

Ed's manner and conversation was relaxed, so the kids and I felt safe in letting our guard down. We all enjoyed the sun and the water although it was too cold out for any of us, except the dogs, to go swimming.

He drank less than usual that day, sticking to beer and leaving the hard liquor alone. The next night, he took us out for supper, and Monday he brought me flowers when he came home from work. He had never bought me flowers before, and so I was hopeful that maybe this time he would follow through on his promise to change.

The next Tuesday evening, supper was over and I was cleaning the kitchen. I heard Ed come in from the garage. I had worked for three hours cleaning it, and I had been waiting with happy anticipation for Ed's pleased response.

He yelled from the door, "What the hell did you do with my drill?"

My happiness drained out as the familiar fear and sadness oozed back in. "I put all the power tools in the cabinet. I thought they would be easier to find if they were all together." I was hopeful he would appreciate my reasoning.

"You thought? You never think, you stupid bitch."

Years later, it was once again in the small hours of the morning when I lay listening, this time for the ATV to drive into the yard. Ed had gone to his friend's down the road to drink. He took the ATV instead of the truck in case the police tried to stop him for drinking and driving. If they did, he could take off across the fields to get away.

I had been in bed for hours but not sleeping when I heard the sound of an unfamiliar vehicle outside, so I got up and put on a tracksuit over my pajamas. There was a knock on the door. I looked through the peephole to see who was outside. Standing in the light was a lady, Jill, who worked in the lounge. I opened the door to see a man standing beside her, holding Ed up. There was blood running down Ed's face.

"We found him lying on the road. It is so foggy and dark we almost drove over him. We didn't see him till the last minute. The ATV he was riding is back there in the ditch," said Jill.

I brought Ed in the house and sat him on the bottom step, and I turned back to Jill. "Thank you, Jill, for helping him. I think I had better take him to the hospital. I won't worry about the trike in the ditch until tomorrow."

Jill looked concerned. "Are you sure you'll be okay? We can go with you if you like."

Shaking my head, I said, "That's considerate of you, but I think we'll be okay."

Thankfully, Connor and Ashley were at their grandparents' for the week. I knew Ed needed to go to the hospital, but I was afraid I would have trouble convincing him.

I said quietly to Ed, "You are lucky to be alive. The hole in your forehead is quite bad. We need to get your wounds stitched right away in order to prevent scarring."

He cared about his appearance. He looked at me as if he had done something wrong and quietly agreed. I got a wet cloth to put on the wound, grabbed my coat and keys and helped him out into the truck. But as soon as I started driving he got belligerent.

"I'm not goin' anywhere. What the hell did you let them in for, you stupid bitch? Go back and get the trike key. We're not leaving it in the ditch."

I kept driving, and I did not respond to his swearing and shoving, hoping he would stop. Finally, we got to the hospital. Once he was around the nurses, he started to behave better.

It took forty stitches for the doctor to close the wounds to his forehead, lip and hip. The nurses gave me instructions on how to clean the wounds to remove dirt and dead skin. The wounds were full of gravel, and they said it would take time to get it all out. By the time we left the hospital, Ed was sober and it was dawn.

As we drove home, I wondered about the harvesting. Ed was in the middle of swathing, cutting the grain, and I knew that with the stitches and scrapes on his face he should not be out in the dust. I would have to learn to swath.

I let him sleep for a while. Then I bathed and cleaned his wounds and brought him mushroom soup to help him get over his hangover.

Later that day, I suggested maybe it would be better if I swathed instead of him, in order to keep his wounds clean. Before the children were born, he would have me ride with him all day on the farm equipment, so I had a good idea of what to do. I had driven the tractor for years and thought the swather could not be that different.

Ed agreed and gave me instructions on what to do. So the next morning I put on my coveralls and drove out to the swather left in the field from the day of the accident. After checking the oil in the engine and the water in the radiator, I climbed up the ladder to the deck of the swather, about four feet off the ground, turned the key and pushed the button to start it. It fired to life and I revved it up a little, engaged the knives and the belts, put it in gear and finished revving it up. I set the table high enough to avoid hitting the rocks. Hanging on to the knob on the steering wheel, I swung into the grain and began my journey around the field.

An hour or so went by and things seemed to be going well when I saw a cloud of dust coming across the field. It was our truck and it was moving fast, meaning Ed was mad. I stopped the swather, stood on the deck, and waited, wishing I could disappear.

The truck skidded to a stop. Ed jumped out and stormed over to the swather. Before I knew what had happened, he grabbed my arm and yanked me off the swather. As I lay in the dirt looking up at him, I heard him yelling and swearing about what I was doing wrong, and it seemed to come from another world.

Viciousness and filth poured out of him. Because of the damage from the accident, his face had swollen to twice its normal size, his wounds were red and seeping, and the black stitches crisscrossed above his eye and down from his mouth. I felt like a bystander watching a scene from a horror show. It was like a curtain lifted; the disguise was removed, and the beast was exposed.

AND THE THUNDER ROLLED

What I fear most is power with impunity.
I fear abuse of power, and the power to abuse.
Isabel Allende

STATISTICS
Violent crimes against women committed by intimate partners increased in the United States from 389,100 in 2005 to 554,260 in 2007.[1]

In Canada, every six days a woman is killed by her intimate partner.[2]

SOMETHING TO KEEP IN MIND

The United Nations Declaration on the Elimination of Violence against Women (1993) defines violence against women as "any act of gender-based violence that results in, or is likely to result in, physical, sexual or psychological harm or suffering to women, including threats of such acts, coercion or arbitrary deprivation of liberty, whether occurring in public or in private life."[3]

ABUSE: THE ACTION OF THE IDEOLOGY

The abuser entices us into his castle with the honeymoon phase of the abuse cycle. Then he slowly draws up the drawbridge, isolating us from friends and family. He has us captive, caught up in his ideology. As it evolves, we descend further into the depths of his fortress—into the dungeons and torture chambers.

In chapter 2, we talked about the abuser's ideal world and the creation of his ideology to achieve this illusion. The abuser's thoughts, emotions and actions correspond to the beliefs, rhetoric and language, and the rules and retribution, of his ideology. His thoughts and assumptions revolve around his illusion of his ideal world. These thoughts generate his emotions, and his emotions produce his language and behavior.

NOTE: Please see appendix A for precautions while still with the abuser.

This is the system of his ideology. The emotional and behavioral aspects of the ideology fashion the accuser and abuser—the rule enforcer.

When the world is not in line with his expectations, what he believes he is entitled to, his thoughts start stoking the fire of his anger. Unfulfilled expectations are a major trigger for his anger. In order to correct the situation, he feels he is justified in implementing his enforcement system to adjust our beliefs and behavior. We are the ones not in line with his expectations. He uses his abusive words and actions to put us back in line and to keep us in line.

Being *king of his castle,* he does not consider his actions abusive. Justification is a cornerstone of his ideology. He believes he is justified in using any measures he sees fit to transform us into his ideal partner. He spins the illusion that the abuse is for our own good or because of his extreme love for us or deserved, convincing us that he knows better than we, or anyone else, what is best for us.

The abuser's belief in his entitlement is at the root of his behavior. Since he believes we are his possession—he owns us—he believes he is entitled to treat us as he wishes. The moment for confrontation is decided, and the abuse tactic is chosen. The abuser has a repertoire of abusive tactics that he implements, sometimes predetermined and sometimes adapted to opportunities that present themselves.

Our actions or comments are triggers for his violence. He could start with an accusation, a criticism, an impossible or unreasonable demand. He waits for us to defend ourselves or question his request, which gives him the opportunity to escalate the confrontation, manipulating the accusations to keep us confused, frightened and hurt. Our hurt stems from the injustice of his treatment and devaluation of us.

> *A common tactic of the abuser is to twist reality so that blame always lies with us.*

The abuser will monitor his words and actions like a boxer, conscious of the timing, rhythm and intensity of each round. His apparent loss of control is an illusion created to excuse his behavior and make it appear that we are at fault for triggering his temper. To gain and maintain control over us requires the abuser to be very much in control of himself and the situation.

Subtle things reveal his self-control: he chooses what to destroy, where and when to "lose" control. Even his control over the noise level of his attack doesn't seem to fit with losing control.

A common tactic of the abuser is to twist reality so that blame always lies with us, reinforcing his superior position in the relationship. He twists expressions such as *It takes two to fight, If you hadn't...,* and *It's because I love you so much* in order to create an illusion, to shift blame to us, to cause confusion and excuse his behavior. In the fights he generates, there is a victim and an aggressor, so there are two people involved; however, there are not two aggressors, as he implies. He chooses to go into a rage with no help from us, and he can calm down just as quickly if the situation warrants. (In many countries, police are now required to determine the initiator when responding to domestic violence calls.)

The abuser often creates limits to his behavior. He will have a concept of behaviors that he considers abusive, and as long as he does not go to that extent, he does not believe he is abusive. Some believe an open hand is okay but a fist is not; some believe hitting anywhere except the head is okay; others believe any abuse except physical is acceptable. However, along the way he becomes desensitized to his current abusive behavior, so he keeps pushing the limits a little further.

Satisfaction requires an escalation of the abuse as the status quo fails to fulfill. He adjusts his justifications, he moves the lines of the limits, and he extends the boundaries of his behavior to achieve compliance. Gratifying his desires through our compliance reinforces the abuser's behavior, and the illusions perpetuate themselves. His successes build his confidence, and the intoxication of power and control leaves him craving more.

The abuser has different beliefs than we do concerning the purpose of the relationship. He believes our role is to satisfy his desires and assumes this is what we should or do believe as well. To us, the relationship is to love, care for and respect each other, believing this is what he should or does believe as well. Therefore, as we interact, events, behaviors and motives are far from what is expected from both parties. He uses aggression to create the reality that he desires, leaving us confused and victimized. We struggle to make sense of and fall in line with his expectations with our thoughts, emotions and behavior.

We apply our own perceptions and reasoning as we attempt to discover a solution. We somehow hope he will have compassion on us and be remorseful for his behavior if we can reveal to him, by some means, the injustice of his actions. Because abusers do not think the way we think, we cannot look to him to discover logical reasons for his behavior or logical patterns to adapt to—he purposely avoids consistency to keep us off balance and off guard.

Compassionate humanity's understanding of logic, justice and mercy is irrelevant to an abuser within the abusive relationship. He creates his own form of logic, his own rules of justice. Mercy is a foreign concept where we are concerned. Devaluing the abused is one of his goals; in his eyes, we do not deserve mercy or compassion. Since he believes he is entitled to treat us as he does, to him there is no relevance in our reasoning as we try to illuminate the truth of the mistreatment. He cannot comprehend the truth.

EXPLOSIVE EMOTIONS

Anger is the ever-present tyrant, the oppressor, the torturer. Even when times seem to be calm, our fear is always there. We know his anger is not gone. It is lurking submerged and will inevitably explode to the surface when we least expect it. Therefore, our vigilance is ceaseless. A better understanding of the abuser's anger will reduce our vulnerability.

We think of emotions as feelings, which they are, but they operate biologically. Biologically, anger produces the need for more anger. Emotions release peptides from the pituitary gland, differently shaped peptides for different emotions. These peptides fit into receptors on our cells. When an emotion is experienced on a continuous basis, more receptors for that specific emotion are created on cells, and receptors for other emotions are reduced. The cells call for the release of peptides according to their receptors. The more anger that is experienced, the more anger receptors are created, which demand more anger in order to release more peptides, and a self-perpetuating cycle is set up. (This is also true on the part of the abused as the cycle of fear is established.)

According to University of Alabama psychologist Dolf Zillmann, "A universal trigger for anger is the sense of being endangered...[which] can be signaled...by a symbolic threat to self-esteem or dignity:...being frustrated in pursuing an important goal."[4] Therefore, we threaten the abuser's dignity and identity as "king" when we are not subservient and submissive. We also frustrate his goal of molding us into his ideal partner. Part of his image includes a perfect spouse. Our noncompliance endangers his identity.

Zillmann also discovered in his experiments that the surge of motivation and drive resulting from perceptions of endangerment "has a dual effect on the brain." First, the burst of adrenaline transforms the anger to rage for an initial outburst. Then, second, it places the nervous system in a state of readiness that lasts much longer (hours or days) where small stimulus will trigger the anger again. We are familiar with this process. We watch the abuser's minor acts of aggression escalate his anger to progressively greater levels of intensity until it reaches a violent rage that refuses to be diffused through the intellect. Zillmann also states, "During rage, the abuser experiences illusions of power and invulnerability."

The constant production of adrenaline becomes addictive. According to Larry Meadows, "The intensity of life becomes more vital than [its] quality. That, in sum, is Adrenaline Addiction."[5]

Another biological aspect that makes anger so desirable to the abuser is the release of endorphins—the natural brain chemical that makes us feel good—after the adrenaline dissipates.

Concern about consequences disappears through the self-justification process. Part of the justification is the abuser's belief that he is above the law where his property, including us, is concerned; he is a law unto himself. No one, including the police or courts, can tell him how to act in his own house or how to treat his property. Therefore, distraction or diversion, rather than reason, in the early stage of anger is the best hope of averting the rage. Turning his thoughts to another subject may possibly cut off the transition into violence.

> *According to Larry Meadows, "The intensity of life becomes more vital than its quality."*

BATTERED AND BELEAGUERED: THE ABUSE CYCLE

The abuser's behavioral cycle is connected to his emotional cycle. It begins with a state of normalcy. Then tension begins to build as he starts to criticize and insult us. The frequency and severity of the incidents in this phase gradually increase until he reaches a tipping point, at which time the abuser explodes into the violent form of his abusive behavior.

After the explosion comes the "honeymoon" phase; a time of treating us with care and consideration and a time of possible remorse for his actions. At the same time, he is promising never to do it again. He is giving his justification to excuse his behavior—his love for us caused it, or we pushed him to it.

He has several purposes for the honeymoon phase. By minimizing the abusive attack, he creates confusion, causing us to doubt our perceptions. He also uses the honeymoon phase to reward our compliance, implying that our good behavior will prevent further explosions of abuse. The honeymoon phase interrupts any thought we have of leaving or seeking help. It also prevents the abuser from being accountable for his actions.

Tactics the abuser uses during the honeymoon phase, such as acts of kindness, promises to change, revealing a vulnerable side or sharing how others mistreated him, keep our hopes alive. Even the absence of abuse when we expect it gives us a ray of hope. If he feels we may leave, he will use the honeymoon phase to convince us to stay or to convince us not to seek outside aid.

The abusive cycle is similar to the abuser playing both the roles of "bad cop, good cop." He plays the bad cop to intimidate us into compliance and the good cop to trap us with deception.

Domestic violence violates human rights. Domestic violence is any treatment that is harmful to us. Often, women feel that abuse only entails physical mistreatment. However, all forms of abuse do damage. The abuser uses abuse to establish and maintain his power and control and to satisfy his anger cravings. He desires our compliance, as it stokes his sense of power. He is able to continue exercising his authority and power by constantly changing his rules and requirements. In his mind, he is then justified in accusing us of "disobeying" them and deserving the abuse. It does not matter how compliant we become; it will not stop the abuse. In fact, it usually escalates.

THE TYRANNY: TYPES OF ABUSE

Power and control, through oppression, are the main objectives of the abuser. However, there is a vast array of abusive

> *Power and control, through oppression, are the main objectives of the abuser.*

behaviors that can achieve that objective. We quite often think of abuse solely in physical terms. However, the psychological damage from abuse is more debilitating. Threatened abuse can be explicit ("I'll kill you if…"), implied ("People who mess with me pay for it"), or demonstrated through destructive behavior to other things or people, sending us the message that we could be next (putting his fist through the wall). Dividing abuse into the following categories will help clarify them: economic, emotional, physical, psychological and social.

Economic

When the abuser controls our ability to generate our own income or restricts our finances, he is abusing us economically and reinforcing our dependence on him.

Financial

When the abuser takes control of all the family money, he is financially abusing us. He may conceal joint assets, waste the family money, run up debt in our name, not allow our involvement in financial decision-making or make us ask for money. He will indulge his desires at the expense of ours. Keeping us financially impoverished or financially dependent on him inhibits our ability to leave him.

The abuser may try to stop us from working or force us to work to supply him with money. He can make it impossible for us to get a job by forbidding us to upgrade our education, denying transportation, preventing us from sleeping, leaving no time to work because of his demands or instilling fear of abuse if we try to get a job. He may sabotage our ability to keep a job by calling us frequently during the day or coming to our place of work unannounced. By preventing us from earning income, he takes away our power and keeps us under his control.

Emotional

All abuse categories, not just the ones in this section, will affect our emotional state. They instill fear and humiliation. They strip us of our self-esteem and self-confidence and leave us brokenhearted.

Verbal

Abusers use their choice of words and their method of delivery to wound and scar. Verbal abuse is limitless, but some examples include:

- unwarranted accusations
- name-calling
- profanity
- sarcasm
- ridiculing
- insulting us, family and friends
- belittling
- demeaning
- teasing
- objectifying
- criticizing
- embarrassing

Many accusations are used to eliminate any thoughts we may have of leaving. When the abuser accuses us of being an unfit mother, it is to instill the fear of losing the children. He attacks our intelligence and competence to undermine our belief that we have the ability to support our children and ourselves. He convinces us that we are undesirable and worthless to instill the belief that no one else would value us. The pain of the verbal abuse erodes our energy, well-being, self-esteem and self-confidence.

Interrogation

Abusers often question us for hours—often the same question over and over. They question us about our real or assumed actions and opinions or the actions or words of others toward us. The questioner holds the power; the one answering is the one in submission. Therefore, the answer to the question is not what they are looking for. It is our submission they want, and the longer the questioning goes on, the more powerful they feel. Also, the longer they question us, the more fuel they gather for their anger.

Intimidation

Intimidation is meant, as the name implies, to instill timidity and frighten us into submission or compliance. The abuse generates hopelessness, apprehension and demoralization. The abuser intimidates us with facial expressions, tone of voice, gestures, destructive behavior, frightening stories and threats.

Humiliation

Demeaning behavior, ridicule and criticism towards us embarrass and devalue us, especially when done in front of others. Forcing us to do or say things against our will also humiliates us.

Coercion

Coercion is using force or fear to gain compliance. Abusing us for a certain behavior coerces us to refrain from doing it again. Threatening to report us to police, child welfare, our employer or other organizations or institutions is another form of coercion to gain our compliance.

Objectification

The abuser belittles us to convince himself and us that we are inferior and worthless and therefore subhuman—an object. He believes this entitles him to treat us as he pleases. He desires some parts of us, hates other parts and never recognizes us as a whole person—body, mind and spirit—with inherent human rights.

Physical

Bodily Harm

Physical abuse includes pushing, pulling, slapping, hitting, kicking, punching, throwing things, restraining, hair pulling, choking, biting, burning, using weapons against, tying up, locking in or out, preventing sleep, withholding food, denying medical help, denying privacy, and anything else that is physically endangering, damaging, disrespectful or forced. Even a simple shove is assault.

Sexual

In the abuser's mind your body belongs to him. Therefore, he expects you to comply with his sexual desires. Sexual abuse includes rape, physically attacking your sexual parts, forcing or expecting sex after abuse, and intentionally inflicting pain during sex. However, it also includes forcing you to perform sex acts you do not want to do, unwanted sexual touching, harassment, controlling reproductive decisions, withholding sex to punish, making you feel obligated to have sex to avoid abuse, treating you like a sex object, forcing any act that is degrading, having an obsession with pornography or having an affair.

Psychological

Our psychological reprogramming is high on the abuser's agenda. At my first meeting with my counselor she asked, as a starting point, what my core values were, what my bottom line was. I sat thinking for a long time, but ultimately I could not think of even one.

At first, I thought that it was to protect my children, but as I thought about that, I questioned if that could be true if I was willing to commit suicide, causing them pain and leaving them for my abusive partner to raise. Either our values, beliefs and opinions disappear through our abuser's enforced ideology, or we bury them too deep to access.

All abuse has a detrimental effect on our minds, but it is the abuser's intent to use tactics in this category to undermine our psychological well-being and attack our values and beliefs.

Mental

Attacks on your mind include threats by the abuser to kill or harm your children, you, himself, or your pets, to damage property, friendships or relationships. It also includes threats intended to instill helplessness, to convince you that you are an immoral, lazy, stupid slob who deserves the abuse, who is his possession. He ridicules your opinions, values or beliefs and elevates his own—expecting you to affirm him.

He plays mind games to undermine your sanity. He denies the facts and your reality, causing confusion; he challenges your reasoning and actions. He vaguely alludes to knowledge of something you have done in attempts to draw out a confession of something unknown to him. You feel he is watching your every move, that he has eyes everywhere.

The abuser dominates your thoughts. Mainstays in the abuser's repertoire are endless rules that apply only to you and that you have no part in negotiating, along with ceaseless interrogation. The abuse desensitizes you, warps your sense of what you think is normal, and your mental health descends into a dark abyss.

Silence

Abusers often use silence to abuse us. They withdraw acknowledgement that we exist. It is paradoxical that this is abuse. It should bring us a measure of peace, and yet we know it is meant as punishment. We know that it signifies that they are very angry with us. Cutting off communication isolates us. Their silence manipulates our behavior as we try various means to placate them. It is once again about power; only they have the power to end the silence.

Responsibility

An inordinate amount of responsibility is placed on us while an inordinate amount of freedom is taken as his right. Every unpleasant task is ours. Every household task is ours. The children's behavior is our responsibility. So are filling out forms, doing errands, paying bills, scheduling, answering the phone, caring for pets, fetching things. The list is endless.

Minimizing

When the abuser minimizes and denies his abuse, we hear:
- Accept it without criticism.
- You are not capable of appropriate discernment.
- You are overly sensitive.
- There is nothing wrong with his behavior.

Placing blame on us exonerates him and punishes us for speaking against him.

Dismissive

Abusers are dismissive. Ignoring our efforts, our feelings, our comments and our questions reinforces the message of our insignificance and their importance. They often uses this in public as a way of telling us to keep quiet; we are to be seen and not heard, and we will later pay for speaking out.

Threats

The abuser uses actual and implied threats. The threats can be verbal, sent through body language or implied through behavior towards property or other people. Destroying property or hurting pets sends us the message that we could be next. Handling weapons while staring at us or reckless driving that frightens us demonstrates that our lives are in their hands.

Stalking

Stalking is an insidious form of abuse that has debilitating psychological effects. It elevates the abuser's sense of power over us, creating fear and a sense of helplessness in us. The most common time for the abuser to use stalking is after a breakup of the relationship, but he also uses aspects of it to keep us under surveillance. The abuser can stalk us himself or by using various channels of communication or technology. It can be done to us, our friends and family or our property; it can include behavior designed to manipulate us into connecting with the abuser.

Stalking's power lies in our fear of the unknown. If stalking is added to the abuser's tactics, we have to consciously monitor our every move and word even while away from him. Evidence of our breaking his rules is a trigger for his anger, and stalking is one of the tools he may use to collect the evidence.

Setups

The abuser will often try to set you up by suggesting an opinion or action, and if you fall for the bait, he has fuel for his abuse. He claims he is testing you and he "gives you enough rope to hang yourself." When he intentionally sets you up for failure, it has a double-negative effect; you are hurt by his deception and subsequent abuse for your failure, and you feel stupid that you fell into the trap.

Social
Isolation

The first act of an attacking army is to take out the adversary's line of communication. That is what the abuser does with us. He denies or discourages our contact with others, especially anyone who could support us, such as friends and family; he restricts who we can see and talk to, where we can go. He monitors and regulates mail, phone and Internet use. To accomplish this, the abuser uses the other forms of abuse: economic, emotional, physical, and psychological.

Extreme Jealousy

The abuser's extreme jealousy is a constant catalyst for his anger. His jealousy is unreasonable and usually unjustified. He expects us to cut ourselves off from half of the population of the world—males—and ensure that they have no contact with us, punishing us if this is not adhered to. He will contrive circumstances to create the opportunity to drive home the message that we are his possession.

Defamation of Character

The abuser will often lie to others about us, trying to limit our options and weaken our support network. It is intended to isolate us from friends and family and may cost us our jobs. It increases our vulnerability, helplessness and dependence on him.

Social Superiority/Male Privilege

The abuser believes in his superiority. He uses a double standard. He believes his role as a male elevates him above the rules and expectations he puts on us. He may use race or economic status to assume privileges denied to us. In his mind, his superior social status is justification for his abuse of us. Our patriarchal society, with its male dominance, reinforces his belief of superiority.

Relationship

When you are in an abusive relationship, all your relationships are sources of stress. Your relationship with the abuser is dysfunctional. To understand dysfunction, it may be easier to explain what a functional relationship is. People in healthy relationships support, nurture, challenge, respectfully communicate with and strengthen each other. The dysfunction of the abusive relationship undermines all of your other relationships.

The abuser uses relationships as avenues of abuse. His infidelity is a way for him to damage the relationship. He abuses your relationship with your children by using them to send you messages, turning your children against you by criticizing you or telling lies about you, threatening to take the children away from you and convincing you that you are a bad parent. He tries to sabotage your relationships with friends and family. The previous description of isolation includes other examples of how and why he damages your relationships.

System

Abusers use institutions to reinforce their power. They may selectively interpret religious writings to justify their subservient expectations and treatment of us. If there is a separation, they may violate restraining orders or child custody agreements, use child visitation to harass or harm the children or us. They may misuse the legal system to circumvent justice by telling lies about us to police, counselors or the courts. They can use tax systems or banking systems to control us.

Spiritual Abuse

Our faith may be a threat to the abusers' domination of us. Since they want complete control and ownership of us, they will oppose our allegiance to God and our recognition of his higher power. Abusers will not want the religious community's support system to be available to us. Therefore, they denigrate it and us for believing in it. They will use abuse to break down our belief system and prevent us from pursuing spiritual growth. They will cut us off from this source of strength and support.

The Tyrant: Types of Abusers

Abusers do not use all of the abusive tactics. There are different types of abusers, and they pick and choose abuse tactics that fit their persona. In his book *Why Does He Do That? Inside the Minds of Angry and Controlling Men,* Lundy Bancroft gives ten broad types of abusers, summarized as follows:

1. The Demand Man—characterized by his exaggerated all-encompassing needs (never yours) and your exaggerated all-encompassing responsibilities (including his).
2. Mr. Right—characterized by his belief in his superior intellect (that he should be praised for) and your inferior one (that you should be punished for).
3. Water Torturer—delivers relentless emotional and psychological assaults in a low-emotion, carefully thought-out manner.
4. The Drill Sergeant—exerts extreme control from head to toe, monitors every move and every word, escalates to physical violence.
5. Mr. Sensitive—has an introspective, gentle, fragile and supportive facade to cover a needy, dismissive, blaming bully.
6. The Player—is a womanizer.
7. Rambo—is aggressive, arrogant, violent.
8. The Victim—has contempt of women; "Women have done me wrong."
9. The Terrorist—believes your life is his, that women are evil and need to be terrorized.
10. Mentally ill or addicted—e.g., paranoid, psychopathic, narcissistic, alcoholic, drug addict; can be any of the types listed; there is an increased chance of dangerous abuse.[6]

Extreme Identity Theft

Abuse is the most extreme form of identity theft. The abuser warps the essence of who we are. We gradually cease to exist; our identity disappears as we modify our essence to avoid the abuse. When we consume an apple, it ceases to exist as an apple and now becomes part of our identity. The abuser consumes us. We become an extension of his identity; we become an entity designed by his desire to magnify his identity.

> *We gradually cease to exist; our identity disappears as we modify our essence to avoid the abuse.*

The abuser's control of us covers every aspect of who we are, from the stray hairs on our heads to the shape of the toenails on our feet and everything in between. He emphasizes our insignificance by coercing us to dress ultra-conservatively. Alternatively, by emphasizing our beauty or sexuality, he flaunts his trophy. His desire is to control how we walk, how we talk, how much we weigh, how we breathe, how we sleep, where we go, what we see, what we hear, who we talk to, what we eat, what we feel, what we read, what we think, what we do, how we do it, and when we do it.

The lists of abuse for the categories of abusers are quite extensive, but they are not all-inclusive, as abusers can transform almost anything into abuse. Just as the abuse can be physical, emotional, psychological, economical or social, the damage the abuse causes encompasses these same categories. Some physical damage is visible or obvious, such as cuts, contusions and breaks, and some physical damage is internal to the organs or brain. All of the various types of abuse cause us emotional pain, in the moment and ongoing. Unrelenting abuse, of any kind, over an extended period eventually causes psychological damage. Our isolation damages our social relationships, and the abuser's control over our finances, assets and careers damages our economic strength.

We undergo annihilation. He consumes us. He gradually kills off parts of our actual identity, replacing them with his ideals. His control is slowly murdering us until, in some cases, he achieves the ultimate control of our lives by taking it.

ENLIGHTENMENT

When we connect the dots of the abuser's ideology—his unrealistic beliefs, his illogical rhetoric, his extreme emotions and his cruel enforcement—we discover the purpose of his abuse and insight into his agenda. Our compliance then becomes a matter of self-preservation while we remain in the relationship, rather than an attempt to discover a solution. We understand that the problem does not lie within us but within the abuser, and nothing we do or say will change him.

When we know the tricks of the illusionist, we are no longer fooled. As we become aware of the abuser's tricks and tactics, it will be easier for us to protect ourselves from them. One of the best ways to begin this is to resist the temptation to defend ourselves. Logic is irrelevant to the abuser, and defending our actions will only give him more fuel to use against us. So disconnect mentally and emotionally.

Staying calm, expressing no challenge to him, either verbally or by body language, helps to disarm him. In general, if you can, keep your comments minimal or nonexistent.

Change the subject to something good about him to put him off balance. Mention a weakness in yourself that is not a soft spot for you or make up a weakness, in order to distract his focus to harmless areas. For example, suppose you are weeding the flower garden when he comes home from work early and he says, "If those plants are going to keep you from having supper ready when I get home, I'm going to rip them all out!"

You could say, as you look down a little surprised at the plants and leave what you are doing, "Yeah, you're right. You always have such a good sense of time. I should watch and learn from you."

He'll probably come back with another softer attack, and you could say, "Yeah, I'm not quick enough to catch on to those kind of things."

This is something like what martial artists use. Instead of resisting or defending against the attack, they flow with the attack to dissolve its power.

Withdraw into yourself. Show less interest in activities, and maybe you will become less interesting to the abuser.

FEAR
is the acronym for
False
Evidence
Appearing
Real

These suggestions may help you loosen the hold the abuser has on you, but the hold fear has on you also needs to be loosened.

Fear is the biggest challenge. It consumes our thoughts and our energy; it saps our strength and our hope; it stifles our creative thinking and our self-confidence. FEAR is the acronym for False Evidence Appearing Real. So we need to examine the evidence and expose the lie. Chapter 8 will help us gain clarity to reduce fear and set our minds free to escape the darkness.

WHAT IF?

A whisper deep within us says, "This is not right," even as our minds struggle to make sense of the illogical web of justification he weaves around his abuse. Even as we convince ourselves of our unworthiness of dignity, as we embrace our victim mentality, we have an unspoken hope that there must be something of value in us, and we long for love.

What would it mean if our intuition was right that something is not right? What is the truth? What are lies?

- Am I human? Do I therefore have human rights?
- Is he really more powerful than me? If so, why isn't he powerful enough to control his anger?
- Am I as weak as I think I am? If so, how could I have endured?
- Is there courage in me? Courage is not the absence of fear.
- Has the constant mental effort required to avoid abuse, to analyze his irrational behavior, honed my mental strength?
- Has the injustice I have endured strengthened my understanding of justice?

If these explanations of abuse and the types of abusers have you concerned that someone you care about may be in an abusive relationship, please go to my website at www.jacquiebrown.com *for tips and resources on what to do to help them.*

You Can Check Out Any Time You Like But You Can Never Leave

I WAS A GHOST SLIPPING THROUGH THE DIM SILENCE OF THE HOUSE. The moonlight softened the darkness as I drifted from room to room. I lived there, but it was not home.

It was the third house we had lived in. My name was on the title below his, and the house was big and beautiful, but the warm, secure comfort that makes a house a home was absent. Instead it emanated cold fear and violence.

I stood in the dark and looked at the blackness of the fireplace, then lifted my eyes to the eagle in the picture above the mantle. I moved the figure on the mantle a little to the side and then moved the pictures on the cabinet into a group as I tried to make the aesthetics of the room feel a little better, tried to make me feel better, but my misery remained. It was 3:00 a.m., and Ed was asleep or maybe unconscious from drinking. It was hard to tell.

I sat on the sofa and contemplated why the color disappeared with the absence of light; why was everything in shades of gray? I looked at the statue on the hearth. She was lovely, made of unpainted gray stone. She was about a foot and a half high, sitting almost cross-legged, looking down at the book in her lap, which had a rose for a bookmark. The only slightly disturbing aspect of her was her eyes. The eyes had no detailing, so she appeared sightless. She reminded me of me, frozen, with her vision focused within and the things she loved lying forgotten in her lap.

I held my hand out in the air in front of me to see if I was shaking. The white form floated in front of me without a tremor. There was something wrong within me. No matter how hard I struggled to will it away, I was powerless to overcome it. I had researched and tried so many things without success. My hand was steady now, so why did steadiness elude me when I needed it most desperately?

It began two years before. It seemed an insignificant thing at the time, a small annoyance, no reason for concern.

Ed and I were at a retirement workshop for employees and their spouses at Ed's workplace. Ed hated anything to do with paper or computers, so he left our administration and finances as my responsibilities. That was the reason for my being with him at the workshop. In addition, everyone else was taking their spouses, and Ed wanted to fit in.

Before starting, we helped ourselves to coffee and muffins. As I picked up my coffee cup, my hand was shaking. A sense of quaking inside accompanied my shaking hand. Throughout the workshop, I was okay holding everything else except my cup or glass. I was quite self-conscious of the trembling and hid it from Ed.

Several months later, it happened again, and again it was in public. Ed, the children and I were heading to the mountains for a family ski trip.

We stopped at a restaurant for lunch. The waitress brought our drinks, and as I reached for my Coke there was a tremor in my hand. I quickly took a sip and put it down. Our lunch arrived, and I cautiously picked up my fork. No shaking. I reached for my glass, and the tremor returned. Fear and disbelief mingled with confusion as I sensed something was not right.

It happened several more times, but only when I was trying to drink when people were around. It was disturbing.

I thought to myself, *Why is this happening, and why can't I make it stop?*

A couple of days later as we sat in the ski lodge having coffee before heading out on our first run of the day, Ed finally noticed my shaking, and I heard the usual derisive "What's the matter with you?"

I did not want him to know what was happening with me. I was already vulnerable in so many areas.

"I'm nervous about the ski runs we are planning to take. I'm not sure if I can do the black diamonds," I said, diverting his attention to the day ahead.

It continued to happen whenever the trigger circumstances were there, lifting a glass or cup with people other than immediate family present. I dreaded it, tried to hide it, and I tried to hide from it.

I could not hide it, or the circumstances that triggered it, from Ed for long. He belittled me because of it, demanded me to stop doing it, told me it was all in my mind and I could stop it if I wanted to. It was a source of embarrassment for him. He stared at my hands and then me whenever we were in public, which magnified the shaking. I could hide the shaking if I held my glass with two hands, but he criticized and insulted me for it, so I usually avoided that option. I tried to time my sips to when no one, especially Ed, was looking. The more it happened, the more I worried about it, and the more I worried about it, the more it happened. It was constantly on my mind.

My social phobia gradually crept into other areas of my life, with an increasing number of circumstances triggering it. It moved from glasses to cutlery; dining out became a nightmare. Then it moved from restaurants to the golf course. Ed enjoyed sports, and since he wanted me with him continually, he taught me to ski and golf. Anger and insults were his teaching style, so learning from him was a humiliating and unhappy process.

Golf courses want to accommodate as many people as possible, so groups of four and a fast pace were the norm. The challenge of performing in front of strangers and being rushed brought on my tremors. As you can imagine, trying to get the golf ball to balance on the tee with trembling hands was a nightmare.

I kept myself between Ed and my ball to hide my difficulty. I could feel the tremor even in my body, and it affected my golf shots. Ed did not like it when I did not golf well. As I missed shots, my tension mounted, and my golf game deteriorated. He harassed me with derisive comments as his anger mounted. I dreaded the tipping point when his stony silence would come. If we were not paired with anyone, he would leave me behind.

Then the trembling progressed to my writing. I went to a workshop on how to analyze case studies for examinations. The room was full of strangers; the desks were tiny and close. I was very nervous and was mortified when my hand started to shake as I wrote. I couldn't read my own writing. I could not even stay between the lines. I felt like crying as I hid my notes from the people beside me. I felt shame and embarrassment when the teacher came around looking at our work. I knew from the past that once the trembling invaded a new area of my life, it stayed. I thought of some of the implications of not being able to write and was devastated.

My fears became reality. Whenever someone was around, or even if I was alone but out of the house, the tremors would come whenever I picked up a pen. I started paying cash when I shopped because I could not sign my name on the receipt. I was Ed's note-taker. "Write this down" was something I heard often, and now he had another opportunity to humiliate me. I was afraid of losing marks on the exams I wrote for my university correspondence courses because my writing was so terrible. I used to receive compliments on my handwriting; now it was a source of torment.

I researched social phobias. I tried behavior modification techniques, prayer and every other remedy suggested, but nothing worked.

After months of this, I recognized a trend; whenever I had even half a glass of wine, my shaking magically disappeared. I let Ed know, thinking that he would want me to use this to prevent his embarrassment because of my condition, but he had something else in mind. This knowledge was yet another tool to use to antagonize and control me. He controlled when I could have a drink, and he would purposely delay or deny me relief.

As I sat on the couch in the dark, I wondered if my shaking would ever go away, if I would ever be normal again. The social phobia had become so debilitating that I was afraid to go out, which compounded the isolation imposed by Ed's abuse. I went to town to buy groceries and alcohol once a week, but I tried to avoid any other outings if possible. As I sat in my sadness, I started to drift into sleep. I jumped awake in fear, realized where I was and reluctantly decided to return to bed.

It was my summer of sorrow, when the despair in my soul descended into apathy. Events ensued that rapidly sent me to the bottom of my pit. It began with my daughter, Ashley, my beautiful, gentle, quiet, timid daughter. She was so afraid of doing something wrong that she chose to do nothing. She and I were close. She also loved her animals, and her room was her refuge, but with everything else she was ill at ease. Ed's abuse did not extend to her, but his abuse of me broke her heart and damaged her spirit.

I remembered the previous fall fighting back tears as I sat and watched the lines on the highway flash by. Ed and I had just left Ashley in Clarion to start her fall term at college, and my heart was aching. I missed her so much already. The music on the country station had been white noise until the voice said Princess Diana was dead. I had left behind my princess the same day the world lost theirs.

I had left Ashley behind that fall, but the next summer I feared I had really lost her. It was hot out. It was the kind of heat that produces thunderstorms. The carpet on the deck was warm under my bare feet. I was holding the downspout we were adding to help drain water away from the house. The phone rang, and I ran into the house to answer it.

I was thrilled it was Ashley, but my familiar feelings of dread started to build at something in her voice.

"Mom, you know last week when we talked about why you wanted Warren and me to wait to get married? Well, I wanted to tell you something then, but I was afraid to. I wanted to tell you that Warren and I had already gotten married."

I did not remember the rest of the conversation. I had gone numb. It was not that I disliked Warren. I liked him, and all I wanted was Ashley's happiness, but Ed hated him. Warren knew it and was afraid of Ed.

Warren had followed Ashley to Clarion when she left for college in the fall, and Ed was not happy about it. Warren had phoned us a few weeks before and asked Ed if he could have Ashley's hand in marriage. Ed said no.

How could I tell Ed that they got married anyway? I could not keep this from Ed. If he ever found out I knew and did not tell him, I would be in deep trouble.

I walked back outside, and he saw on my face that something was wrong, and as I told him I watched anger flood his expression. Then the tidal wave of his rage tumbled down into my deep well of sorrow as tears poured out from the wound in my heart.

Why would she ever want to come home again and have her husband receive the abuse she had watched her mom receive for so many years? I had lost her.

The days went by, and each morning I woke with the sense that something was wrong. Then I remembered, and my eyes would sting with tears. My ache got stronger and my despair deeper.

Ed knew he could not undo this. His diminished power and control over Ashley heightened his abuse and control of me. His loathing and his seething anger were unrelenting through the summer. Then another wave hit.

It was time for the local rodeo, and Ed wanted us to go. He wanted me to go so he could drink and I could drive home. However, thoughts of the rodeo led my mind to a happier thought: Connor was going to meet us at the rodeo. He also lived in Clarion, where his sister was going to college, and he was coming home for a visit.

I missed my children tremendously, and I was excited about Connor coming home. Connor and I had a secret language. Since Connor was very intelligent and knowledgeable, we often carried on a conversation within a conversation that was over Ed's head, inserting words laden with hidden meaning. Ed suspected we were doing this but couldn't quite grasp it.

Although I felt a bit guilty that we were having fun at Ed's expense, it brought me a sense of closeness and camaraderie with Connor. He has always tried to protect me from Ed. He understood and hated Ed's abuse of me.

I was hoping Connor's visit would go well, as Ed and Connor's relationship was volatile. Sometimes they enjoyed each other's company, but often they ended up in fights, especially when they were drinking. Ed still wanted to control Connor, and Connor had passed the age of accepting it.

All day I was cautious and compliant as I tried to avoid anything that would upset Ed. The hours dragged by as I waited for Connor's call or arrival. It was 5:30 p.m. The evening rodeo performance started at 6:00 p.m., and Connor had still not contacted us.

Ed said, "I'm not waiting any longer. He knows where to find us" as he took the truck keys off their hook. I grabbed my bag and followed him out the door.

The rodeo grounds were not far from our farm. Ten minutes and we were there. We found a seat in the grandstand, and I was thankful the forecasted rain held off. I watched the crowd more than I watched the chuckwagons as I scanned the people watching for Connor. It was a small-town crowd, and it was interesting to see people we knew dressed in their western clothes and cowboy hats.

The teams and time raced by, and I had given up the possibility of Connor coming. The races were almost over, and it would not be worth the admission price for Connor to come. The last heat was thundering around the track as I worried about the drive home. Ed had drunk continuously since we came, and he had been drinking all through the day prior to our coming.

Ed was belligerent when he had to let someone else drive. Handing over the control of the vehicle never sat well with him. He would snap orders and yell at my driving decisions. Sometimes he grabbed the wheel or stepped on my foot on the gas. I never knew what to expect and was dreading the drive home after.

The chuckwagon races were over, and as we followed the crowd out, Ed's cell phone rang. I strained to hear his comments, wondering if it was Connor, but the crowd was too noisy, so I watched his expression to gauge what effect the call was having on him. He hardly said a word, and as the lines around his mouth tightened, so did my heart. Whatever the message was, he was not happy.

We drove home in silence, which added to my sense of foreboding. As we drove down the gravel road and approached the house, a fire engine left our yard. Fear replaced my foreboding. *Why was a fire truck here? I don't see any smoke. Have they already put the fire out? Was Connor involved? Is he okay?*

I drove up the driveway and saw a police car parked beside the garage behind Ed's company truck. I parked to the side of the police car. We got out, and Ed stopped at the officer's door and knocked on the window.

To myself I thought, *What are you doing? Your attitude is going to antagonize him.* But I would not dare say it out loud.

I just kept walking, back through the basketball court around to the deck and the French doors that opened into our kitchen. As I walked through the door, I saw Connor by the fridge.

He was devastated and said, "I burnt up Dad's car."

I hugged him and said, "It doesn't matter. It doesn't matter. All that matters is that you're okay. That's what is important."

After a minute or so I asked, "What happened?"

Connor had brought a friend from Clarion with him, and they had run out of gas a mile from home. They walked to our house and took our old car out to the fuel storage tanks to get some gas. As they drove, flames started shooting out from under the hood of the car. They jumped out and raced back to the house to get water, but when they returned the whole car was engulfed in fire. They went back to the house and called 911, which brought the fire engine and the RCMP.

I was still trying to calm and reassure Connor when I heard the door open behind me. As I turned, I was unprepared for the dark rage on

Ed's face. I expected concern and compassion. His eyes were riveted on Connor behind me. He lunged for Connor before I could process what was happening, but I stayed between them and tried to stop Ed from reaching him.

As we wrestled, understanding and disbelief came to me. *He is actually angry at Connor for the loss of the car.*

Ed threw me out of the way, and I landed on the coffee table. I stumbled to my feet and interjected myself between them again, trying to reason with Ed to stop. He was swinging and grabbing around me, trying to attack Connor as we moved through the dining room and into the living room. Ed's frustration and anger at my interference escalated until he slapped me and shoved me into a chair. His rage was so focused, he had not said a word throughout the attack, and now he stood fuming, his eyes blazing at each of us in turn. Then he abruptly turned and stormed out through the attached garage.

Connor and I were frozen in numb silence for a moment. Then he explained that his friend Roger had been in the officer's cruiser giving his statement when Ed and I parked by the house.

We had bought the car that was now in cinders from Ed's brother as a second vehicle and paid very little for it. I could not fathom how Ed could place the disappointment of the loss of that car above the relief and thankfulness that our son was alive. Unknown to Connor, Ed had disconnected the gas line filter in the car while repairing it, so gas was shooting into the engine as Connor drove.

I explained this to Connor and saw relief replace the fear and pain. He thought for a minute, then said, "I still need to go out and give my statement to the police. I need to see how Roger is doing too."

As we stepped out onto the deck and approached the garage, we saw that another officer had come. I saw Ed jump at Connor's friend, Roger, grabbing him and pushing him backwards. One of the officers pulled Ed off and the other said, "Ma'am, can you please get your husband under control?"

I thought to myself, *Are you crazy?* but instead of answering I tried to send the officer a signal by shaking my hand *no* down by my side so Ed could not see, before I escaped back into the house.

Confused and helpless, I wondered, *What do I do? What do I do? This is so bad and getting worse by the minute. How do I diffuse the situation to minimize the damage?*

It would take months to soothe away Ed's anger, and he would never forget this. He would use this as justification to ignite his fury whenever he craved a rampage.

A jolt of fear went through me as I heard the door to the garage open in the hall.

"Get out here," Ed barked.

I went through the hall, into the garage. We had a three-car garage, and we usually parked the truck in the doublewide part while the singlewide part was a workshop. It was all one larger open area with a window on the far side. That night the only thing in the doublewide part was the ATV, the quad.

"What the hell happened to my quad?" yelled Ed.

"I don't know," I said in fear.

Mud was caked on the wheels of the ATV and splattered on the rest of it, long grass was wrapped around the axel, and the chemical sprayer was missing from the back. I had a dreadful feeling it had something to do with Connor.

"What the f— do you mean, you don't know?"

"I was with you; how could I know?"

Ed hissed, "You stupid bitch" through his teeth as he came towards me. I retreated out of the garage back into the house and out through the kitchen to find Connor. I saw a flurry of movement by the garage, and I was shocked when I realized it was Ed and the two officers wrestling.

One of the officers said, "You are under arrest for spousal abuse and resisting arrest" as he twisted Ed's hands behind him, handcuffed him and pushed him into the back seat of the patrol car.

My mind reeled at the implications of what he said. I turned and ran around to the far side of the house and stood on the grass crying, looking up at the stars. I felt the warmth of the stucco on my back as a strange mixture of fear and peace filled me as I cried. The nightmare had ended for the evening, and there was an odd, small seed of hope in me. The abuse was no longer a family secret.

I wondered, *Has a turning point come?*

Yet at the same time, dread and fear built within me as my thoughts turned to Ed's possible reaction to all of this.

Connor and I talked through most of the night. In the morning, we both agreed that it would be better for me if he and Roger went back to Clarion before Ed was released from jail.

Over the next few weeks, Ed's lawyer worked to have the spousal abuse charge dropped, leaving only the resisting arrest charge. Eventually he succeeded. At the trial, Ed's lawyer convinced the judge that the whole incident was a comedy of errors with Ed as the victim, and the judge pronounced time served, Ed's night in jail, as his sentence. He was free to return to life as usual, and he did.

I sank lower into misery. Both Ashley and Connor avoided coming home. I was relieved they had escaped, but I grieved the loss of light and hope their presence brought. Now I faced the gloom of my endless oppression in isolation.

Then the next sorrow came. This time it was my dad.

My dad and I were still close, even though we seldom saw each other. I always believed that if my dad knew about the fear and torment I lived with, he would come and rescue me. He would once again save me like he saved me from the train long ago.

Mom called, and I knew by the sound of her voice that something was wrong. Doctors had diagnosed my dad with bladder cancer.

My soul cried in anguish, "No. Please don't let me lose my dad too; don't let me lose my dad."

Operations were scheduled. The doctors, Mom and Dad were optimistic. I prayed. I always prayed, but the prayers I wanted answered the most seemed to fall into a desert where they wither and died unanswered. Yet I knew God was listening, loving and sovereign, even if I didn't understand my pain.

The operations went well, but improvement was slow.

My other friend and protector, my yellow Labrador retriever, Sam, was not feeling well either. He had trouble getting up. He moved very slowly when he did move, and he had lost his appetite.

I whispered "No" in my heart again.

One day, I could not find him anywhere on our acreage, and I doubted he would go anywhere else on our farm. I suspected he could be next door. The house was sometimes rented, but it had been empty for a while. I knew Ed would not want me over there looking for Sam in case someone came, so I gathered the courage to ask Ed to go look for him.

I stepped through the garage door. Ed was rummaging through the can of bolts as I said, "I can't find Sam anywhere. He hasn't been feeling well, and I am afraid he may be at the neighbors'."

"I don't give a damn where he is," Ed snapped without looking up.

I was nervous and quiet for a bit, and then I tried again. "I think he's really sick, and I don't want him to be alone."

Ed turned to me and yelled, "He's going to die, and so is your f— dad going to die."

His words slammed into me, and I staggered out the door in shock. I needed distance. I felt a desperation to escape, but escape what? How could I escape the loss of my loved ones?

I couldn't go find Sam, so I walked down the hill, through the field of alfalfa. It was waist high. Its flowers were various shades of purple; the small leaves were deep green. Honeybees buried their heads in the blooms in search of the sweet nectar. But the loveliness magnified my dark despair.

I was walking towards the horse trough. Bell was the only horse we had now. There were two graves not far from the water trough where we buried her mother and her sister. The mound still had not settled from where her sister, my horse, was buried a couple of years before. I missed her.

Bell was not at the trough, so I waited, not wanting to go look for her, not wanting to whistle for her in case Ed heard, and not wanting to return to the house. I hoped she would come so I could pet her and feel her affection as she nudged me with her head. I waited a long time, but she did not come, so I started back up the hill. As I came over the crest, I saw Sam following Ed on the path from the neighbors'. Sam's head was down at his paws, and each step was an effort.

Ed agreed we should take Sam to the vet. He was too heavy for one person to lift and he could not jump, so we put him on a rug and used that to lift him into the truck. At the vet's, I petted and soothed him and tried to avoid the thoughts in my mind. The vet suggested we leave Sam overnight.

My tears dripped on Sam's nose as I brushed his soft velvety ears. Sensing this could be the last time I looked into his gentle eyes, I whispered goodbye.

The vet called in the morning. He said Sam had cancer of the stomach and would not live. We could bring him home to die, but the vet said he was suffering and recommended euthanasia.

Sam was gone. I lost my friend. We buried him with our horses.

My dad's health continued to decline. Then on July 13th, just after his 69th birthday, my mother called to tell me that Dad was full of cancer and was not going to make it.

Anguish overwhelmed me, and I sank to the floor.

'No, no, please no. Don't take another loved one away. Not my dad."

I needed to see my dad before he died, and, taking a rare stand, I decided I was going to Clarion with or without Ed. I no longer cared if Ed went into a rage or not. I called Ed at work. As I told him what was happening he sensed that my despair had pushed me beyond his control, so, to maintain the reins of control, he said he would be home and would take me to Clarion.

The seven-hour drive seemed never-ending. Ed's anger had been quietly building. I could feel it in his short, terse comments that seemed out of place with death so close.

We finally pulled into the parking lot of the hospital. I got out of the car, unsure of what to do. Ed came around the car and walked towards me. The anger in his eyes burned into me. He slammed the car keys into my hand and said through clenched teeth, "I got you here. You're on your own now."

I leaned against the car, looked up into the sky, and cried deep sobs from the depths of my soul. Ed's abuse was somehow welcome, as I wanted to experience my grief alone.

I did not want to go into the hospital, and yet I needed to see my dad as soon as possible in case I missed my chance to tell him how much I loved him. My limbs were like lead as I forced myself to turn towards the hospital. As I looked at the front doors a few yards away, I saw Ed with my brother and sister. Underneath my pain, there was a small sense of satisfaction knowing that they saw how Ed treated me and Ed would know that they knew. From his comment to me, I thought he was going to go find a lounge somewhere and leave me on my own, but with my siblings watching, he needed to try to protect his image.

I went to my siblings and cried with them. I followed them up to Dad's room. My mom was outside the door. I held my mom as we cried. We waited for the nurses to finish.

I rushed to my dad as soon as the nurses opened the door. I held him and cried more tears. His arms came around me, and the first syllable of my name escaped from him in a breath of a whisper. My sister told me he had been incoherent, but I knew he knew it was me. I did not want to let him go. I held him and held him. I had missed him for years, and I did not want to miss him anymore. It hurt so much.

I slept in a chair by his bed and held his hand through the night. In the morning, he took a final breath and was gone.

My dad was gone and would never come and rescue me; he would never hold me safe in his arms again. I felt like I did not belong in this world either.

As we arranged for the funeral, it began to snow. It was July, and it was snowing. I believed in my heart that it was snowing because the world was cold and sad because my dad was no longer in it.

We buried my dad in a beautiful place in the foothills of the Rocky Mountains, overlooking a valley. I wished I could die and stay with him, but instead I faced the long drive "home"—seven hours with Ed to return to my dungeon.

The trip passed mostly in silence as I struggled to keep from crying in my despair. Gravel crunched as it was crushed under the tires when we drove up the driveway. It matched my soul; I was crushed.

I had lost my daughter. I had lost my son. They were far away, and I couldn't go to them. My Sam was gone, and my dad was gone. I felt there was no one who needed me to hang on, to keep myself together, and I just wanted to escape. I had spiraled to the bottom, and I no longer wanted to be in this world. I wanted to go to Heaven.

I often sang this song:

Don't it make you wanna go home?
Now don't it make you wanna go home?
All God's children get weary when they roam
And God how I wanna go home.

The days went by in a fog, and the nights brought my tears. I went to a room by myself, to my daughter's empty bedroom on the second floor. I sat on the bed, rocked myself and cried deep sobs from the depths of my soul.

"I wish I was dead. I wish I was dead," I repeated in rhythm to my rocking. Through the blur of my tears I saw Ed in the doorway.

"You pathetic bitch. Your dad is dead. What the hell are you doing?" I looked in disbelief at the anger on his face. I was too broken to try to understand it. I looked out the window and continued to cry as he continued to yell at me. After a while, the door slammed shut. The night passed.

The days passed. I withdrew from the world into my misery. I visualized myself overboard in the dark in the ocean. A storm was raging, the wind drove rain in my face, and the waves billowed over me. The thunder boomed, and in the flash of the lightning I saw the ship I fell from slip away from me into the dark. I thought to myself, *I could swim, but what is the point?*

I no longer cared. I knew there would be no rescue from this dungeon, no rescue from my oppressor. I no longer fought the tremors of my phobia because I no longer waited for Ed to allow my relief. Alcohol was the magic elixir of my relief, and I kept that elixir hidden and close.

There was a tiny bottle of vodka in my pocket, one in my sock, and another in my bra. However, I saved these as a last resort; instead, I used the bigger bottles hidden in the unfinished basement walls, behind the cleaning supplies in the laundry room and in the upstairs linen closet. I also carried the tiny ones in my backpack that I took with me everywhere except golfing, so I put some in my golf bag. I palmed them

83

into my pocket and drank them in the washroom. I did this when I went to write my exams as well. And I drank before I tried to cut Ed's hair in the morning because it would be a disaster if I shook then. It was like magic, and I felt like I had control since the timing was now in my hands instead of Ed's—another illusion. I was getting deeper and deeper into alcohol's grip.

All of this eventually led to more than a bottle of vodka drunk in secret each day and at least a bottle of wine drunk with Ed. I slipped away to my hiding spots and gulped the vodka down quickly to avoid being caught.

I was now what is called a functioning alcoholic. I did what was required of me and worked very hard to hide my state. I stayed quiet and still as much as possible until I was allowed to go to bed. But first, before bed, I wrote a note for myself describing what happened that night and whether or not Ed was angry. Then I hid it in my makeup case for morning.

I woke in the morning and tried to recall the previous night. I could not, so I went searching for my note and hoped that I could read the writing and that there was enough information to help me remember. I needed to know how cautious to be around Ed and how to answer for my actions the night before. Even though alcohol numbed my suffering, it had become a beast.

Another beast also consumed me. I thought it was my friend. No one knew, especially not Ed. I did not want to share it or lose it. It was a refuge, a comfort, a branch that kept me afloat in the raging river. It was the eating disorder bulimia, which developed years before. I did not recognize it for what it was until recently. Little did I know that it was deadly.

But then, I wanted to die. Which one would succeed: Ed, alcoholism, bulimia or me?

six

WE ARE PRISONERS OF OUR OWN DEVICE

Vanity of vanities…all is vanity and a striving after wind.
Ecclesiastes 1:1-14, ESV

*If you realized how powerful your thoughts are, you would
never think a negative thought.*
Peace Pilgrim

STATISTICS

Across studies of U.S. and Canadian women receiving services for domestic violence, rates of depression ranged from 17 percent to 72 percent, and rates of PTSD ranged from 33 percent to 88 percent.[1]

SOMETHING TO KEEP IN MIND

If shackles are clamped around our ankles, they will damage us. As the shackles rub on our ankles, they create sores. Our bodies will try to compensate and protect themselves. Blisters, lesions and deformities form. Infections damage the ankles' function and could end up destroying us.

This is similar to what happens to our minds when we are shackled in abuse. The mind adjusts its thought and behavior patterns, and it adjusts its brain chemical balance in an attempt to survive. These adjustments often cause depression, disorders and addictions. Just as the blisters, lesions and deformities destroy the ankle, the depression, disorders and addictions destroy the mind, and each of these, if left long enough, may destroy us.

> *Then the abuser plays the tune, and we begin to perform the dance of the abused through the minefield.*

THE DANCE OF THE ABUSED

The abuser enters the garden of our life under subterfuge and lays a minefield. Then the abuser plays the tune, and we begin to perform the dance of the abused through the minefield. It is much more deadly than the typical analogy of walking on eggshells.

Outsiders reading this may say, "You don't have to perform the dance. You can choose not to; you can choose to leave." There are complicated reasons why we stay, why we behave the way we do, and why we indulge in self-destructive self-soothing in our attempt to cope.

WHY WE STAY

There are many reasons why it is so difficult for us to "just leave." Fear is an obvious one. The abuser uses threats to keep us bound. Other obvious ones are isolation from support and resources, and our escalating commitment to the relationship the longer we stay. A less obvious reason is the phenomena of the Stockholm syndrome. Stockholm syndrome is a counterintuitive protection mechanism that develops involuntarily from our survival instincts.

As time progresses, all of these factors deteriorate our capacity to choose to leave.

Stockholm Syndrome

The discovery of Stockholm syndrome happened during a bank robbery where the hostages bonded to and helped the hostage takers, making it difficult for the authorities to free them. Subconsciously, the hostages felt that their best chance for survival lay with pleasing versus antagonizing the hostage takers. This is also the pattern evident between the abused and the abuser.[2] The abuser gradually takes control of the abused person's existence, and her well-being is dependent upon him.

Stockholm syndrome develops when certain symptoms and conditions are present. The abuser begins the courtship with the honeymoon phase of the abuse cycle, which sets the stage. Positive feelings towards each other is the first condition.

The tension-building phase of abuse begins to disempower us. Belittling by the abuser decreases our self-esteem and elevates the esteem of the abuser. We support his beliefs and behavior, and we feel compelled to defend and protect the abuser from the criticism and actions of others.

Because of our allegiance to the abuser, we resist support or rescue from family, friends or authorities. We feel helpless and powerless, and we are unable to contemplate detachment or escape. These are all symptoms of Stockholm syndrome.

These symptoms develop when certain conditions exist. The first condition is our belief, on a conscious or unconscious level, that our psychological or physical existence is threatened. As stated earlier, these threats can be direct, implied through his words or implied through his actions. We believe these threats, and our fear ensures our compliance.

Occasional acts of kindness during each successive honeymoon phase of abuse are also conditions of the syndrome.

Isolation ensures we are exposed to nothing but his ideology and belief system. This prevents us from discovering the truth.

The last condition of the syndrome is the belief that we can never leave.

And so we stay.

Isolation

Isolation is another method the abuser uses to frustrate our escape. At the start, it comes as subtle hints—"I think it is a stupid waste of time when women talk on the phone all day." Soon, any outside contact escalates into serious trouble for us.

> *He reinforces our isolation with lies about what awaits us outside his castle.*

He bullies us while we are on the phone and abuses us as soon as we get off. He implements the silent treatment or openly insults visitors and abuses us after they are gone. We are in trouble for using the Internet or for reading books he doesn't approve of. Even parent-teacher interviews or school field trips for our children pose a threat to us. Therefore, to avoid abuse, we avoid communicating with anyone but the abuser. Even our communication with our children is in his control.

He reinforces our isolation with lies about what awaits us outside his castle: rejection, corruption, immorality and danger. We accept his beliefs and view the outside world as a threat to our safety and well-being.

Mobility is the other area the abuser uses to enforce our isolation. He may prevent us from getting a driver's license, refuse to own a second vehicle or refuse to allow us to drive. He may refuse to allow us to use public transportation, convincing us that it is too expensive, too degrading or too dangerous. He will reinforce the idea that it is unacceptable to go anywhere except with him.

We gradually come to believe that we cannot survive without the abuser. A threat to the abuser is a threat to our survival; removal of the abuser is removal of our survival. This, along with fear of retribution from the abuser if we try to leave, is why we are terrified of help from friends, family or those in authority.

And so we stay.

Escalating Commitment

The longer we stay with the abuser, the more our commitment to stay escalates. Early in the relationship, while he is in the honeymoon phase, we may have talked to others about his wonderful qualities. Then as the relationship changes and the abuse becomes apparent, we are reluctant to tell people of the change or to admit that we made a mistake. So our pride keeps us committed.

Then, as we spend time together as a couple, our finances become intertwined. Abusers often control the finances. If this is the case, he controls the bank accounts, the credit cards, and the purchase and sale of assets. These assets are usually solely in his name. Sometimes he gives us an allowance; sometimes he makes us ask for money. We have to account for every penny we spend. He will make our getting or holding a job difficult and will control the money we make if we do have a job. The wealth and its accumulation, including the family home, are in his control. All of these increase our commitment to stay in the relationship.

The more cycles of abuse we go through, the more emotional investment we have in the relationship. Going through difficult times together strengthens the bonds of a relationship. Every honeymoon phase strengthens our hope and our loyalty.

The longer we are in the relationship, the more likely it is that we will have children together. With the children comes the bond of parenthood. Now our love and commitment to our children escalates our commitment to and dependence upon the abuser.

Our escalating emotional, family and financial commitments strengthen the chains that bind us, dig us deeper and entangle us further in the web. As we discussed in cognitive dissonance, the more our commitment escalates, the more we need to justify why we stay in order to create agreement within ourselves. If we do finally recognize our plight, we feel we are in too deep to escape.

And so we stay.

Threats

The abuser uses actual and implied threats to demonstrate that our life, and all we treasure, is in his hands. He uses the power of these threats to keep us trapped in our dungeon.

And so we stay.

HOW WE ADAPT

Fear is our taskmaster as we unconsciously submit to the ideology. We develop many strategies to avoid pain as we adapt to the abuse. We avoid behavior that angers him, we avert trouble-causing circumstances and we engage in activities that please him.

Avoid Behavior that Angers Him

The abuser gradually trains us not to engage in behavior that angers him. The phone is the easiest line of communication with the outside world, so it is important for him to cut off or control this line. We soon avoid or hide our phone calls to avoid his insults and badgering. He questions us, in a rage for hours, after he gets the phone statement or checks the recent calls. He may force us to answer the phone and then yell at us for talking, or he may hang up the phone when we are in the middle of a conversation with someone else. He may refuse to let us have a cell phone, or he may use our cell phone to increase his surveillance of us. So, we fear the phone.

We also face a barrage of questions, accusations and abuse when we go out. He monitors our activities. Our errands should only take a certain amount of time. We should only put a certain amount of mileage on the vehicle and only use a certain amount of gas. He may force us to call him before we leave and call him when we get home. He may call unexpectedly during the day to see where we are and what we are doing. He may come home at unexpected times to catch us unaware. His friends and family watch us. So, we fear leaving the house.

Information is power. The abuser is the one who holds the power, and so the abuser is the one who controls the information. He does not want us exposed to viewpoints that are opposed to his, and so he monitors our reading. If reading material is allowed in the house, it must meet his approval. Internet use is monitored or denied. He attempts to control our mind by controlling what goes into it. So we give up reading.

Another attempt to control our minds and our means of escape is to discourage further education. Acquiring an education will reduce his power and control over us because it opens up employment

And so we give up our education dreams.

opportunities, reducing our belief of dependence on the abuser. He may discourage us from pursuing further education by his degrading comments and attitude towards our education, or if we are already acquiring an education.

He may sabotage our assignments and exam preparation. He is also against education because it costs money and reduces the time we are available to him and his desires. In his mind, he not only has to keep us powerless and submissive, he also needs to maintain his elevated position of having the superior intellect. And so we give up our education dreams.

Since the abuser controls the finances, he may allow us a career so he can enjoy the money it provides. If he allows us to have a career, it must not take precedence over him, his desires and his career. It gives them more power. But often abusers will make it difficult or impossible for us to have or keep a career by engaging in activities that cause our dismissal or cause us to quit. And so we give up our career dreams.

We engage in many other activities to avoid the abuser's anger. We stay in the location he wants us in: not leaving the room he is in, not leaving home when he's away, not leaving the restaurant, not leaving the store, not leaving the vehicle, not leaving the hotel room, not leaving the waiting room. We avoid changing the temperature, the channels, the music and the lighting.

We watch our words to avoid his anger; we avoid words or phrases he dislikes; our opinions never differ from his. We take his side in every dispute with others, including the police. When speaking, we avoid any tone or volume that he dislikes. We only talk to people he allows, and we keep the conversation to a minimum.

This micro-monitoring of our behavior to avoid his anger is relentless and exhausting. As we give up pieces of who we are, we become a hollow shell.

Avert Trouble-Causing Circumstances

Averting trouble-causing circumstances is another area that consumes us. Anything that goes wrong in the abuser's world is an opportunity for him to engage in rage and take it out on us. Although the children soon learn to walk on eggshells as well, our minds and actions are constantly anticipating and correcting any of their misbehavior to protect the children and ourselves from the abuser's anger. We try to ensure pets behave, that items are in their places, and that things are working properly, all to make the abuser's life smooth. We make sure nothing is in the mail that will anger him, and we shield him from unpleasant topics and news. We avoid association or conversation with anyone who could inadvertently cause trouble for us, including our relatives. Of course, this is an impossible task, and we often pay the price for falling short.

Engage in Activities that Please Him

Another way we modify our behavior is by engaging in activities that please the abuser. We try to dress in a way that will not antagonize him, although this is a challenge because something he likes one day will be the source of insults the next day. Yet, dressing nice requires discretion as we do not want to look too good or attract unwanted attention.

The more submissive, subservient and obedient we are, the less likely the abuser will flare into a rage. Or so we hope. He likes us gentle, quiet and agreeable. Meals must be ready when he comes home and the house kept the way he likes. But, we know to do our work when he's not watching if we want to avoid shouts of orders and insults…because everything we do is wrong. We accept the fault for all his outbursts and mitigate the aftermath by doing something special for him. He demands our loyalty and expects our praise.

HOW WE ARE AFFECTED

Domestic violence is destructive, and the destruction is vast. It not only affects us as victims, but it also affects our families, our communities, our cities and our countries. It has destructive consequences for every aspect of our society, from our health-care system to our education, legal, political and economic systems. Since all the destruction domestic violence causes are too immense to cover in this chapter, I will focus on the damage to the victims. The abuse of anything causes damage, and it is no different in our case.

> *The most destructive process is the psychological damage that keeps us bound to the abuse.*

The physical trauma that victims of domestic violence go through is horrific in and of itself. However, if we had not undergone the psychological and emotional trauma first, the physical abuse might have been limited to a few isolated incidents, convincing us to leave. The most destructive process encompasses every aspect of the essence of who we are and has the potential to, literally, destroy us virtually undetected. It is the psychological damage that keeps us bound to the abuse. Complex Post Traumatic Stress Disorder (C-PTSD) is often at the core of the psychological damage.[3] Complex PTSD is also a catalyst for several other destructive mental and physical health issues.

Complex PTSD

A woman suffering in a relationship of domestic violence is similar to a soldier's experience as a prisoner of war. Both undergo prolonged exposure to traumatic experiences and both can develop C-PTSD.

Causes of C-PTSD

Exposure to a stressful situation releases surges of stress hormones to help us deal with the situation. However, if the situation is traumatic and overwhelms our ability to cope, this helpful process can turn destructive. For an event to be traumatic, we usually perceive it as unjust and a threat to our survival, although we may not be consciously aware of coming to these conclusions.

When we are unable to cope with a traumatic event, PTSD can develop. According to Judith Herman, if the trauma is repeated over an extended period, if the victim feels powerless against the violation and betrayal, and if there seems to be no escape, as in the case of domestic violence, then PTSD takes on additional aspects.[4] Complex PTSD is used to label PTSD with the following symptoms:

- Confused, disturbed emotions
  —Suicidal thoughts
  —Occasional, unexpected, explosive anger
  —Passive-aggressive behaviors
- Psychological disruption
  —Forgetful of the traumatic experience
  —Detachment from life (dissociation)
  —Detachment from body (depersonalization)
  —Hyper-vigilance to potential threats
- Self-condemnation
  —Shame
  —Guilt
  —No self-worth
  —Feeling different from others
- Consumed with thoughts of the abuser
  —Considering the abuser all-powerful
  —Fearing the next round of abuse
  —Fantasizing about either revenge against or allegiance with the abuser
  —Fantasizing about escape from the abuser
- Loss of meaning of life
  —Hopelessness
  —Loss of faith
  —Loss of identity
  —Despair

Physiological Process

There are physiological explanations for the destruction and chaos in our inner world. The unrelenting stress of domestic violence has a biological effect on our minds and emotions. The brain requires the proper levels of the chemicals adrenaline, cortisol, serotonin, dopamine and norepinephrine,. These chemicals work together in symphony to respond to stress, to feel good, and to maintain emotional well-being. When stress is so traumatic that it overwhelms our ability to cope, a biochemical imbalance is created among these stress hormones and neurotransmitters.

In the early stages of the violent domestic relationship, our adrenal systems will respond normally to the stress with the proper release of stress hormones to deal with the situation. However, in an abusive relationship, a stressful situation is not a one-time occurrence. It is relentless. This constant state of emergency prevents cortisol levels from declining the way they should, and cortisol buildup is damaging. It damages the hippocampus area of our brains where memory is stored. It also depletes the formation of serotonin and damages the cells' ability to absorb it. We need this chemical to give us our sense of well-being. Cortisol also depletes our dopamine levels, which we need in order to feel pleasure, and elevates our norepinephrine, which triggers our fight-or flight (or tend-and-befriend, which will be discussed later) response.

The Damage Done

It is difficult to fathom the destruction to our lives that results from too much or too little of the chemicals that our brains rely on. According to Carole Warshaw in *Psychological Aspects Of Women's Health*, a study in 1987 found that 81 percent of women who had been treated for psychiatric disorders reported histories of abuse.

Serotonin Loss

When serotonin levels start to decline, we become forgetful and find it difficult to concentrate. As it continues to decrease, our thoughts begin to race uncontrollably. This disturbs our sleep and creates fatigue. Then it affects our appetite for food—we either lose it or crave carbohydrates—

and our appetite for life—where we lose interest in everything, including pursuits we used to enjoy. As the serotonin levels decline further, so does our self-esteem and self-confidence. This multiplies the damage to our self-worth inflicted by the abuser.

With severe serotonin loss, our thoughts race uncontrollably and the content becomes disturbing. Depression develops. We avoid decisions as our confusion intensifies. We may fantasize about escape from the abuser and our life situation.

Low levels of serotonin contribute to the development of addictions, disorders, phobias and anxieties. We numb our emotions and hide from our feelings in a desperate attempt to ease our agony.

In addition to the mental and emotional effects of low serotonin, there are also physical effects, such as changes in body temperature, aches and pains, muscle cramps, and bowel and bladder problems.

Depletion of serotonin can also cause learned helplessness syndrome.

> *Suicide may seem like our only means of escape.*

According to Martin Seligman, "When an organism has experienced trauma it cannot control, its motivation to respond in the face of later trauma wanes. Moreover, even if it does respond and the response succeeds in producing relief, it has trouble learning, perceiving, and believing that the response worked. Finally, its emotional balance is disturbed; depression and anxiety, measured in various ways, predominate."[5]

Learned helplessness syndrome creates an over-dependence on the abuser and the belief that we are incapable of taking care of ourselves; it creates a sense of helplessness in us.

The destructive effects of declining serotonin levels spiral downward, culminating in suicidal thoughts and possible attempts to end our lives. This may seem like our only means of escape.

Dopamine Loss

Dopamine is the chemical responsible for feeling good, feeling pleasure and a sense of well-being. Elevated levels of cortisol cause dopamine levels to decline. This decline in dopamine, along with the decline in serotonin, also contributes to depression. The depression increases stress, which in turn generates more cortisol in our system, creating a never-ending cycle.

Elevated Norepinephrine (Noradrenaline)

Another chemical affected by stress is norepinephrine, related to adrenaline, which creates the fight-or-flight reaction. With elevated levels of norepinephrine, we become anxious, hypervigilant, nervous, and uncomfortable with crowds and confined spaces. It also interferes with our ability to sleep and concentrate.

Elevated levels of norepinephrine also stimulate the fight-or-flight response. Most of us are familiar with the term fight-or-flight as it pertains to stressful situation. However, according to *UCLA News*, UCLA researchers led by Shelley E. Taylor found that men often react to stress with a "fight-or-flight" response, but women are more likely to manage their stress with a "tend-and-befriend" response, protecting and nurturing their young (the "tend" response) and seeking social contact and support from others—especially other females (the "befriend" response).[6]

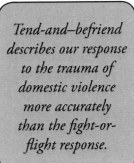

Tend-and–befriend describes our response to the trauma of domestic violence more accurately than the fight-or-flight response.

Tend-and–befriend describes our response to the trauma of domestic violence more accurately than the fight-or-flight response. In light of C-PTSD, the learned helplessness syndrome and Stockholm syndrome, neither fight nor flight would be considered a possible means of protection from the abuser. In fact, the opposite is more likely. Since we suffer from Stockholm syndrome and believe there is no escape, we do not perceive flight as an option. Our fear, our inferior strength and our learned helplessness rule out fighting as a viable protective response. In addition, the debilitating symptoms of C-PTSD leave "tend-and-befriend" as our best option to protect ourselves from the abuser, the tending in hopes that our nurturing of him will transform him into a compassionate, considerate person, and the befriending to mitigate and minimize the violence.

OTHER DAMAGE

The state of constant crisis causes other damage throughout our bodies. When we are faced with repeated, long-term trauma, other systems in our bodies adjust in response to the situation. The immune system, sexual drive, sleep, cell reproduction and organ function are all suppressed, and our appetites are increased in an attempt to maximize our resources to protect ourselves.

When our immune systems are suppressed, we can develop lupus, rheumatoid arthritis, osteoporosis, fibromyalgia, irritable bowel syndrome, skin problems, allergies, chronic fatigue and infections.

The constant terrorization we experience within our abusive relationships has devastating effects on our health and the essence of who we are as individuals. At a time when we need to be performing at our peak to avoid or deal with the abuser's unpredictable violence, we are robbed of our mental, emotional and physical stability and instead suffer confusing, debilitating symptoms. Our decline creates additional justification, in the abuser's mind, for increasing his violence against us.

HOW WE RESPOND

"You can check out anytime you like, but you can never leave." This line from the Eagles' song "Hotel California" is a haunting analogy of our circumstances. In desperation, we "check out" as we self-soothe, self-medicate, self-destruct, in an effort to endure or escape.

In attempting to alleviate the pain and escape our fears and survive the torment, we develop addictions, disorders and phobias. The stress-induced chemical imbalance is a strong contributor to these.

Addictions

According to Teresa McBean, "A helpful way to view addictions is to understand that they are behaviors we start out doing because it feels good and is helpful in some way to our life, but these behaviors end up taking over our lives and result in negative consequences."[7] Using less judgmental, more compassionate terminology for the definition may give us the courage to address this problem instead of hiding in denial and fearing shame.

The C-PTSD discussed earlier has a link to our addictions. C-PTSD causes the depletion of the brain chemicals that give us pleasure and a sense of well-being. This depletion creates a desire to feel good. A behavior we engage in to satisfy this desire has the potential to become our addiction. Our addictions can be drinking alcohol, doing drugs, smoking, gambling, watching soap operas, shopping or any behavior that brings pleasure.

Addictions damage the physiology of the brain, which then keeps the addictions self-perpetuating. As we engage in the activity, the release of chemicals registers in the brain as a pleasurable experience. However, as the brain gradually undergoes the process of addiction, it eventually sends out an over-abundance of chemicals, which bombard the receiving cell until the cell is damaged and no longer receives the pleasure messages, and the chemical supply is depleted.

This process also damages the connection between the part of our brains where the cravings originate and the part of our brains that helps us understand the consequences of our choices. Therefore, the cravings are never satisfied, the consequences are never comprehended, and we are now addicted to the behavior.

> *Addictions harm the parts of our brains that regulate the memories and emotions that give us a sense of well-being and meaning to our lives.*

Addictions also harm the parts of our brains that regulate the memories and emotions that give us a sense of well-being and meaning to our lives. Because the behavior helped us feel good in the past, we continue the behavior in a futile attempt to recreate the feeling, and we entrench a neural pathway in our brains we cannot escape from; we never attain the feeling of well-being we seek.

A visual picture of this is animal pacing in captivity. In the wild, the animal walks to find food, to find water and to find a mate. Walking is a behavior that brings desirable outcomes. She is now in a cage, but in her desire to feel good she starts to walk and comes to a barrier. She turns and starts the behavior again and comes to a barrier. However, because walking brought pleasure in the past, she continues the behavior, seeking the pleasure, and in so doing entrenches the addictive behavior. It is no longer a search; it is a compulsive repetition of the exact same movements in the exact same tracks.

And so it is with us. We are in captivity. We are tormented, and in order to soothe our suffering, we self-medicate with our addiction of choice and never escape.

Disorders

The psychological damage flows into our emotional damage and manifests itself in self-destructive disorders. There are many types of disorders and many suggested causes, but victims of domestic violence commonly suffer some more than others, C-PTSD being chief among these. The symptoms of C-PTSD, described previously, are also contributing factors for other disorders. Several of the various symptoms, both psychological and biological, of C-PTSD are on the list of causes for eating disorders and anxiety disorders.

Eating Disorders

> We form our beliefs of inadequacy through society's propaganda and through the abuser's rhetoric.

Eating disorders, which include anorexia, bulimia, and compulsive eating, begin in the mind; they begin with what we believe about our environment and ourselves. The illusions we believe of ourselves (see chapter 2) as well as the self-condemnation aspect of C-PTSD create low self-esteem, one of the contributing factors of eating disorders. We form our beliefs of inadequacy through society's propaganda and through the abuser's rhetoric—we have to be thin, we have to be beautiful—and we internalize the message that we fail to measure up.

Another contributing factor is a traumatic relationship involving past or present abuse. The trauma we go through in domestic violence is mentally, emotionally and physically overwhelming. The trauma leads to feelings of fear, worthlessness, helplessness, loneliness and anxiety. We want to numb our emotions as we attempt to cope, and eating disorders numb our emotions. They also give a sense of control that the abuser has robbed us of.

Brain chemical imbalance is another contributing factor to eating disorders. The eating disorder is an attempt to satisfy the craving to feel good caused by the chemical imbalance from C-PTSD.

For the compulsive eater or the bulimic, eating perpetuates our existence (I eat therefore I am) while the abuser is annihilating our identity. For the anorexic, not eating diminishes our existence. As the abuse destroys our identity, we want to hide, to disappear, and this is, in essence, what we are doing in anorexia. We are starving for the love and nurturing that humans need. We compensate for our lack of love by eating, which brings a sense of comfort, or by not eating, which brings a sense of accomplishment.

Eating disorders release endorphins, which counteract the anxiety caused by the loss of serotonin and the elevation of norepinephrine. Endorphins are a natural opiate that produce sensations of peace, pleasure and euphoria. Our bodies naturally release endorphins to anaesthetize debilitating pain. For example, when injured in an emergency we often do not feel the pain until the crisis is over. Endorphins are also responsible for the "runner's high" after pushing the body to extremes. However, it is not only pain that releases endorphins; eating, sex and touch also release endorphins, still as protection, but in these cases it is to ensure our survival as a species.

The endorphins released from the eating disorder behavior help cocoon us against the ravages of domestic violence, and we become addicted to it. However, the eating disorders themselves are destroying us as they damage every biological system in the body and lead to death if not stopped. Once an eating disorder has begun, the chemical effects as well as the behavioral reinforcement create a perpetual destructive cycle, which is extremely difficult to escape.

Anxiety Disorders

There are many anxiety disorders, which include personality disorders and phobias. Personality disorders usually have some of the symptoms of C-PTSD and include disorders such as antisocial personality disorder, avoidant personality disorder and borderline personality disorder.

Phobias are of three types: fear of open or public places (agoraphobia), fear of people (social phobia), and fear of things (specific phobia). Phobias, like anxiety disorders, stem from exaggerated fears beyond what is warranted. We respond to our fear emotionally and behaviorally. Emotionally, our fear takes on panic proportions, and we will engage in extreme irrational behavior in order to avoid what we are afraid of. We understand we are being irrational, but our reactions are automatic and uncontrollable. Our phobias become debilitating as they take over our lives.

Any disorder can be triggered or exacerbated by domestic violence. We all mentally assess danger in order to determine appropriate action, but with anxiety disorders, something goes awry. When faced with a situation that presents a risk to us, we exaggerate the possibility of a negative outcome, which triggers our fears. Our fears may be based on real life experiences or on hypothetical scenarios. Each time we capitulate to our fear and avoid the situation, the fear is entrenched and escalates.

There are environmental and psychological stimuli associated with fear, and soon even the stimuli trigger our fear. The stimuli can be external, such as a slammed door, or internal, such as an elevated heart rate, which may or may not be related to something fearful.

The biological aspect of anxiety disorders involves elevated levels of norepinephrine. As we learned, elevated levels of norepinephrine produce anxiety, nervousness and discomfort and stimulate the fight-or-flight response, or the tend-and-befriend response. However, when we are the victim in the middle of a violent episode, none of those responses are available to us, and our sense of powerlessness also contributes to the anxiety disorder. Elevated norepinephrine also increases our heart rate, breathing and temperature, which is why these can also trigger an anxiety attack.

> *Our anxiety is insidious and gradually creeps into all areas of our lives*

Our anxiety is insidious and gradually creeps into all areas of our lives. With domestic violence, our fears are very real and founded. However, as we try to anticipate the violence and try to avoid it, the anxiety disorder gains a foothold, and as it grows it destroys our lives.

It is stated in *Anxiety Disorders: An Information Guide*, "When depression occurs in someone with an anxiety disorder, it is of particular concern since these two problems in combination increase the person's risk for suicide."[8]

Substance Abuse

Substance dependence or abuse commonly develops to cope with the mental health disorders brought on by domestic violence and to escape the pain caused by the domestic violence itself. "Recent research indicates that 55 percent to 99 percent of women with the co-occurring conditions of a disorder and substance dependence have experienced trauma from abuse and that abused women tend to engage in self-destructive behaviors."[9]

The presence of the disorder and substance dependence together makes treatment very difficult. Alcoholics Anonymous and similar support groups for drug addicts would be a challenge for us to go to while we are still in the abusive relationship since the abuser would not want us free from our addiction or to be around supportive people. Our addiction reduces our power and reinforces his.

Attending one of these groups is also a challenge for us even when we are out of the abusive relationship, since we fear publicly sharing our story because of our low self-esteem and high self-condemnation. In addition, we are adverse to being vulnerable in the presence of male attendees.

On the other hand, treatment for C-PTSD, anxiety and personality disorders often involves cognitive behavior techniques that expose us to what we fear in order to eliminate it. However, the stress of this treatment can trigger our addictive behavior.

With dual mental health problems, both should be treated in unison to prevent further damage and to speed recovery. However, therapists often encourage achieving stability in one mental health issue before treating the other, so neither is effectively treated.

> *At the time we developed the addiction and disorder, they helped us survive or cope, like holding on to a log as we are swept down a rushing river.*

At the time we developed the addiction and disorder, they helped us survive or cope, like holding on to a log as we are swept down a rushing river. When we come to a point where we seek help with our mental challenges, the river may have brought us out into a lake, and now as we try to push our log in front of us as we swim, it is hindering our progress. But as we persevere, eventually we gain the strength to swim to shore.

FUNDAMENTAL HUMAN NECESSITIES

There are many lists of what people consider fundamental human necessities. The following is a compilation of a few of these lists:

- Subsistence
- Affection
- Relaxation
- Participation
- Protection
- Understanding
- Identity
- Freedom
- Transcendence or dreams
- Creativity
- Appreciation
- Recognition
- Love
- Security
- Self-esteem
- New experiences

If these are necessities, we are perishing. We long for these, but we cannot depend on someone else to provide them. The seeds to produce these are within each of us. They are ours to give to others and, just as importantly, to ourselves. When we give them, they multiply back to us.

COULD WE CHOOSE DIFFERENTLY?

There is a common thread running through why we stay, how we adapt and how we cope. That thread is our mind. It creates the tapestry of our life. Our tapestry is being torn and worn faster than we are able to mend it. We strive after the wind in vain. The ways we adapt and cope keep us busy stitching and keep us bound to the same dreary, damaged tapestry. Can we let this tapestry go? Can we begin a new tapestry where we can choose the rich colors and beautiful patterns and weave a work of wonder?

seven

THE DARKEST HOUR IS JUST BEFORE DAWN

I LOOKED AT THE BLACK SLURRY LIQUID IN THE GLASS THE NURSE WAS encouraging me to drink.

"It's charcoal," she said.

"Maybe it's better than having my stomach pumped, but I'm not so sure." I drained the glass and handed it back to the nurse. As I looked into her eyes, I saw compassionate concern.

"Why would you do this to yourself?" she asked in a gentle voice.

I could not forget her words. They troubled me.

I thought, *What a strange question. I'm not doing anything to myself. I'm trying to do something for myself. I'm trying to escape. She doesn't understand…or is what she is implying true? Am I hurting myself?*

She checked my vital signs again, then left me for a while. I would have loved to lie on the bed a few feet from me, but instead I remained on the examining table and waited.

The lights were dim, especially in the hall, since it was so late at night. It was quiet. I liked hospitals. I felt safe and cared for. Since we lived in a small community, the hospital was not busy. It was a pleasant new hospital with native etchings on huge glass panels. Paintings, plants, heritage pictures and soft leather furniture added to the warmth.

After I told the emergency ward receptionist that I had swallowed a handful of pills, she took me straight into an examining room ahead of the other two people sitting in the waiting room. Ed brought me to the hospital, but they did not let him in the examining room with me.

It was not that long ago that I was here in the hospital for them to stitch up my cheek after Ed threw a steel travel mug full of whiskey and cola at me. Maybe that information came up on my file when they admitted me this time and that is why they did not want him in with me. Whatever the reason, I was grateful for the peace.

I had waited so long for a change in Ed's beliefs, values and behavior. In spite of his promises, he became more entrenched in his ideology with every passing day, with every passing year and with every passing decade. Apathy was displacing my hope. I wished I was no longer part of Ed's world, but I had made a vow "For better or for worse." The "worse" was never ending, with "better" nowhere in sight. Of the long litany of conditions in my marriage vows binding me to Ed, the only condition to free me was death: "Until death do us part."

Sitting in the dim quiet of the hospital room, the words to a song whispered in my mind. I thought back to when I had heard it. It was late at night, and I was listening to satellite radio on the computer in the den. Ed must have been at the bar, because I would not have been doing that if he was home. It was strange that I was listening to music at all, because I usually kept the house as quiet and still as possible when I was alone. I had lived with the chaos and violence for so long, and I craved peace and stillness.

A song came on about leaving, and part of the refrain was "Got that get away feeling."[1] As I listened, the words resonated down my deep well of sorrow to the bottom of my soul. The longing for that song to be for me brought sorrow and tears.

Since leaving was not an option for me, I chased every thought of leaving out of my mind, but that song seemed embedded in a secret place, and my spirit would sometimes recall its haunting refrain.

As I sat in the hospital, time slipped by in peaceful silence until, too soon, the nurse said I was free to go. Free to go? Free to go back to my dungeon. I reluctantly returned to the emergency waiting room. Ed was there to take me home.

At home, I went upstairs and sat in my daughter's old room. I floated in a fog, not wanting to move.

Ed yelled up from the living room, "Get down here and phone your mom. Tell her what you did."

This was too strange a command for me to make sense of. Why was he ordering me to call my mom? He hated my mom and hated when I talked with her. And there was no way I wanted to tell anyone what I had done, especially my mom. What was he up to? What did he want from this?

Fear started to spread through me. His actions were out of character. It was a fear of the unknown, of not knowing how to prepare for what was to come. I remained still and silent, sitting on the edge of the bed, looking out the window. The dark sky was starting to turn indigo, and the stars were slowly disappearing as the morning began to make its presence known. I still had my pajamas on under the tracksuit I wore to the hospital. I thought of changing and putting on my makeup before I drew insults from Ed. I was avoiding a decision about his command, hoping that he would drop it.

He yelled again from the landing, "Get down here and call her, or I will."

I sat frozen in confusion, trying to determine what to do or what to say. My mind raced, looking for safe ground, avoiding a decision.

What seemed like an eternity passed, then I heard Ed talking. I could not believe he had called my mom. I struggled to hear the words or at least the tone, but I was too far away. The conversation was short, and soon I heard footsteps on the stairs.

At the door he said, "She thinks you should see a shrink. You're f—— crazy, and I want this behavior stopped now."

I quickly agreed before he changed his mind. I had a feeling he would regret allowing me to share what I was going through with someone, but I hoped his pride would prevent him from going back on his decision. Just the thought of a crack in my isolation was a soothing balm.

I pondered what just happened. His call to my mom and his agreeing to counseling was so strange. He had insulted psychiatrists in the past, calling them quacks, and any poor performance by the kids or me he saw as an insult to him—he was embarrassed if we were less than our best. Then the reason dawned on me: it was the same reason he took me to the hospital, the same reason he beat me the first time I tried suicide—he did not want to lose his obsession, and his anger was no longer having the effect he expected. He spent many years creating his trophy. He had molded and chiseled, getting just the right look, just the right attitude. "She is always there when the craving for a rage comes, and it is so satisfying when her pain finally shows; the longer it is drawn out, the better. Then there is all the cooking, cleaning, shopping, gardening and administration…not to mention all the other ways she satisfies. I made her who she is. She is mine, and she does not die until I say she dies.'

I began counseling. My counselor, Rita, asked what was troubling me.

I said, "I'm a suicidal alcoholic having trouble dealing with the death of my dad." Then I waited to see which of those three she chose to start with. My bulimia was not something I was willing to share with anyone, not even a counselor. She chose the alcohol.

By this point my drinking was tearing me apart; I desperately wanted to be free of its stranglehold, and yet I was terrified to be without it. I would have no defense against my shaking. I would be vulnerable and exposed. Alcohol also eased the pain of the abuse. It created the illusion of a different existence, as my fear subsided and the tension eased. But I knew drinking produced more pain and a deeper pit. Alcohol was as destructive on the body as it was on the mind and emotions.

Rita assured me she was not there to tell me what to do. She was there to listen, support, to help me discover what was best for me. The story of my relationship with Ed slowly emerged as I shared with her the history of my drinking.

The tears flowed as I revealed my heart. It was such a relief to feel safe and to be able to cry without being humiliated for it. It was such a comfort to feel someone's compassion instead of condemnation and to be able to tell someone what was happening in my life.

Going home, I planned what to say to Ed. I knew he was going to ask, and I needed to somehow work it around the truth, because he had the ability to sense if I was being honest or not. However, if I revealed everything, I would not only face his angry abuse, but he might refuse to let me go to counseling again. So that evening at supper I waited for the questions.

We were sitting at the island in the kitchen watching the television in the family room. Ed had not said anything since he came home from work. I wondered about his silence, but he was ready to eat with me, so he did not seem mad. I put dinner out, and he helped himself, then sat there not eating. My mind scrambled to figure out what he wanted from me. *What's in front of me that he doesn't have yet? The salad dressing.* I passed him that, but he ignored me. *The salt and pepper?* I passed those, and he took the pepper mill and ground some on his dinner. I felt a sense of relief that it was not the start of a confrontation.

"So, what did you tell your shrink?" Ed asked while he kept his eyes on the television.

"About missing Dad," I said as my heart started to pound.

"I suppose you told her everything about me," he said as his expression started to get darker.

"We focused on Dad and some things about me," I said. *Will he be able to tell I'm sidestepping his comment?*

"What goes on between you and me is none of her business," he stated with icy finality.

I quickly agreed with him. I wanted to reassure him so that he did not take this opportunity away from me. To be let out of the dungeon, to be free to be able to share my fears and pain with someone, was like being drenched with rain and chilled to the core of my soul as I wandered lost in the dark and then seeing a candle in a window. As I approached, I was welcomed, brought to the warmth of the fire, wrapped in a soft blanket and given a mug of something warm and sweet. After so many years of isolation and pain, I could not believe that this amazing gift was for me, the gift of sharing the things in my heart.

Ed did not talk to me the rest of the night, but his body language indicated that he did not seem to be angry. After a few more drinks and a few more television shows, I thought it might be safe to attempt to go to bed. I got up and went over to him. I kissed him on the cheek as I was trained to do and suggested that I was going to bed. He ignored me, so I understood that to mean I was free to go.

With relief, I slipped into bed, thankful that I did not have to go through an interrogation and thankful to have a time of peace in bed by myself for a while.

I was allowed to continue my counseling, but as I revealed my fear and pain, my depression remained. Rita wanted to put me on antidepressants, but she could not until I reduced my drinking to two drinks a day for a week.

I tried. Each morning I said, "Today I will not touch a drop; I will not touch a drop." I was determined, but not for long. Something triggered my shaking, and even as the alcohol was pouring down my throat, one part of me said, "No. Don't do it," while another part of me said, "I can try again tomorrow." Then I waited in happy anticipation of the warm fuzzy feeling the alcohol would bring. But tomorrow was the same, and so was the day after.

Rita had left it up to me to tell her when I was ready to start antidepressants. Finally, I made it a week with only two drinks a day except for a couple of three-drink days. I let her know I was ready. She wanted to set up an appointment with the psychiatrist, who was the only one in our town who could give me the prescription.

I was confused. "Can't you give me the prescription?"

"No, it has to be a doctor," Rita said.

My voice trembled as I asked, "Is the doctor a lady?"

"No, he's a man," Rita replied.

I was terrified and torn. I was anxious to try the medication, but Ed would be enraged if I saw a man alone, regardless of whether or not he was a doctor.

Earlier when Ed found out the only surgeon in our community was a man he said, "You better never need one, because you're not seeing him if anything happens to you."

I asked Rita if she could see the doctor with me, thinking Ed might agree to that.

"I'll talk to the doctor next time he comes and see if it would be acceptable to him."

A week later, she let me know that she could come in with me to see the psychiatrist. Then I had to decide the best time and way to approach the subject with Ed. When I finally got up the courage to ask, he was angry and made comments about psychiatrists just wanting to get women on the couch to take advantage of them. I reassured Ed that I did not have to discuss anything with the doctor and that Rita would go in with me. The doctor just needed to write the prescription. Ed finally relented, and I started on my medication.

However, sticking to the two drinks a day was sporadic and then impossible. Soon I was back to drinking in secret as much as I did prior to starting my medication. Mixing alcohol with the medication nullified its effect, and I noticed no improvement in my depression. However, I was reluctant to admit it because I did not want anyone to know that I was drinking too much again. When I was drunk and behaved strangely, I blamed it on the medication.

Ed used my mental state as yet another reason to denigrate me. He did not believe my state had anything to do with his treatment of me. He believed I could be better if I wanted to be and that my weak character was the problem. I believed this as well as I struggled to do what was right, as I struggled to escape this monster that was consuming me.

A year went by, and I was still trying to deceive myself and everyone else that I was getting better, but deep inside I knew I was in trouble. I prayed in anguish for God to take my alcoholism away. I knew he had done it for others; why wouldn't he do it for me?

Maybe it was my fear that was blocking me from receiving God's deliverance. Maybe it was my imprisonment in the dungeon of abuse.

Then one morning as I reflected on Ed's rage the night before and my drunken tears, a radical thought came to mind: *Maybe if I'm away from Ed for a while I can quit.*

The thought filled me with both terror and hope. I had never gone to see any of my family without Ed, and even with him the visits were years apart. From the start of our marriage, he had belittled me with "Why don't you run home to Mommy and Daddy" whenever I cried, so it was a matter of my pride, at the start, not to go home. However, Ed soon taught me I was not allowed to visit anyone without him, and visiting was something he disliked.

I waited several days for Ed to be in a mood where it might be safe to test the waters. I posed the hypothetical question of going to see Mom for a few days.

My fears turned into reality as the angry assault began and progressed into waves of fury rolling over me. I shrank into my inner hiding place and brought the fog up around me as the storm raged. He took the easy way away from me. Then, I faced the hard question: *Do I go anyway, even if it is against his will?*

That was the most terrifying, defiant decision I had ever contemplated in our marriage, maybe in my life. I was desperate for deliverance from the chains of alcoholism, and I felt God telling me I needed to take this step. To me, the step felt more like Neil Armstrong's "giant leap for mankind." The courage to do this was beyond me, but I decided to go to my mother's, 400 miles away. Next, I needed to determine how and when.

It seemed like another person making the travel arrangements. The previous fall we had bought a four-wheel-drive truck that was his pride and joy. I could not take it; Ed would be livid. He would also be enraged at my going such a great distance in the truck on my own. It would create unlimited potential for me to end up in dangerous situations and for others to influence me without him there to screen it.

A solution presented itself a few days later. The mom of Ashley's friend was going to Albertville, which was halfway to my mom's. I had relatives in Albertville who could help me take a flight to my final destination. There my mom could pick me up.

I talked to my friend. She was somewhat apprehensive since she was familiar with Ed's anger, but she knew I needed help and agreed. The rest of the pieces fell into place, and I anxiously waited for the day.

The morning I set off on my dangerous adventure, I left Ed a note saying I had gone to my mother's for a while.

Terror and excitement overwhelmed me, and by 10:00 a.m., before my ride to the city came, I had already drunk half a bottle of vodka. I was hoping not to drink once I reached Mom's, so I took plenty of alcohol to last until I arrived, my final chance to indulge. I stashed all my convenient little bottles in every nook and cranny I could think of so that I could gulp them down in the washrooms on my journey.

It felt like I was in another world as I sat on the floor of the airport along with all the other passengers awaiting delayed flights…me in an airport by myself!

"Where are you flying to?" I bravely asked the young lady beside me.

"I was visiting my family on our farm. Now, I'm heading back to college."

I could not believe I was talking to a stranger without the fear of Ed's judgmental insults to keep me silent.

Our flight was finally cleared for takeoff. I boarded and buckled up. The ground raced by outside the window, and I felt a thrill as the wheels left the ground and we were airborne. The flight was short, less than an hour, and as I entered the busy terminal, I was delighted to see that my daughter had come with my mom to pick me up. I was very drunk by this time, so tears came easily, but I knew I was with people who loved me dearly and wanted what was best for me. I felt very peaceful and protected.

Ashley drove us to Mom's and stayed to visit for a bit. Soon after she left, I went to bed in an antique bed with homemade quilts, in bed by myself! Terror was not sitting in the other room, soon to join me. There was only serene quiet, as my mom had gone to bed as well.

The next morning I wanted something to drink so bad that I was in agony. I felt quite ill, which was unusual. Because I had drank for so long, I had not had a hangover in years. I had anti-nausea medicine with me because I sometimes used it to sleep. As I tried to remove a tablet from the package, I shook worse than I ever had before. I had to ask my mom to help me as I did my best to disguise my tremors.

Mom and I were quite comfortable together. We read and talked. Later that morning, I took her car to the store for groceries. Mom does not drink, so there was no alcohol in her home, but I knew there was a liquor store close to the grocery store. The craving got more powerful the closer I got. I debated and drove and debated some more. "Am I going to turn in? No, no, no, don't look, keep it out of your mind.'

I was past the liquor store and on my way back to Mom's. I was overjoyed and sad at the same time—a victory and a lost opportunity.

We were meeting Ashley and my niece, Sarah, for lunch. I was still not feeling well but looked forward to seeing the girls. As soon as I was seated at the table, I could feel the tremors inside me, even without trying to lift something. I felt like crying. This enemy had been with me so long, and I wanted to be free of it. I was craving a drink too, but since I knew I was not going to have one I knew there was no relief for my shaking.

I struggled with my knife and fork, picking them up and then putting them down again, hoping the shaking would ease. I decided to go ahead and try to eat, but my knife fell to the floor because I could not hold on to it. Shame filled me as I tried to hide it. *Why didn't I order a sandwich that I could eat with my hands?*

My self-consciousness and struggles kept me from enjoying my time together with these special ladies as much as I wanted to.

Ashley knew about the shaking of my phobia, and I sensed her compassion. She is an amazing woman. She cares for people deeply and expresses it. She often gives people small gifts and cards and writes gracious, loving words in her cards. She is wise and thoughtful, always thinking of creative, significant ways to help. She is generous with her time and attention. The peace you feel in her presence washes healing over you. But she is also courageous and adventurous. I felt very fortunate that she was my daughter. I was sad I couldn't spend more time with her.

However, Sarah did have a few days off from work. My sister, Sarah's mom, and her family were moving, and we agreed to go to my sister's in a couple of days and do some packing. I was looking forward to helping.

The day after our lunch, I waited in excited, terrified anticipation for my mom to leave. She was going with a seniors group on a trip and would be gone all day. My excitement was over my decision to fast and pray.

I had been quite frightened when Mom told me she was going to be gone for a whole day. If I was left alone, I doubted if I would have the strength to resist my cravings. Then I realized it would be a perfect time to fast and pray. But I was terrified that I might fail and give in to the cravings. I hoped my prayers could carry me through.

In the morning, I went with Sarah to my sister's, who was at work. Sarah went upstairs, and I went to work in the kitchen. When I entered the kitchen, the table was covered with bottles of alcohol from the men working the night before.

Drinking in secret had become a part of my life, and normally I would have rejoiced at the opportunity to indulge in alcohol, but as I looked at it, there was no desire to have any of it. The craving was gone! I was amazed and delighted and asked God, "Is this true? Is this for me? Have you given me this gift?" A line from Psalm 40 came to my mind: *"I waited patiently for the LORD [to help me]; he inclined to me and heard my cry. He drew me up from the pit of destruction, out of the miry bog, and set my feet upon a rock, making my steps secure"* (Psalm 40:1-2 ESV).

I put all the alcohol up in one of the cupboards and set to work on the rest of the kitchen. Mom picked us up after, and we went for lunch again. And another miracle—my shaking was gone, too!

Actually, if I had thought of it, I might not have had the courage to pray for deliverance from alcohol, since that was what I had been using to stop my shaking. But God in his loving mercy set me free from both.

I had called Ed a few times. He would make a few snide remarks and terse comments interspersed with long silences. I resisted the impulse to fill the silences and kept my comments short and neutral. After a few minutes, he would hang up on me.

After a week at Mom's, I flew home and met Ed's wrath at the airport. But the peace and joy I had because of my freedom from alcohol and my social phobia elevated me to a different place. Ed's anger no longer lodged in my heart. It passed right through me. I maintained my peace in the storm, knowing the storm would eventually pass.

When I told Ashley and Connor about my escape from the agony of alcohol, they were happy, proud and amazed, especially Connor, who knew, more so than Ashley, how far gone I was. He had found my hidden bottles on several occasions, but he was never judgmental and he kept my secret. They were probably also torn between relief, skepticism and hope.

I could not wait to see my counselor, Rita, again. On my next visit, I told her my good news. She was amazed and pleased. She said, "I have never had a client work so hard and accomplish so much in so short a time."

It did not seem short to me.

Then she said, "I respect your decision to remain with Ed, but as long as you do, there is only so far your recovery can go. I've decided to put you on maintenance, and we'll schedule your visits every two months instead of one."

I did not want to let go completely, because I still had my bulimia to deal with, but I was not ready yet. I kept this to myself however, because I was not ready to share it.

A few months later at my meeting with Rita, I asked to borrow her book on eating disorders, which was an easier way to let her know I had another struggle to deal with than telling her outright. The book was fascinating and disturbing. I learned that eating disorders had a tremendously complex interrelation between the biological, psychological and emotional processes. I also discovered that Ed's abuse was at the core of my disorder. What was most disturbing was the deadly effect it had on every system in the body. Fear gripped me as I read about the damage it did to the heart and what the symptoms were. I'd had a problem with my heart for years, and I thought back on an episode that had happened several months before.

This was before I had stopped drinking, and I had drunk quite a lot before I went to my appointment with Rita. When I arrived, my heart started racing and would not stop. This symptom happened every few months and had started twenty years before, a few years after my eating disorder started. It was nothing new to me and usually stopped after a minute or two, so I ignored it. But it wouldn't stop, so I told Rita about it and she sent me downstairs to the emergency department. They put me on an ECG and tried several things to return it to normal. The doctor knew I had been drinking and would not give me any medication. It lasted two hours, and I was worried. Finally, my heart rate slowed to normal, and they let me go home.

Then reading Rita's book about eating disorders, I understood that my heart condition was probably caused from the eating disorder. I read of many more damaging conditions that could develop, but the one that frightened me the most was cancer of the esophagus.

I talked to Rita about my disorder at our next session. It just so happened that the hospital's mental health department had received funding to include a traveling eating disorder specialist in their services. Rita asked if I would like to talk to her. My heart was saying "no," but my head moved me to say "yes" even though I was not at a point where I was willing to give it up.

I prayed about it and felt I should do whatever they asked of me. The eating disorder specialist, Karen, joined Rita and me for my next session. Karen was one of the most gentle, compassionate ladies I had every met.

She said, "This is not about getting you to stop your behavior, since it is serving a purpose in your situation. But what I would like you to do is have your doctor give you a physical exam to assess any damage caused by the disorder."

This was frightening for me, since I did not want anyone to know, and the circle was getting bigger. Also, my doctor was Ed's doctor as well. I did not know where my disclosure would lead, but I had decided to do what they asked so I agreed.

My doctor was very understanding, and she asked how my relationship with Ed was.

I said, "He has high expectations of me." But when I started to cry, her suspicions were confirmed that Ed's treatment of me was at the root of my disorder. Her concern and encouragement brought relief and hope.

I had done as my counselors asked and felt good about it. My fears of facing the bulimia began to dissipate. I returned in my mind once again to the beginning of the eating disorder. When my eating disorder started, I thought it would be an occasional occurrence, but the frequency continually increased, and so did my concern. It controlled my waking thoughts.

As a bulimic, I was either avoiding food, buying food, preparing food, eating food or getting rid of food. I had thought bulimia was my friend until I tried to escape, until I tried to quit and discovered another tormentor held me captive. I could not quit. It ruled, abused and consumed my identity as ruthlessly as Ed did.

I tried to overcome it by not eating at all, and I became anorexic. Then the craving for food would build, and bulimia would return. Over time, I disconnected from my unbearable emotions and my external senses in order to bring soothing relief to my world. I felt like I was in a fog or a cocoon, and I had trouble concentrating and trouble making decisions.

My eating disorder controlled my hidden life, Ed controlled my external life, and my inner world was in turmoil.

I believed I was unworthy. I was full of shame and guilt. My eating disorder isolated me further by hindering my friendship with God. I was trying to hide from him too. Even though I knew in my mind that he loved me, I could not feel it in my heart.

As I tried to come to grips with the eating disorder, I was full of fear. I was not ready to give up my "lifeline" yet. I always needed time to gather information and analyze it before I was willing to take action, but I didn't know if I would ever have the strength or courage to let it go. Then I remembered that God had helped me overcome alcoholism. Maybe it was possible to overcome the eating disorder as well.

Free Your Mind and the Rest Will Follow

> *"Man's mind, once stretched by a new idea,
> never regains its original dimensions."*
> Oliver Wendell Holmes

STATISTICS
Economic consequences of intimate partner violence in the
United States:

- The cost of intimate partner violence exceeds $5.8 billion each year, $4.1 billion of which is for direct medical and mental health services

- Victims of intimate partner violence lost almost 8 million days of paid work because of the violence perpetrated against them by current or former husbands, boyfriends and dates.

- Approximately 50 percent of employed battered women are harassed at work by their abusive partners.[1]

SOMETHING TO KEEP IN MIND

We want freedom; we want clarity. Our very first action step towards this is to go to the playground and swing.

For now, let's imagine ourselves in a beautiful park. The day is warm. There is a sea of emerald green grass. At the edge of the park, peonies, pansies and petunias line the black wrought-iron fencing. Islands of trees flow through the park with burgundy leaved shrubs and the varied green hues of the aspens and oaks. The fragrance of the purple lilac blooms sweeten the air, birds soar against the soft powder blue sky, and the golden sunshine warms our hair. At the center of the park is a playground, and we are sitting on a swing with warm white sand at our feet.

> *Developing successful habits to move higher in our purpose is like swinging.*

We lift our feet off the ground, and we start to move our legs. We swing slowly at first, and it requires a lot of work. We pump our legs back and forth, and we don't get very far. But with each pass, the arc is a little higher and it requires a little less effort. The rhythm becomes smoother as we go with the flow. As we sail forward, we lean back and reach our feet to the sky until we hesitate at the top of the arc. Then as we start back, we curl our feet under, lean forward and watch the ground zoom beneath us until we once again hesitate at the top of the arc. Higher and higher we soar, laughing as the wind blows our hair and clothes one direction, then the other. We are full of joy and exhilaration.

This is the beauty of repetition, the beauty of perseverance, the beauty of rhythm. Developing successful habits to create the life we want is like swinging. It is all about rhythm.

1. We sit on the swing. The swing is now supporting us. It is our purpose, even if we don't know what it is yet.
2. We hold on to the ropes. They connect us to the Higher Power. They are the two-way communication in our relationship with God.
3. We take our feet off the ground. This is our step of faith.
4. We begin to move in rhythm, back and forth, to start the swing in motion. The rhythmic movement is the choices, the small steps, the actions we take that start us on the path, the plane, the trajectory of what we want to create or change.

As we start our rhythm, as we start to swing, it takes a lot of effort to produce very little movement. But as we repeatedly apply our effort, we swing higher and higher. When we persevere, the amount of effort required diminishes the higher we go. The higher and faster we go, the more thrilling it is.

This is what happens with our life when we follow the repetition and rhythm of the swing. And as we take ourselves to the playground to plan our escape, to plan our new life, a step will come to mind. If we take one small step or question one belief, the momentum will carry us until it is time for the next step. We only need to start one pass of the swing at a time.

The Paradigm Shift

"I understand I'm being abused, but I can't leave." Somehow, that doesn't quite feel like the truth. Is it fear that is trying to extinguish the flicker of hope? "He'll kill me if I try to leave; there is no way I'll be able to support myself; no one will ever love me; this will be so hard on the kids; I'll lose my friends and community and maybe my job." On the other hand, maybe pride is the issue. "Am I

> *DANGER:*
> *Please see appendix B for precautions after leaving the abuser.*

being a quitter? If I hang in long enough he'll see the light; my family and friends will see me as a failure; my church will see me as a sinner."

We are the managers of our lives. Even if we have abdicated it to someone who is running it and ruining it, we are still ultimately responsible for it.

Our beliefs and our value systems elicit our emotions and actions. This is our paradigm, our perceived reality. To change what we believe of ourselves, the relationship, and the possibility of leaving will require something of us. Someone once said, "You have to open your hands and let go of what you are holding on to before your hands can receive something new." There are perceived costs and benefits to an abusive relationship, and if we analyze these to become enlightened, we loosen the hold of the lies keeping us trapped.

Opening our minds to possibilities is frightening. We may be familiar with the saying "The devil we know versus the devil we don't know." We somehow feel our chances are better with the status quo. But the fact is, we know for sure the repeated pattern of abuse we live with now. The probability of a miserable life is 100 percent right now. What is the realistic probability of a miserable life if we leave? It has to be lower than the 100 percent of our current circumstances, so what do we have to lose?

Right now, we are afraid; we are resisting change, restricting possibilities and repressing potential. But we are told if we change our perception we change our reality; we shift our paradigm.

So it all begins with our mind. As the song says, *"Free your mind and the rest will follow."*[2] We start with our thoughts, and then our emotions and actions will follow naturally.

How do we set our minds free? If we open a crack to let a sliver of light into the darkness, enough light to allow a possibility in to ponder, we will feel our paradigm start to shift. Be willing to draw back the dusty drapes, swing the windows open and soar free.

DRAWING BACK THE DUSTY DRAPES

We learned in chapter 2 about the lies and the illusions that are the basis of our fears. We learned in chapter 4 about the abusive rhetoric and behavior that destroy our health and well-being, our self-worth and self-confidence. We learned in chapter 6 about the psychological and emotional damage caused by the abuse. The lies, abuse and damage create the destructive paradigm that blocks out light and life.

In order to draw back these drapes and let the light in, we must first recognize and question the thoughts and beliefs that keep us in the dirt and darkness.

We do not deal much in facts when we are contemplating ourselves.
—Mark Twain

Cognitive Dissonance

In order for the bonds to develop between us and the abusers, we retrained our minds. If our thoughts and beliefs (cognitions) are in disagreement (dissonance), it creates inner conflict and discomfort. This is cognitive dissonance, so we realign our thoughts to be in agreement with our beliefs.[3]

For example, we think, "It is wrong for him to hit me, therefore I should leave.'

We also think, "I can't leave, because I can't support the children and myself."

To create agreements in our minds, we subconsciously adjust our thought to be "He had a right to hit me, because I shouldn't have done what I did" or something similar to justify why we stay. The abuser is usually supplying us with these reasons, and this is how we become part of his ideology and refuse to see reality.

Another thing that causes cognitive dissonance that keeps us trapped is the fear of our insufficiency. The abuser soon destroys any past trust we had in our capabilities. Every tiny thing that he thinks we do wrong

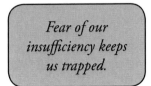

Fear of our insufficiency keeps us trapped.

he magnifies, and anything that we do right, or well, he belittles or dismisses. Therefore, because we cannot have both faith in our capabilities and belief in his indoctrination, we sacrifice our self-confidence to create accord in our beliefs; we believe we are incompetent.

The language the abuser uses to humiliate, intimidate and coerce us, along with the physical violence, sends us the message that he must hate us, because everything about us ignites his rage. Then the honeymoon phase comes to create the dissonance. Here he tells us how wonderful we are, how much he loves us, how sorry he is for his behavior and that it will not happen again. Therefore, to create accord in our thinking, we excuse the abuse and cling to the hope that his words of love and promises of change are true. He keeps us on a mental and emotional roller coaster, always disoriented, never grounded.

Fears and Illusions Associated with Leaving

We often lack confidence before entering the relationship with the abuser, and once in the relationship, self-confidence is destroyed. Lack of confidence paralyzes us with fear because we fear that our skills, abilities and resources are insufficient for us to survive on our own. We also believe the abuser will thwart any attempt we make to start a new life without him, and we doubt our ability to escape and protect ourselves from him.

- The children need their father.
- Family and friends tell me to stay.
- It's his drinking or drugs that cause him to be abusive.
- The abuser needs me.
- The abuser threatens suicide if I leave.
- The abuse is deserved.
- The abuse will stop eventually.
- I have no opportunities.
- I have no resources.
- I have no skills and abilities.
- I am afraid of threats and retribution.
- I am afraid of losing our children.
- I am afraid of failing.

Perceived Benefits Associated With Staying

We may talk ourselves into staying by looking at the enticements that we are allowed and because we are uncomfortable with change. Another part of us is struggling against giving up on the relationship.

The following is a list of perceived benefits associated with staying.
- Shared goals
- Time to spend with our children
- Joint family and friends
- Less lonely
- Position within the church or other organizations
- A desirable lifestyle
- Established roles
- Free of job responsibilities
- Free from decision making
- Allowed to hide from the world
- Economic security
- Expenses are lower for one household than for two
- Pleasures of the honeymoon phase
- Familiarity (the devil we know)
- Easier to indulge disorders and substance abuses
- Shared history

Even contemplating whether any of these are an issue with us draws open the drapes and sheds light on them.

Swinging the Windows Open

As we swing open the window to fresh winds, they dispel the illusions and perceptions that keep us trapped. They create clarity to reveal the truth that will set us free. To determine if our perceptions are true or false we need to take a look at our beliefs and values.

Dispelling the Fears and Illusions

Here we address the fear and illusions that we listed previously associated with leaving.
- Your children need a live mother more than an abusive father.
  —The children's highest priority is the need to be healthy and safe.
  —If the children remain under the abuser's influence, they will likely be trapped in the same cycle when they marry. It is up to you to break the destructive cycle.

> *63 percent of male youths between the ages of 11 and 20 who are serving time for homicide have killed their mother's abuser.*[3]

—Abuse damages their development.

—The abuser has a negative impact on their character, which affects who they become.

• Outsiders cannot fathom the damage sustained in abuse and are not in a position to advise you to stay. As you have read in previous chapters, an abusive relationship is very complicated and destructive.

• Alcohol does not cause violence; it is the excuse he uses to be violent.

• Why does he need you?

—You are not one of his possessions to be used as he sees fit.

—The definition of codependence is "taking on the responsibility caused by another person's problems…the codependent is understood to be a person who perpetuates the addiction or pathological condition of someone close to them in a way that hampers recovery…through direct control over the dependent, by making excuses for their dysfunctional behavior, or by blunting negative consequences."[4] Not allowing the abuser to deal with the consequences of his choices prevents him from being responsible. You do not help him by saving him. ***However, changing this pattern may be dangerous for you if you stay.***

• When he says he will commit suicide if you leave, he is using emotional blackmail. You are not responsible for his life. It is his choice what he does with his life. You cannot forfeit your life and your children's lives because of his unethical manipulation.

• No, you never deserve abuse, regardless of your words or actions. You deserve to, at least, be treated according to international human rights. You also have the right to individual self-fulfillment. You are not responsible for the abuser's choices or his behavior; he is.

• Abuse is more likely to escalate rather than stop if you stay in the relationship.

—According to Lundy Bancroft in *Why Does He Do That?* "It is more common for abusers to stay the same or get worse than it is for them to make…changes."[5]

—Because he is sorry afterward doesn't mean he will stop.

- You can brainstorm potential opportunities with counselors, people you know, or online. Opportunities are endless when we are creative.
- In most Western societies, we own half of the net assets built up during the relationship regardless of whose name they are registered under.
- There are abundant resources, city agencies and Internet sites, such as Kijiji or Craigslist, that can supply us with everything a household needs; there are programs to save for the down payment on a house or to start a new business; to get an education there are scholarships, grants, bursaries and loans.
- The unknown is frightening because we believe we do not have the skills or resources to overcome obstacles we may face.
   —Read of others who have surmounted obstacles and the unknown.
   —Take an honest assessment of your skills and qualities.
   —You can acquire new skills.
- How serious are the abuser's threats?
   —Are they a bluff?
   —Are the consequences of his threats worse than the consequences of staying?
   —How much more cumulative damage will you suffer over time if you stay? The more damage you sustain, the more challenges you face when you leave. So, sooner is better than later.
   —If his threats are real, what are your protection options, e.g. safety plan, restraining order, distance and time, exposing his threats to friends, family and the public?
- Is there proof that you are a good parent? Is there proof that the abuser is an unfit parent? (Gather evidence that may be needed. Keep a diary and save receipts.) It is more likely the children will be taken away if you stay in an environment that is unsafe for them than if you leave.
- Many small successes are more likely than total failure.
   —Is there benefit in failure? Everyone has failure. Walt Disney went bankrupt many times before he was finally able to pursue his dream.
   —Failure is never permanent. Most likely, you have the skills and intelligence you need to survive without him. Surviving without

him takes less skill than surviving with him. If you think you are short on skills, you can find a way to improve the ones you have or gain new ones.

Dispelling the Perception of Benefits

This is a challenging area, because dispelling the myth of the benefit leaves us with cognitive dissonance, and then we must choose between the truth and the myth in order to create resonance.

- Shared goals (Perception):
  — Are the shared goals yours or his?
  — What life will you have, even if you arrive at the goal?
  — You can create new goals to reach your own dreams.
- Time to spend with your children (Perception):
  — You will be free to interact with your children as your true self.
  — You will relieve your children's suffering.
  — Your children will no longer feel helpless to help you.
  — Your children will be less likely to perpetuate the cycle of sons becoming abusers and daughters choosing abusers.
  — Leaving will prevent further damage to their development.
  — How will your children thrive if you leave?
  — Safe to be themselves
  — Experience the relief that comes with peace
  — Opportunities to choose their own future
  — Opportunities to achieve their potential
- Joint family and friends (Perception):
  — Your family will always be your family.
  — His family you may or may not have to let go of for your safety's sake or because of their loyalty to the abuser.
  — Friends will remain friends if they are true friends.
  — You will make new friends as your life transforms.
  — You need to surround yourself with good healthy people in order to heal and grow.
- Less lonely (Perception):
  — You may fear being alone if you leave, but there are many like-minded people to become friends with.

— People care.
- Your position within your church or other organizations (Perception):
  — There are many worthy organizations and causes to become involved with.
  — You take your skills and experience with you, and there will always be new opportunities to get involved.
- A desirable lifestyle (Perception):
  — You cannot assume your lifestyle will deteriorate.
  — Your current lifestyle will be considered for divorce rulings, splitting net assets as well as income 50–50. Currently most spousal support in Western society is for an indefinite length of time, calculated using the length of the relationship and the income of each person.
  — Being free from the abuse will change you for the better so your desires will evolve, and so will your lifestyle.
  — Consider all the ways your lifestyle will improve.
  — You will not have a lifestyle if you no longer have a life.
  — Is your current lifestyle worth your children's suffering now and in the future?

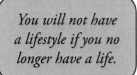

You will not have a lifestyle if you no longer have a life.

- Your role has been decided (Perception):
  — Pursuing your dreams and desires gives you back the identity that was stolen from you.
  — Your role should be to develop your true identity that the world needs.
- Free of job responsibilities (Perception):
  — Although you do not have the responsibility of going to work each day, you also do not have the power and freedom a career offers.
  — Abusers sometimes require us to work while they stay home and control our money.
- Free from decision-making (Perception):
  — You will no longer pay such a high price for decision-making mistakes.

— Mistakes are how we learn and grow.
— If you reframe mistakes to look for positive results, your fear of decision-making will diminish.
- Allowed to hide from the world (Perception):
    — Hiding from the world is hiding from life; choose life.
    — Hiding from the world hides your light.
    — Hiding from the world hides you from its gifts.
- Economic security (Perception):
    — Security is an illusion if you are in an abusive relationship. Security means safe from harm.
- Expenses for one household are lower than for two (Perception):
    — What part do you and the abuser play in creating the expenses and debt?
    — Usually the abuser is the biggest contributor to the debt, so postponing leaving will deteriorate finances further.
    — You will control the expenses and debt when you leave.
    — You have honed your caution skills living with an abuser, and you can apply those skills to your finances when you leave.
    — Credit counselors can develop a manageable plan for your debt payments.
    — Part of your expenses will probably be covered by spousal support.
    — If necessary, declaring personal bankruptcy will give you a fresh start.
- Pleasures of the honeymoon phase (Perception):
    — You know what follows the honeymoon phase.
    — You can create your own honeymoon when you leave.
    — You can pamper and treat yourself when you choose, and you should choose to pamper yourself often.
- Familiarity—the devil you know (Perception):
    — Familiarity has its benefits, but so does adventure.
    — As Helen Keller said, "Life is either a wonderful adventure or it is nothing."[6]
    — As you taste adventure, you can transform the ones you enjoy into the familiar by repeating them regularly.

- Easier to indulge disorders and substance abuses (Perception):
  — Leaving will help you overcome the substance abuse or disorder out of necessity.
  — Leaving also removes the overriding cause of the addiction or disorder, making it far easier to be free of it.
  — Your self-destruction is reason to leave, not stay.
  — There is help available.
- Shared history (Perception):
  — Abuse is not meant to be part of your history.
  — Leaving allows you to create a new history filled with following your dreams.

You need to be cautious to keep the abuser from sensing your paradigm shift and any decisions you make around leaving until you have prepared the way. Chapter 10 discusses the details of preparing to leave and may be helpful in shifting your way of thinking.

During this time of pondering, you must guard your words, especially if you are using substances, since they loosen the tongue. Anything you say or write could make its way to your abuser. It may even be through well-meaning people who don't understand the implications.

Soaring

As we swing open the windows, we let the fresh wind blow away the myths and illusions, and our spirits starts to soar. When the light of truth comes, illusions lose their power; when the myths no longer hold us spellbound, we are empowered.

Working through the beliefs, values, misconceptions and perceptions of your current paradigm may bring more confusion than clarity at first. However, as you consider and evaluate each aspect of how and why he abuses you, how and why you react as you do, and why you perceive you cannot leave, the truth will become more evident, and your paradigm will begin to shift.

Even when you start to recognize truths in your mind, believing them in your heart will take time but will come with practice. Just try it. Test it. You can reframe your fears in optimism and find something

> *As our paradigm shifts to one of truth and enlightenment, it will empower us to dream and plan.*

positive, some benefit. When you feel fearful, you can think of at least one action, no matter how small, that you can take to reduce the fear. Remember that courage is not the absence of fear; it is taking a step in spite of the fear. Whenever a fearful thought enters your mind, you can replace it with a positive empowering truth, and soon your thoughts will transform your emotions, and you will believe.

> *Watch your thoughts; they become words.*
> *Watch your words; they become actions.*
> *Watch your actions; they become habits.*
> *Watch your habits; they become character.*
> *Watch your character; it becomes your destiny.*
> —Author Unknown

Preventing fear from paralyzing you is similar to the expression "Don't look down" when you are afraid of falling. Do not focus on the fear. Instead, focus on the desires of your heart, on the gifts you will give to the world, on the people you care about and who care about you.

We need a paradigm shift to leave and to thrive. As our paradigm shifts to one of truth and enlightenment, it will empower us to dream and plan. We will be set free to soar into the joy and beauty of our hope.

GOT THAT GET AWAY FEELIN'

With a Broken Wing
With a broken wing,
She carries her dreams.
—Martina McBride

THE INTENSITY OF MY THOUGHTS BLOCKED OUT THE NOISE OF the vacuum. *I had no idea all eating disorders were so deadly. What am I going to do?*

I don't know if I want to give it up.

I don't think I can give it up.

Was I saying I'd rather die than give it up?

Maybe I was.

Since researching and talking to my counselors about my eating disorder, questions and concerns crowded my mind. I understood that Ed's abuse was at the core of my destructive disorder. I knew his arrogance and anger were at the core of his identity. After so many years of violence and promises, I had no faith in him changing.

Through the glass of the coffee table I saw the brush of the vacuum move back and forth as I debated with myself. *As long as his violence remains, my disorder remains. The disorder will eventually kill me. What am I going to do?*

All of a sudden, a thought came to me that was so foreign and beyond anything I would think that I wondered how it ever entered my head.

Maybe I could tell Ed that I had this eating disorder and that it caused many life-threatening complications—it was most likely the cause of the trouble I had with my heart. I could explain to him that his abuse and control were at the core of my eating disorder and that I needed him to give up his control of me or I would have to leave to overcome the disorder. If I explained it to him, maybe he would understand; maybe he could change his character, and I wouldn't have to leave.

This was a bizarre thought for anyone with an eating disorder to contemplate, let alone someone in my position, where the negative control was so extensive, intense and long-term. You did not tell anyone; the disorder survived and thrived on secrecy. If I did tell Ed, he would take his control of me to a higher level, which was exactly opposite of what people with an eating disorder need. What they need is more empowerment in their lives, not less. I had always been terrified of Ed finding out, which made my thoughts of telling Ed so bizarre.

The thought of leaving was equally bizarre. As soon as that thought entered my mind, I shook my head in confusion and fear. Ed would never let me leave. I was never supposed to leave. I took a vow. Even if I did leave, where would I go? How would I survive?

All week I struggled with my dilemma, going in circles and down blind alleys trying to find my way out of the maze.

When I met with Rita and Karen again, I explained that Ed's psychological and emotional abuse of me was getting worse. I shared with them the thought I had of telling Ed about my eating disorder and possibly leaving to get better if he did not agree to change.

I was startled by their body language, which showed shock and resistance. Then Rita said she did not think that telling Ed about my eating disorder was a wise thing to do. "If Ed knew that he needed to either change or lose you, there is a good chance that he would become desperate. He would not relinquish control to you, and he would not accept losing you. Therefore, what are his remaining options?" she asked.

I knew in my heart the conclusion to which her questions were leading me.

Over the next while, I contemplated whether or not to tell Ed about my eating disorder. He had always considered it lying if I hid things from him, and for all the years of my bulimia, I had felt guilty about it. Telling him would lift a burden from my conscience, but I knew it would add a burden to my existence.

There was a new television series I liked about women overcoming adversity. That week there was an intriguing woman on. She had short red hair and a black patch over her eye. She had been in an abusive relationship, though she did not consider it physically abusive. She decided she needed to leave and told her husband that she and the children were leaving as soon as the school term was finished.

That evening he went up to the bedroom with a gun and shot her several times. One of the shots was in the face, and he left her for dead. However, she was not dead. She made her way into the kitchen, where her son called 911. In the meantime, her husband had forgotten his briefcase and went back into the house to get it. He saw she was still alive, so he grabbed a butcher knife and started stabbing her. The police arrived by that point and arrested him. She survived but lost an eye and became a victims' rights representative for the federal government.

Watching this show, along with reading the heartbreaking fate of Nancy in *Oliver Twist,* dramatically answered my question about whether or not to tell Ed. I knew I had to keep any mention of my eating disorder and possible leaving a secret.

As usual, the closer the weekend came, the more my fears and tension increased. Friday arrived, and so did Ed's drunken rage. However, Sunday brought a dark twist.

"I cou' kill 'er... bu you can't kill som'un who knows so much…or can you?" I heard Ed mutter this as I came down the stairs. I froze in disbelief. I did not feel fear; instead, I had an otherworldly sense of being an observer of events in a dream.

The walls framed the entry to the living room. I could see the edge of the couch, and Ed was slouched there with his chin on his chest, talking to himself.

It was morning, but he was drunk already. He talked constantly when he was drinking. If I was not there to listen, he talked to himself. In this state, he was oblivious to anything that was not within three feet of him. I hoped he was unaware of my presence on the staircase behind him. I stood there stunned for a moment and then a little panicked as I quickly tried to decide what to do. Did I want him to know I overheard what he said, or should I avoid him until his mind moved on to something else?

I decided it would be best if he did not know I overheard him, so I slipped into another room and listened and waited. Soon, he was mumbling to himself about something else, so I knew he had not detected my presence.

Was it me he was talking of killing? I sensed that it was. But what did that mean? He had been abusive for many years, but he had never said anything about killing me. In fact, he wouldn't even let me kill myself. I knew he enjoyed saying outrageous unconventional things to shock people and to let them know that he said and did whatever he wanted. Yet talk of killing was beyond outrageous. It was beyond the law. How could he say something like that?

The next weekend brought more disturbing comments. Saturday, Ed was out feeding our old horse, Belle. As he approached her, she staggered around backwards and fell on her side, hitting her head on the ground. She did not get up. Hours later, she was still not up, so Ed called the vet to come and put her out of her misery. As I thought of losing another friend, sadness washed over me.

However, the vet said he could not euthanize horses when the ground was still frozen because they could not be buried quickly enough. He offered to come and shoot her instead, but that evening when he arrived, Belle was up again. Ed decided to let her live, and I let my sadness go with relief.

Sunday afternoon was sunny and warm for spring, and Ed moved his drinking out onto the deck. As usual, I was expected to keep him company, even though it had been a couple of years since I quit drinking. For some reason, I always felt more vulnerable and uncomfortable outside. As I sat and listened, I wished I could go in the house and clean or something.

Like Belle, our Husky dog, Tundra, was also getting old. He was lying in the sun beside us on the deck. He lifted his head at the sound of a bird and struggled stiffly to his feet.

Ed said to him, "I might have to get a second gun for you, Tundra."

He knew the incident with Belle would come to my mind.

Then he turned to me and said, "And a third gun for you, but I'll give you a running start."

My heart started pounding as the implications of what he said sank in. I was afraid to look at him. I pretended I didn't hear him as I reached down to pet Midnight, our lanky black cat curled up by my chair.

Ed repeated, "And a third gun for you, but I'll give you a running start."

Because he had repeated it, I knew he was looking for acknowledgement, and I did not want to arouse his anger, so I glanced at him but said nothing.

Something was shifting. My essence, my energy, seemed to be siphoning out of me, leaving me more vulnerable, more defenseless. He had stolen something vital, but what? He seemed to sense it as well; his calm assurance as he changed the subject brought a picture to my mind.

I recalled the scene of Saddam Hussein's hand on the head of the boy hostage, terror in the boy's eyes; the televised message to the world was clear without saying a word, without showing any violence. Watching it, people could sense the deadly implied threat.

Another week went by. It was Friday night, and we were watching a movie called *The Italian Job*. One scene began with a man standing and holding the handle of an axe. He slowly lowered the head of the axe, with the blade pointing upward, down onto a coffee table in front of another man. The scene switched, and I heard the character speak the ominous words "Don't mess with a Ukrainian."

Ed was Ukrainian, and he said with a smile, "A Ukrainian will straighten them out."

The next day as we left for town, we stopped first at the shed, where we had frozen scraps for Tundra. Ed went into the shed. He came out with the axe and mimicked the scene from *The Italian Job,* the blade of the axe pointing upward.

He looked at me and calmly said, "Does this scenario ring a bell? Don't mess with a Ukrainian."

I stayed silent and registered no emotion, but inside I no longer doubted the message he was sending me. This was not just another outrageous comment to make me uncomfortable; something had changed. Ed had developed a new pattern of abuse. Now every weekend and occasionally during the week, he made comments that contained implicit references to killing me. Along with this behavior, he had reduced his outbursts of rage and destruction. He had discovered a very effective combination. He felt the power, and I became even more quiet and compliant, even more invisible.

Ed went a step further.

Once again, he had been talking and drinking for hours in his traditional place, with his back to the sink in the kitchen. As I sat on the sofa in the family room, listening to him from the other side of the kitchen island, I was grateful that he preferred me to be seen and not heard. I gave the occasional nod of agreement and allowed my mind to reflect on whether or not he would actually kill me. It was like an unspoken conversation, always murmuring below the surface of every spoken conversation. I sensed that I had left the dungeon of torment and was in the corridor to the death chamber.

I felt as if he had been reading my mind when he answered my silent ponderings with his next sentence: "You know I could kill someone. You've seen me kill animals before."

I remained silent and cowering whenever killing comments rose to the surface, like avoiding eye contact and easing away from a growling animal. However, vivid memories came back to me as I thought back on our recent trip to the city.

We came upon a car stopped by the side of the highway. The driver was out of his car, trying to drag the deer he had hit off the road.

Ed pulled over and got out to help. I put down my sun visor to watch them in its mirror. After talking to the driver, Ed came back to our truck and opened the back door of our extended cab.

"The guy can't even put it out of its misery. He was just going to drag it into the ditch and let it suffer," he said with anger and condescension in his voice as he pulled out an axe from behind the seat.

As he strode back to the animal, I turned away, but I heard the crack as the axe made contact with the skull of the deer.

As a hunter, Ed had shot many animals, but as he stood at the sink and stared at me, waiting for his message to sink in, I was sure that he intended me to recall that scene on the highway. He was letting me know that he was capable of following through on his comments about killing me.

I left the subliminal conversation and returned to our surface one. "You always have compassion for the animals, never wanting them to suffer," I said in support as I tried to divert his thoughts away from me.

"You'd be shocked if you knew what I was thinking," he stated in that superior way that people do when they have a secret they intend to keep to themselves.

I recalled that my counselor said, "Once someone gets to the stage of verbalizing death threats, they have already contemplated and developed the concept in their minds."

Maybe I wouldn't be shocked at what he was thinking.

Sidestepping the comment, I asked a question that I hoped would steer the conversation to safer ground. "Have they decided who will be responsible for the hurt wildlife out at work?" I asked, pretending his last comment went over my head.

I was hoping to prevent his anger from exploding. It was almost midnight, and I thought an acceptable amount of time had passed for him to allow me to go to bed. I just had to maneuver him into a calm state first. He liked to talk about work.

"We are supposed to call a Fish and Wildlife officer, but they take too long to get there and the animal suffers, so most people still call me," he said.

"How is the remediation site coming?" I asked.

He was now off talking on a safe subject, and soon I was able to go to bed. He would stay up drinking, and I silently prayed that his inner conversations would not turn dark.

Later that night after Ed was finally asleep, I tried to sort out the implications of all the thinly veiled death threats and their progression. But I remained frightened and confused. Maybe my counselors could help me understand.

For my next appointment Rita, my psychologist, was sick, so Karen and I met alone.

I started by saying, "Ed's behavior is changing. He has not been very physically abusive. It has mainly been emotional and psychological abuse, but he has started to say bizarre death threats."

As I told her about the threats of the last month and a half, I watched her face fill with apprehension. "What do you mean by 'not very physically abusive'? Can you tell me about some of the abuse?"

I told her about the time Ed woke the kids up to make them watch the beating he gave me because I tried to commit suicide. I only got a few words out at a time, before I needed to stop, hold my breath and look at the ceiling as I fought back the tears. After that story was finished, I justified his actions, "But he only did that because he loved me so much and didn't want to lose me."

My words sounded hollow, and I saw in her eyes that she also knew the truth I had discovered: I was not allowed to escape.

She gently said, "Can you tell me more?" encouraging me to tell her about more stories of shoving, choking, kicking and hitting. My words were broken and mixed with tears. When I heard it spoken, it did not sound as insignificant or as seldom as I had imagined in my mind.

"I know this has been hard for you to say. You may think that you have betrayed a trust, but by concealing Ed's behavior you are betraying yourself," Karen said. "You have already made the connection, in past weeks, between Ed's treatment of you and the eating disorder. You also learned a little of how destructive an eating disorder is, not only physically, but also psychologically and emotionally. However, it is not only the eating disorder threatening your life."

Karen then asked, "Do you have a safety plan?"

"Well, if it gets bad I thought I would phone our neighbor to come and help. Or if I feel it is best to leave, then I would go to an aunt's apartment," I cautiously said.

"The aunt's apartment would be good because, for security, you have to be let in, but calling a neighbor to come and help could jeopardize their safety," she said. "Have you told Rita about this yet?" she asked.

I shook my head "no."

Karen then stated, "I feel it is important for you to share with Rita what you've shared with me. Can you do that?"

I nodded "yes" as my sobs subsided. We made an appointment to meet at Rita's next available opening.

When I joined Karen and Rita at the next appointment, we were in Rita's new office. She was going to start focusing on child psychology and was not taking on any more adult clients. Her new office was a child's dream; there were costumes and cars, puzzles and a sandbox, children's books and dolls and of course stuffed toys. At the top of a shelf I saw the little stuffed mountain goat named Cliff I had given Rita because she usually ended our sessions with "Onward and upward."

The eerie scene unfolded as I related my horror stories to Rita among the cheery, colorful children's toys. She listened quietly and patiently as I cried my way through it again. After I finished, I told her of the new twist on Ed's behavior. He was now treating me better, but it was forced. His underlying attitude had not changed, and his comments about killing had increased.

Rita explained, "I have never tried to give you advice or influence your decisions or choices, but in order to protect your life, I would be negligent if I was not forthright. You are in a very dangerous position right now. Both Karen and I sense a real change in you, and I'm sure Ed senses it as well. That is why his behavior has changed. He knows he is losing control of you, and he is starting to get desperate. He is using good behavior to entice you into staying, while at the same time, he is terrifying you with talk of killing you—he is using death threats to tell you what he will do to you if you try to leave him."

She leaned forward, rested her elbows on her knees, took a breath and said, "The fact that he is not physically abusive on a regular basis, coupled with his disregard of authority, evidenced by the episode of his resisting arrest, makes him more lethal than if he beat you all the time."

She stopped to let me think for a bit. I sat in stunned silence. All my intuition was telling me it was true.

She started again. "Karen told me your safety plan, but I think you need to include more things."

I had only told Karen about outside help. I did not know a safety plan meant everything I did. So I told them about hiding the keys to the gun cabinet, hiding the bolt to the gun in the closet, keeping keys on me and hidden outside and hiding the garage door opener. I told them about turning the volume up on the phone in case I needed to put it on speakerphone during an emergency, about the emergency bag I had packed in the closet with his and my stuff in it so that he wouldn't be suspicious if he found it. I told them that there were two ways out of the basement, four ways out of the main floor and one way out of the upper floor, not counting the windows, and that I had reviewed the best ways to escape for different scenarios.

Rita said, "Well, I am a lot more relieved to hear this plan. I was worried about your other one."

As we ended the session Rita said, "Stay safe."

Driving home afterwards, I thought to myself, *If what they are saying is true, if I really could be killed not just threatened, what does that mean? What do I do?*

All day, thoughts and scenarios played in my mind. Then at 4:00 in the afternoon, a jolt of fear brought me back to reality. I thought, *No, no, I don't dare think about what Rita said now. Ed will be home soon. I need to get back into a normal frame of mind, or he will sense something different about me. If he gets suspicious and starts questioning and assuming, I don't know if I will be able to pretend everything is normal.*

Things were so unfamiliar now, and I didn't know where his rage might take him. So I stored these things up to think about at a safer time.

The next morning after Ed left for work, I pondered all the disturbing issues: the danger my counselors believed I was in, their concern about Ed learning of the eating disorder, the health dangers I faced because of the eating disorder, Ed's death threats and my vow to remain married.

I had always taken my marriage vows seriously. I believed I was married "until death do us part." I had resigned myself to being married to the beast for the rest of my life.

Had the beast now put on the black hood of the executioner? I remembered a comment Ed once made, "If I can't have you, nobody will."

I questioned whether God wanted me to stay until I became a statistic and Ed became a murderer. If I stayed, hoping for the best, it could be too late to choose. It seemed if I stayed I would die from either him or the eating disorder. But I sensed on a deep level that God was speaking to my soul, telling me to leave, and I said, "If this is what you want me to do, you need to make it very plain to me."

If there was ever a time I desperately needed to hear from God, it was now. On a television show, I heard an author, Brad Jersak, speak about how to have a conversation with Jesus. So even though I had been praying for years, I decided to try what he said.

I was alone in the house, and I found a comfortable quiet spot—in Ashley's old bedroom on her bed. I closed my eyes, and the walls of the dungeon faded. I slipped into another dimension.

I took myself far away to a warm, safe, tranquil place. I visualized my meeting place. The meeting place I chose to imagine was a library. It was in a beautiful home, my dream home, where I lived all by myself in peaceful solitude. The library had a high ceiling and wood panels on the walls with bookshelves to the ceiling. There was one of those funny ladders attached to a rail, ceiling and floor, that slid across the shelves so that I could reach the books on the highest shelves. I could smell the wood of the fire that burned in the fireplace; I could hear it crackle. Heavy forest green velvet drapes framed the tall window on the end wall. Raindrops ran down the windowpanes. I could hear the wind blowing and see the lilacs swaying. I was sitting on a deep, soft burgundy sofa waiting for God to join me.

Mentally, I knew Jesus loved me and wanted what was best for me, but I could not feel his love for me in my heart. I had a difficult time understanding why he would want anything to do with me. But I chose to go on faith that he did love me and would come and talk with me. I took a deep breath and invited him into my imagination. I sensed his presence beside me.

Now for the next part of the exercise, to ask Jesus what he wanted to tell me.

"Jesus, what would you like to tell me?" I whispered.

Immediately, the scene in my imagination switched, and I was in a rocky wilderness, and Jesus and I were on horseback. Everything was dry and pale and dusty. There was a line of rocky, barren hills to our right, and we looked across the desert-like wilderness along the base of the hills and saw the way we were to go. Then the scene disappeared.

I was surprised and wondered what it meant. The desert scene did not come from an intentional thought on my part. I would never have imagined that as a place I would want to meet with Jesus, so I felt there was some significance to it. I was left with a sense of peace and trust.

Coming back to an awareness of where I really was brought back my anguish, confusion and fear. I wanted to understand the meaning of the wilderness, the meaning of being on horseback. I believed it was a message, an answer to my confusion, but I could not figure it out.

I decided to set aside a day to fast and pray to try to understand what it meant. I returned, in my mind, to the wilderness where Jesus and I were on horseback. Once again I asked, "What would you like to tell me?"

This time I was surprised when I sensed the words, deep and gentle, almost audible, "Follow me."

I somehow sensed there would be a protected journey, and I asked, "Where are we going?"

I heard no answer.

As I sat on my horse in my imagination, I quietly said, "I'm not getting a map, am I?" I really wanted a map.

I always needed a map with me even if I knew where I was going. Any venture beyond the front door was always frightening for me. On the other side of the door, there were so many people and events beyond my control that could trigger Ed's abuse. If I did have to go out, maps were my friends.

They were a part of my protection. I was expected to be the navigator when we traveled. So they protected me from Ed's rage for my giving wrong directions. They helped me find the way home when his drinking and anger brought chaos. I carried lots of them with me in my backpack that I took everywhere (I was told only old ladies carried purses).

I had road maps, city maps, park maps, ski hill maps, and I even had maps of each shopping mall we used. I always needed a map; they were my security blanket.

Jesus remained silent.

Then the scene disappeared. I wanted Jesus to tell me more. I wanted more answers. I wanted to know what to do, but I couldn't bring the scene back.

I went to find the little booklet I read most mornings that gave me insight and inspiration for the day. I opened to that day's date, November 5. The title was *Marching Off the Map*. My heart leapt and I held my breath as I read the words again—*Marching Off the Map*. Jesus answered my question about the map. Then I understood that he knew where I was going, and I just needed to trust and follow him.

I was both excited to read the passage and afraid to read the passage because I knew it was going to speak to me about following him. The passage was about Alexander the Great marching off the map of the known world at that time. Maybe Jesus did not give me a map because where he was taking me was beyond my ability to fathom. The content of the article was about God telling Abraham to leave his home and his lands and go to a land that he would show him.

After reading this, I knew God was honoring my request for him to make it very plain if I was to leave. He was telling me that I was going to ride out of the wilderness with Jesus.

Inside me, a mist seemed to blow away, and I perceived with a strange blend of peace, trepidation and excitement that a turning point had come. Was my escape imminent? Could I ride away from the beast?

The swirling chaos of thoughts came together and revealed leaving as my inevitable choice. And so I decided to heed the voice that had said "Follow me," even if it meant to follow "off the map" of my world.

At this point, I understood in my head that I must leave, but there was still fear and hesitation in my heart. Because I knew I had to leave, I began to prepare in spite of my fear.

When I saw my doctor for an annual checkup and told her that it was not safe for me to stay with Ed any longer, she asked in her calm, quiet voice, "What is happening?"

I told her of the death threats, and I saw her shake as a shiver ran down her back.

She said, "When the hair on the back of your neck raises and your instinct tells you to run, you run. You don't try and figure it out."

It was the middle of winter, and I told her my nearest neighbor was half a mile away. She looked worried as she continued the checkup.

Before I left, she said, "The marriage is no longer alive. Now you have to focus on keeping yourself alive."

It was another confirmation from a trusted source that I was doing the right thing in leaving.

I had many questions about "who, what, why, where, when and how," but not very many answers. I knew God was the "who" that was going to help me, and I knew the "why" was to save my life, but I didn't know the "what, where, when or how." Over the next while, as a question came up, God would answer it, and I would take a step. Then the next question would come up. This was how I methodically prepared to leave.

My first question, raised by what my doctor told me, was "Am I to leave immediately and take nothing, or am I to prepare longer and take the things that are important to me?"

God answered this with someone on television who spoke about Moses. Moses was to lead his people out of bondage into the land that God showed Abraham. This resonated in my heart because it was a continuation of my "marching off the map" story. God told them to take their valuables, so I took that to mean for me to pack what I should take and to arrange our affairs to run in my absence. I understood I was not just to run now, with only the clothes I was wearing.

My next question was "How do I pack without Ed suspecting what I am doing?"

A week or so later I went down the stairs to the basement. The floor looked darker and shinier than it should. When I flipped the light switch on, I saw water, a couple of inches deep, covering the floor. My heart sank at the thought of cleaning the mess up. The floor was carpeted, and there were boxes, bags, boots, and sports equipment soaked by the water. I had to move the furniture to lift the carpet. As I was thinking of where to begin, Ed came down.

He yelled a stream of curses and shoved me out of the way. He waded through the water and grabbed a corner of the carpet.

"Get over here," he ordered.

I stepped into the water and waded over to help him. I reached down and rolled the wet, cold, rough burlap backing of the carpet. My hands were too small to keep up with him. He snapped and shoved and swore at me as we carried the sodden carpets and everything else up to the garage. We shoveled and mopped up the water from the floor. I was drained from the hours of cleaning and the hours of his yelling. Exhausted and stifling my tears, I crawled into bed.

The next day Ed was at work, and I sorted through the mess. Some of the boxes had books and clothes in them that needed to be discarded because they were damaged, and some could be kept.

As I went through this process, I thought to myself, *If I buy some plastic containers, our things won't be ruined if it floods again.* Then it dawned on me. The flood would help me with my packing problem.

I could use the flooded basement as a pretext for buying lots of containers, and I could pack things according to what I wanted to take or leave behind.

Joseph M. Juran suggested and named the Pareto principle, also known as the 80–20 rule. For clothes, we wear 20 percent of our clothes 80 percent of the time. So I decided to take only the 20 percent I wore. There was another rule, keep nothing unless it is beautiful, useful or treasured, which I also kept in mind as I decided what to take and what to leave. I wanted to take the textbooks from the distance education university courses I had been taking to help me with the farm accounting. I also wanted to take the special dishes and blankets my mom gave me and treasured pictures and mementos. There were many difficult choices, but I wanted to travel as light as I could. I was taking nothing that could be replaced inexpensively and nothing bigger than I could carry myself.

In the meantime, I was having trouble deciding where I should live. I thought about staying in the town near where we lived or going to the next closest city, but being that close to Ed was terrifying. I didn't think I should move to Clarion, where I had family living. That would be the first place Ed would look for me. Then I heard Lianna Klassen speak of her album called *Out of Borderland*. That caught my attention, since God had asked me to go beyond the borders of the known world. I watched this beautiful red-haired lady in fascination as she told her story. Line after line, she restated things that God has been saying to me.

She lived in a city on the coast, and God had asked her to move over the mountains to the city of Clarion. He told her that she was so used to where she lived that she could not see the danger she was in.

I knew God was speaking directly to me and telling me that "Yes, it is Clarion that I want you to move to." The question of "where" was answered.

Money, of course, was a big question. I was confident I would be able to find a job when I moved, since Clarion was booming and people from all over the country were moving there because there was so much work. However, I knew I would need some money in the beginning. Then one morning I realized that I could use some of our home equity line of credit. It was a loan; it was not Ed's money. It was secured with the house that was half mine, which Ed would be using all for himself. That gave me some peace of mind, but I knew I could not take it out until the last minute.

As I thought about future costs, I heard a conversation between my sisters-in-law about wisdom teeth that kept my nephew from work and cost thousands of dollars to have pulled. I recently had one wisdom tooth out, and the dentist said there was no room for the remaining three if they started to come through.

Since I was currently on a health plan that covered many extra health costs, I needed to get as many health issues as I could looked after before I left. I had my eyes checked and ordered new glasses, I had my feet checked and ordered new orthotics, and yes, I talked to my dentist about having my last three wisdom teeth removed. Not a pleasant thought, but better before than after I left.

As I continued to prepare to leave, I kept wondering about different options for how and when to leave. Should I find someone to drive me? Should I take the bus? Should I drive partway and then fly? Should I take our truck or should I rent a vehicle? I was reluctant to involve someone else, as there might be hard consequences for them. Taking the bus would be too difficult if I wanted to take my things with me. I didn't want to leave Ed without a vehicle, so I decided not to take our vehicle. Also, the police said that since it was registered in his name he could report it stolen. The more I considered it, the more my best option looked like renting a vehicle.

Then to decide when to leave. I still needed to have my wisdom teeth out. I also wanted to wait until after I did our taxes, since Ed's and mine were connected because of the farm partnership, even though we rented the land out. *Maybe I should leave the first part of March. I should have all the tax slips by then.*

I went in to have my wisdom teeth out, and it was not as bad as I thought. The care and concern of the dental staff touched my heart, and they gave me pain-killer medication to take every three hours.

Ed had his own remedy for my pain.

"I could cut your head off and throw it in the river," he suggested, and I wondered if I would live long enough to leave.

It was then the beginning of March; I had not been able to eat solid food for two weeks, and to my delight, neither had I had a bulimic episode. In my heart, I started to believe that I would leave that beast behind as well.

I received the final tax slips, but we also received bad news. An uncle of Ed's had died. Ukrainian weddings and funerals were big events, and all the relatives went. On one level, the delay added to my stress, but it also gave me a chance to see all the relatives who had been part of my life for many years. I knew I wouldn't see them again, so the funeral held deeper sadness for me than anyone realized.

As Ed and I sat in a lounge after the funeral, the news came on an overhead television. Four Mounties had been shot trying to apprehend a suspect on a farm. As I watched I heard Ed's comment in my ear, "Make sure you don't call the cops. You never know what might happen."

The funeral was over; our taxes were filed. I knew that there was nothing left that I needed to prepare. If I stayed any longer, it would be at my peril. Ed had a meeting on March 15, and he was the presenter. He wouldn't be coming home unexpectedly. I booked a rental vehicle in my dad's name, for the Ides of March.

It Is Still Unwritten

Perhaps the most important thing that has come out of my life is the discovery that if you prepare yourself at every point as well as you can, with whatever means you have, however meager they may seem, you will be able to grasp opportunity for broader experience when it appears. Without preparation you cannot do it.

—Eleanor Roosevelt

S TATISTICS
A woman's attempt to leave was the precipitating factor in 45 percent of the murders of a woman by a man.[1]

SOMETHING TO KEEP IN MIND

Three things to keep in mind while preparing to leave:

1. Safe—What will I need to be, do or have to stay safe?
2. Secure—What will I need to be, do or have for my future security?
3. Sorry—What will I need to be, do or have to avoid regret after I leave? For example, make sure you don't leave behind your mother's sapphire ring.

PREPARE THE PATH: THE 5 WS AND HOW

> SAFETY IS
> PARAMOUNT!
> *Before taking any action, you must think through the consequences of each step to minimize its detection, maximize its benefit and ensure your safety.*

Our mind is free from the tricks of the illusionist; now, it is time for physical liberation. Preparing for our actual escape from the dungeon can be a terrifying and exhilarating time, or we may just be numb and operating on autopilot. In either case, it is extremely important to maintain a heightened vigilance.

According to statistics, the time just before and just after leaving is the most dangerous time for us. This is true whether or not the abuser has typically been physically abusive. Often abusers sense something has changed even if we try our best to conceal it. We should already have some safety precautions in place, but if not, it is imperative that we implement them now before we begin to prepare for our escape.

The first element of our plan is the preparation. This will vary depending on how much time, resources and liberty we have. The better prepared we are before we leave, the more control, safety and opportunities we will have after we leave.

Most of us are familiar with the "five w's and how" used to analyze and investigate. The five w's are Who, What, Why, When, Where. Once we decide to leave, before we take any steps, the process of leaving and creating a new life needs to be planned and implemented. The "five w's and how" will help us do this systematically. We also have the added challenge of doing this without raising the abuser's suspicions.

WHY PREPARE?

Think of preparing as a precious gift you give to your future self for which you will be extremely grateful. The more opportunity you have to prepare before you leave, the safer you will be after you leave and the better position you will be in to maximize your success. As part of your preparation, you need to review and practice in your mind. Practice both the leaving process and the first things you need to do after leaving. If it is safe to do so, actually practice aspects of preparing, like packing, to assess the time and resources you need. Practicing will help things go smoother and swifter when it comes time to leave.

Before you can prepare, you need to assess where you currently are and where you hope to be. Analysis of your current strengths, weaknesses, opportunities, and threats (SWOT) will help you assess the situation.

> When planning and analyzing, it may be safer to do it in your head than to have it written out for the abuser to find.

After this, you can create your ultimate vision of what you would like your future to look like. Dream as if anything is possible. What would you dream if there was nothing to prevent you from having it?

When you look at your dream, it may seem unattainable. However, each step you take, no matter how tiny, builds mass and momentum. You gain strength and clarity as you climb. You need to keep your dream in your heart as you step into your future.

Strengths, Weaknesses, Opportunities and Threats (SWOT)

Our strengths and weaknesses pertain to us; opportunities and threats pertain to our environment. Strengths can include a variety of things. We all have special individual talents. We may know them, we may have lost sight of them, or we have yet to discover them. Living with an abuser develops strength in us. It improves our planning skills; it helps us see and evaluate consequences; it builds endurance, perseverance and patience. It helps us see other people's perspectives. It helps us to be independent problem solvers and troubleshooters.

On the more practical side, an element will be a strength if we have it and a weakness if we do not. These elements include a stable career, financial resources, education, transportation, health, safe accommodations and a network of people to help.

Opportunities and threats exist beyond us. Opportunities are the ways available to achieve a strength, such as the ability to earn an education online without having to physically attend classes, a friend willing to give us driving lessons, a community health organization offering free counseling, or a relative offering us a place to stay if we leave.

Beyond the obvious threat that the abuser poses, external threats are situations or events that would contribute to our weakness. These could be a downturn in the economy, a move away from family and friends, rising tuition costs, or cancellation of programs that help us.

When you have your SWOT list, look creatively at it and determine ways to build your strengths, eliminate your weaknesses, take advantage of opportunities and mitigate threats. Even if you do not yet have faith in achieving your dream, if you keep taking steps, both small and large, your faith will grow as you make progress and see possibilities materialize.

Your Ultimate Vision for Your Future

For your vision of the future, your fear may cause you to think small. However, you need to resist the lies of shame, inadequacy and worthlessness that may restrict your dreams; there is no harm in creating an incredibly beautiful vision. It will bring you comfort, encouragement and strength, as well as creating a haven in your mind until it comes true.

However, your vision is of greater importance than this; it is the catalyst for creating your new life. A wholesome foundation to build your life on should consist of love, security and dignity. These may be foreign concepts to you now, but they will grow with each small step you take.

Most of us, when we are in an abusive relationship, just want our partner to change, to stop the abuse. Our first choice is not to leave. However, if our vision is to be free to become the amazing person we were created to be and live the abundant life that comes with living our purpose, we have to honestly assess if that is possible if we stay in our current environment.

Your vision must not require someone else to complete it. It does not empower you to dream "if I had a wonderful husband" or "if my kids would just stay out of trouble." Dreams that will empower you are ones such as gaining good health, receiving a diploma, discovering and employing your talents and making a difference in the lives of others.

Your vision is your hope. Hope means desire with expectation. As you hope, your desires are transforming into reality.

Steps Forward, Steps Upward

Depending on where you are now, you may need to take a few steps or many steps. When you break your dreams down into small manageable steps, what seems insurmountable becomes a series of simple actions. Whether or not you have decided to leave yet, there are many steps you can, and should, take.

You should implement as many safety steps as you can. In addition, your every action and utterance can have far-reaching consequences that may make your life more challenging if or when you decide to leave.

Covering your tracks (leaving no trail of evidence for him to find you or interfere with your life) may take extensive preplanning before you leave, or it may be relatively simple. It will depend on the level of danger you anticipate, how resourceful and persistent you perceive your abuser to be, the likelihood that he will hire a private detective to locate you, the likelihood that you will be successful

> *Your every action and utterance can have far-reaching consequences that may make your life more challenging if or when you decide to leave.*

in keeping your location confidential. If you keep your current job or share child custody, this may be difficult. Suggestions for covering your tracks are incorporated into the various sections that follow.

Each section describes many possible steps to implement. The steps do not necessarily have a certain sequence or time frame to follow. You could start with the easiest and work towards the more challenging ones, or you could complete them section by section. You can work in whichever way is best for you, always keeping safety in mind. Some steps may not be safe for you to take while you are still with the abuser. Remember that every step is a celebration.

Resources to Assist Your Ascent

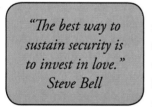

"*The best way to sustain security is to invest in love.*"
Steve Bell

As you move towards your vision, some resources are essential and some resources are helpful. Resources are highlighted in the Who, What and Where sections. They include people, places and things: people from your past, present and future; places to live, learn and earn; things to improve quality of life and security. However, your most valuable resources are the intangible resources of faith, perseverance and courage.

Love, security and dignity will grow as you take each step and interact with your resources.

WHO CAN HELP

You may need to keep all your thoughts and plans confidential, or you may use a support system of people to help you. On the one hand, the fewer people who know, the less chance of someone, inadvertently or with the best intentions, revealing your thoughts or plans to your abuser, which could jeopardize your safety or your efforts. Also, keep in mind that you may put in jeopardy whomever you bring into your confidence. If your abuser discovers they have helped you, they may be in danger of his retribution.

On the other hand, the more assistance you have, the easier it is to prepare your escape and your future. The number of people willing to help is surprising. It has surprised everyone I know who has undergone the process of leaving her abuser. People willing to help may be from your (or your children's) past, present or future.

Who from Your Past?

People you may not think of to help may be your best sources. A close childhood friend with whom you lost touch would probably be very moved if you asked for help, and the abuser might not think of them since they are from your past. Alternatively, a coach, distant relative or even a favorite teacher may be honored to help in the leaving process. These people would not come up on the abuser's radar if you have not kept in touch with them. If your relationship with the person from your past was important at one time, chances are that they will still care about you. You shouldn't be discouraged. If one says "no," be persistent; try someone else. However, you need to protect yourself and be cautious about what information you give in case the abuser finds out.

Who from Your Present?

Many people and organizations may be potential sources of help. Any organization or person who works to improve the quality of life for various groups of people will probably care about helping an abused person or will know of resources or other people who can help. You do not necessarily have to know this person. In fact, not knowing them may be to your advantage, as they will be less likely to sympathize with your abuser.

The following is a list of potential people or organizations that may offer varying degrees of assistance:
- Boys and Girls Club
- Church
- Community and Family Support Services
- Counselor
- Crisis shelter
- Employer
- Family

- Friends
- Government social services
- Lawyer
- Media
- Medical professionals
- Peers
- Police
- Schools
- Sports, business and general interest organizations you, or your children, belong to
- Women's groups
- YMCA
- YWCA

These sources can also refer you to similar or connected organizations in your future location. Sometimes, an organization that you thought would help will let you down. Don't be discouraged; just try another one.

Who in Your Future?

To prepare your path before you arrive in your future location, you can tap into the same list of people and organizations from the last section.

Churches can help you in several of your areas of need. The larger the church, the more resources they have available to assist you. They can help with a place to stay, food and career guidance. They may pay for personal counseling out of their benevolent fund, and they will be able to help with the needs of your children. They can also direct you to other agencies that you will need.

If you call emergency shelters in the city where you are going, they will be able to provide information on other resources available. Also, if you look at the website of the city itself, it will have many programs and guides available.

What Will You Need? What Do You Have?

If you walk through your current daily, weekly and monthly routines in your mind, you will be able to make a list of what you use on a regular basis. You can use this list in preparing to leave and to arrange for similar services where you are going.

Stuff

You can use the occasions when you do errands as opportunities to take things to leave with a trusted person or in storage, if that's feasible (remember, liquids may freeze). Some things to store outside the home are things you will need immediately if you leave suddenly: personal hygiene products, a couple of sets of clothes—business and casual— shoes, coat and sleepwear. You should also take extra vehicle, house, mail and safety deposit box keys, money, a credit card (preferably not in the abuser's name), copies (not as good as the original, but better than nothing) of deeds, health records, driver's license, passport, birth certificate, education certificates, government ID, marriage license, etc.

Some things you cannot take out of the house because the abuser will notice them missing. At home, you can organize drawers and closets and store things according to what you want to take with you and what you will leave behind. This will streamline the leaving process and unclutter your mind. However, you need to try to have everything appear unchanged in order to avoid raising the abuser's suspicions. Plastic storage bins are great; they are easy to carry, easy to stack and easy to open. You can plan how many storage containers or suitcases you need and know where they are. If you imagine or practice the packing, you can estimate what you need.

Name Change

It is possible to change your social insurance or security number if you have left an abusive relationship. This will prevent your abuser from using this to find you or for fraudulent purposes. The federal

> *It is possible to change your social insurance or security number if you have left an abusive relationship.*

161

governments in both Canada and the United States have a procedure for doing this.

Only changing one form of identification can connect the two names on your credit report and nullify your efforts to change your identity. Some places, such as educational institutions, need to maintain the connection between your two names in order to verify that it is the same person receiving the credits towards your program. You can contact these institutions and explain how vital it is to keep this information confidential and have your file flagged with a warning that your life is at stake and under no circumstances is the information to be given to another party.

- Decide early if you want to change the name you will use in the future, as this affects all future transactions.
- A name change will make it harder for the abuser to locate you.
- Consider choosing a common new name; the more common the name, the harder to find you.
- Your maiden name is always your legal name, and you can start using it immediately.
- You should use your old name or maiden name for divorce documents, not your new name.
- If reverting back to your maiden name, you can use your birth certificate and marriage license to change your driver's license and passport. They will need an actual physical address for the driver's license, which may be dangerous; consider using a relative's.
- If you are legally changing your name to something other than your maiden name, there are forms at registry offices to do this; however, be aware that the name change may be published for the public.
- Paper or electronic trail—to cut this off, cancel and close accounts in our old name and old address, and reapply in your new name and new address. If you only do a name change and keep the same account, the abuser can trace you through credit checks.
- Keep a government-issued photo identification with your old name on it in case you need to prove who you are.
- Begin your job search with your new name.

Utilities

You should avoid putting utilities in your name, as the abuser can call disputing something to get your address.

• Phone
  —Keep phone number unlisted.
  —Block number from displaying.
  —Block any numbers from your phone that he uses.
  —Give someone else's number as a contact on the forms you fill out.
  —When you first leave, do not give your number to family and friends. They will not have to lie, and they cannot give it by mistake.
• Internet
  —Cancel your name from accounts.
  —Change the password for your e-mail and discontinue using it. The abuser may be using it to monitor you. Create a new e-mail address.
  —If you have files and documents in your computer that you want in the future, one way to have access to them anywhere regardless of what computer you use is to e-mail them to a new e-mail address. Make sure to delete the sent message.
  —Use cloud computing.
  —If you want copies of paper documents, you can scan them in, then e-mail them. Again, make sure to delete the sent message and possibly the scanned document.
• Television
  —Cancel your name from the account.

Mail

• Consider if you want your mail forwarded to a friend or family member's address.
• Apply for a postal box in the city where you are going.
• Some courier businesses have postal boxes that allow for parcel delivery, which are unavailable if you have an ordinary postal box.

- Arrange a change of address with an effective date a week or more prior to leaving.
- When filling out forms, consider ahead of time which address to use, a postal box or a friend's.
- Caution needs to be taken to ensure that your forwarding address is not disclosed to the abuser.

Finances

The abuser often controls the household finances. Part of maintaining control is to convince you that you are incapable of understanding finances, of responsibly handling money, or not entitled to know about the income, expenses or investments. These are all false. We can all learn to budget and make wise choices with money. Do not be overwhelmed by thinking it is too much or too hard to learn. Just learn about one piece at a time; any financial learning will be beneficial no matter how small, and eventually the little pieces create a picture, and you will be delighted with your accomplishment.

Even though you may not have access to the money or information on your household finances, you can still educate yourself. The areas you should learn about are budgeting, banking, debt and investments.

Budgets

Budgeting is a powerful tool that the majority of people underutilize. Budgets can turn dreams once thought impossible into reality. You can create a hypothetical budget to approximately mirror your current household financial situation if you do not have access to actual information. Or you can create a budget for your future circumstances after you leave. Knowing how to budget will be an important key to surviving and thriving once you leave.

To create your budget, start with the income. If you plan a career change, research on the Internet, at the library or by contacting trade organizations to find what the average wage or salary is for that occupation. Go to the government website to see what the tax deductions are for that salary, and subtract that from the income. This will give you an approximate take home pay.

Next, gather information on the monthly expenses. Expense categories include housing, utilities, transportation, groceries, clothing, supplies, health, education, childcare, vacation and entertainment. The largest expense is housing.

If the expenses are higher than the income, you need to find ways to cut costs or increase income.

If you plan to rent, you can find out through papers or the Internet what rentals are for areas you are considering. To qualify for a mortgage, you need to have worked for several months at the same job and have a down payment saved. Mortgage brokers can shop for the best mortgage for you.

Research utility costs for telephone, heating, electricity, water and sewer. Find out from the city what property taxes would be if you bought. For vehicle costs, what would the range of payments be for a vehicle like the one you would like? Check on the Internet for insurance quotes. The number of miles the vehicle is driven a month will determine monthly fuel costs.

You will go through this process for all your expenses and after you have an approximate amount for your expenses deduct them from the monthly income. If the expenses are higher than the income, you need to find ways to cut costs or increase income. If you do this exercise on your current finances and the income is greater, the excess is probably being invested or spent by the abuser on things you do not know about. If the expenses are higher, he could be building up credit charges to maintain a lifestyle he cannot afford that you will be partly responsible for.

Banking

If your name is connected to any bank accounts, you can obtain a personal bankcard that you can use to access all your account information at the bank, over the Internet or by phone. This also applies to any credit cards if you are either the primary card holder or a supplementary card holder. You can go into the bank branch and arrange for your bankcard. Ask to pick it up at the bank instead of having it mailed.

If you open a personal bank account in just your name, it will not show up on your abuser's Internet bank profile or bank statements. However, you have to consider what address you give them as they may mail information.

You can visit a bank to educate yourself on various aspects of banking, regardless of whether or not you have an account there. You are a valuable potential client. A financial advisor will talk to you free of charge to help you understand what banks have to offer and how to do various banking activities.

You can also go to bank websites to see features of checking and savings accounts. Many other websites also offer banking education. You should not let your lack of knowledge be a deterrent; people will love to help you learn. Compare features and their costs at various banks to choose one that fits the best for the least cost.

The basics of banking are
- Deposit income (checking and savings accounts)
- Pay expenses (e.g., rent, credit cards, utilities)
- Pay loans (e.g., car, house, education)
- Invest (to build wealth)

Until you build a good reputation with the bank, checks you deposit will have a few days' hold on them. If you pay bills or loans late or overdraw your account, you will pay a penalty. Penalties are an unnecessary drain on your finances and detrimental to your credit rating, so it is important to do your homework to avoid this.

When you leave,
- Open a bank account in your old name (the one the abuser knows you by) at a branch far from where you plan to live.
- Any banking that involves the bank account of the abuser should be done as a transfer from the account opened in your old name (this will hide the location of the transaction).
- Avoid using joint accounts with the abuser if at all possible; the location of the transaction can be traced by the abuser.
- Open a new account in your new name for your new-life banking.

- Do not transfer from one account to another; instead withdraw and deposit.
- You must not do any transactions that mix old and new names and old and new accounts (not just bank accounts, but all accounts).
- Don't leave an electronic trail or paper trail that connects your old identity and your new identity.
- Use cash as much as possible, even when paying bills at the bank.
- Avoid using only the bank branch close to you; instead use a variety of branches.
- To help you build your future pay yourself 10 percent of what you earn, and live off the remaining 90 percent.

Debt

Keep in mind that when you divorce you share jointly all the debt, including the abuser's, as well as all the assets. Abusers often charge up a lot of debt on our credit cards, especially when we leave. If there is a possibility that the abuser will do this, you should remove your name from, cancel or freeze any debt instruments, such as loans or credit cards, when you plan to leave. Have the bank or credit card company stop any further charges on them and only allow payments.

> *Abusers often charge up a lot of debt on our credit cards, especially when we leave.*

One of your most useful economic resources is a home equity line of credit against the house you are leaving. This can potentially provide thousands of dollars to use to get established in a new location.

You need to keep in mind that a home equity line of credit is a loan secured by the house. Alternatively the abuser can also withdraw thousands on it, leaving you jointly responsible for the debt. It is debt that will be calculated in the divorce process. If it cannot be frozen when you leave, you may want to withdraw the balance available, but it must be handled wisely.

If you decide to use this option, you should withdraw or transfer the funds to another account as soon as you are about to or have just left, since the abuser may see the account activity.

167

Access to funds will be important to you when you leave, and so a good credit rating will be important. Your credit rating is a measurement that institutions use to decide if they will allow you credit, such as for credit cards, cellular phone plans, car loans and mortgages. Institutions enter information about your bank and credit activities, such as how much debt is available to you and how responsibly you handle it.

Having no credit rating is as limiting to you as having a bad credit rating. However, your activities can be tracked through your credit rating, so the benefits of creating a good credit rating, through the wise use of credit cards and diligent payment of bills in your name, needs to be weighed against the ability to hide your whereabouts and activities.

If the abuser is in any way connected with acquiring a credit card you use, such as the use of his earnings to qualify or a supplementary card in his name, then he can obtain information from the credit company, including your change of address or phone number and where the card has been used. Even if he is not connected with the credit card, he can use information from it as part of a credit check on you that will show name and address changes as well as any organization that has done a credit check on you for such things as mortgage application, cell phone purchase or other credit applications.

Also, credit rating agencies, like Equifax, have all your various names, addresses, bank information and every place that does a credit check on you. If the abuser knows your social insurance number and information on two of your bank accounts, like preauthorized payments or payroll deposits, he will have access to your credit report since the system is automated.

Most likely, you will not qualify for credit cards or a mortgage until you have worked at the same job for six months.

Investments

If you have a spousal RRSP in your name, you are the only one who has access to this fund. This is something to keep in mind if there is an emergency. However, you will have to pay taxes on the amount you withdraw. Before you leave, make copies of important documents in your current safety deposit box and remove anything you want to take with you.

It is often quite difficult to obtain your share of the house value. It is usually the largest asset available to you, whether the house is in both names or only the abuser's. If the abuser is living in the house, he does not have any incentive to sell it and give you your share. The abuser is living in a bigger home than he could afford if he paid you your share. He is living in your half of the home and should, theoretically, be paying you rent for using it. He is denying you the funds to buy your own home, so he is still controlling an important part of your life. He may believe you will go back to him if you become destitute.

Withdrawing funds from the home equity line of credit and putting it in your separate bank account will secure your share of the home and provide you with funds until the divorce is settled. This loan will be offset against the value of the home in the divorce settlement.

> *The most important investment you can make is in your education.*

He will have an incentive to pay the interest on the loan since the loan is secured by the house and he will not want the bank to repossess it if he defaults.

Any investments you make should be very safe ones, since your circumstances are volatile. It is wise to have three months worth of living expenses saved and readily available. However, this may be something you need to work towards if you do not have it now. You may need to have access to your investments on short notice if you need to move suddenly or if you lose your job. Some investments are very difficult, time consuming, and costly to gain access to. So ask questions before investing.

The most important investment you can make is in your education. You can never lose your education. Over a person's life, she will earn 70 percent more if she has a degree. Student loans are available from the government and financial institutions. They are a source to support yourself as well as an investment in your future when you leave.

Employment

Prior to leaving, you must think about getting a job, even if you know it will be difficult to keep because of his abuse or because you decide to leave. If he prevents you from accessing this income, it will still have several other benefits. The process of creating your resume can be quite time consuming and will require information that is more readily available before you leave. You can also collect evidence of your accomplishments (presentations, awards, proof of skills and qualities, etc.) to put in a portfolio. These will then be up to date if and when you do leave.

If you have not or cannot get paid employment, volunteering is also beneficial.

Employment will give you experience that will be beneficial in obtaining positions if you have to leave your job when you leave the relationship. It will allow you to apply for a credit card in your own name without using the abuser's income to qualify. If you use the abuser's information on the application as part of the qualification, he can cancel it or use it to monitor your activities if he finds out about it. When you leave, your own credit card can be a source of emergency funds.

Employment will also generate employment insurance and federal pension contributions that will be beneficial in the future. It also creates retirement contribution room. A registered education savings plan could be used to upgrade your education when you leave.

Employment can also create a network of people to help either in your personal situation or as references for future jobs. It may also provide a transfer opportunity to facilitate leaving.

If you have not or cannot get paid employment, volunteering is also beneficial. You can use these people as references, and you can include this as job experience on your resume. You can also take an upgrading course.

As you can see, in addition to the income earned from employment, the residual benefits are also very useful.

After leaving:
- Use your new name for job searches.
- Choose references carefully, as past employers or coworkers may inform the abuser of your new employment or sabotage your efforts.

• Grants are also available to start new businesses.

Housing
You need a place to live, and there are a variety of options:
• Women's emergency shelters
  —First line of defense, supplying accommodation, food and guidance for a few weeks
• Second stage housing
  —Available after leaving a crisis shelter, but often there is a waiting list
  —Supplies a home and possibly counseling for a period from a few months to a year or more
  —May be subsidized, and some have extensive safety systems
• Organizational Programs
  —Finds you something temporarily but will also put you in a program where they will match your funds five to one to save for a down payment on a house or to start a business
• Become a nanny or live-in housekeeper
  —A job as a nanny or housekeeper will supply you with a home and give you the opportunity to upgrade your education
• Partner with another mother
  —Your housing costs will be lower
  —One could look after both sets of children while the other works, and vice versa
  —Share one vehicle as well as other household items
  —Someone else as support for you and your children
• Remaining in the home and removing the abuser
  —Legal system may force the abuser to move out of the home
  —Requires you to prove he is abusive
  —Costly for you
  —You would be more vulnerable to the abuser
• Entering a rehabilitation center for substance addictions
  —Will supply accommodation and help for a short period of time
  —Helps you overcome a huge obstacle to thriving on your own

- Supported housing for the mentally ill (however, be cautious, as this could affect custody of children)
  —An option to heal mentally
  —Support of professionals and other clients
- Friends and family
  —With people you are comfortable with and who care for you
  —First assess the danger to them
- Going on a mission's trip
  —Help in a needy part of the world
  —Change your life perspective
  —Abuser would be challenged to find you
- Rental places
  —Shared accommodation to keep your name off a lease
  —Won't be alone
  —Inexpensive
  —Flexible mobility
  —Utilities included in the rent will prevent utility company credit checks and accounts in your name and prevent an electronic trail

Health

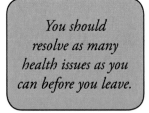

You should resolve as many health issues as you can before you leave.

It is important to consider your health before you leave. You should resolve as many health issues as you can before you leave. You can get your dental work up to date. Having your wisdom teeth removed might be a good idea. It is costly, and you need recovery time. Your eyes should be tested and your glasses updated. You should think about taking advantage of any benefits such as orthotics, braces and any other health devices you can think of that are available through a health benefits plan that you may not have access to in the future.

Things to consider:
- Health plans of the abuser
  —You may be covered under his plan for a time period after you leave

—Prevents a wait period if you change to your own health plan
—Copy his health and dental group plan number and policy number when leaving
—Claims may need to be signed by the plan holder (the abuser) before being reimbursed; others may be paid directly through the insurance company
—Access through an Internet account if you know the password
—Consider name connection between the two plans and if they need to contact the abuser
• New family doctor; this may be arranged before you leave
• Upgrade your health coverage to avoid dental or medical emergency costs
• Obtain counseling

Insurance

• If you are on the vehicle insurance policy with the abuser
    —Staying on the policy will ensure a lower premium when you take out a new policy because there will be no break in coverage
    —Check if staying on will have any cost or liability if you are leaving and no longer using the vehicle
    —Who receives payout if damaged?
    —Check if you can stay on even if you do not have a vehicle after you leave
• If you are on the insurance coverage of anything you are still part owner of, for example, the house,
    —Who receives payout for a claim?
    —Check for liability if the abuser destroys property
    —What costs or obligations?
• Take out tenant insurance if renting
    —Very inexpensive
    —Covers your liability. If you do not have it and you cause damage to other people or their property, you are liable for the cost of the damages (for example, if you cause fire or water damage)

Taxes

- Moving expenses may be tax deductible if moving to start a new job, so keep receipts.
- Contact the government prior to filing to change name, address and especially bank deposit information, as you do not want your tax rebate deposited in your abuser's account.
- Past income tax returns, if the income is low, are proof of income to receive discounts that are prorated according to your ability to pay, such as city recreation programs or second stage crisis housing programs.

Education

- Assistance may be more readily available prior to finding employment, so research this first if planning education upgrades.
- You can improve your education before leaving to create a valuable asset to take with you.
- Take all your academic transcripts and your children's.
- Registered retirement plans can often be used for education without paying the taxes.
- Taking one course at a time may be less expensive and easier to accommodate than going back to school full-time. Distance education is great for this.

Child Care

It is not illegal to leave an abusive home with the children, but contact the police or a lawyer and verify the procedure. Leaving one jurisdiction and moving to another may have different requirements.

- Crisis nurseries are available to look after children for a few days.
- Safe visitation programs can be used if the abuser insists on child visitation.
- Education facilities often have daycare.
- Watch for employers who offer daycare.
- Churches often have solutions.
- Seniors could be excellent child caregivers.

- Babysitting courses may refer their students.
- Trade babysitting services with other single mothers.
- Rotate through family and friends as babysitters.
- Some jobs allow children to come with you (for example, school bus drivers).
- Ask in the neighborhood.
- Start your own daycare at home.

WHERE DO I GO?

You may be tempted to stay close to the familiar; however, he will watch for you at all the places he knows you go. If you are in the same city as he is, it will be easier for him to find you and to connect with you if he does.

Where will the abuser expect you to go? He will most likely go to your friends and family first, to look for you. So you are adding an element of danger for them if you decide to move in with them when you leave. This does not mean you should not go to them. Maybe they are confident that they can keep themselves and you safe. But you should seriously consider all consequences, in light of the abuser's potential desperation.

> *The farther you are away from the abuser, the more planning, time and costs are involved for him, and the less likely it is that he will come searching for you on a drunken urge.*

It will be easier to sever connections with your old life and start over in a new city. However, you should weigh all of this against the resources and opportunities available in your current city.

Usually distance is in your favor and creates some security. The farther you are away from the abuser, the more planning, time and costs are involved for him, and the less likely it is that he will come searching for you on a drunken urge.

Researching where to go will make the transition less challenging. Employment, transportation, education and accommodations are usually easier to obtain in a larger community. You can research the demographics such as job growth, crime rate, weather and other relevant information on websites such as the top ten cities to live in. You can also research the attitude of the city justice system towards domestic violence.

If you have no vehicle, towns without a public transit system will be a challenge. It will also be easier for your abuser to find you in a small community, since there are limited places for shopping, working and recreation.

WHEN DO I LEAVE?

Remember, there will never be a good time to leave. There will always be something coming up. However, something coming up may be to your advantage. He will not be expecting you to leave at that time, and it might keep him preoccupied. He will never be in the optimum frame of mind. Plan to leave when you have a large window of time available.

If you can practice packing, you will have an idea of how much time you need to leave the house. The police may agree to oversee your exit.

When He's Away

If he is going to be away from home for several days, this would be the ideal time to leave. However, he may have someone secretly watching you. Another good time is if he has some important work or personal commitment coming up. His mind will be focused on it and less than usual on you. Also, he will not expect you to leave at a time that would be the most inconvenient for him, since he believes he has you trained to always put his needs first.

Before Scheduled Activities

The end of the school year may not be a wise choice. If the abuser has any suspicions that you may be leaving, he will be in a state of heightened vigilance at this time. Choosing to leave during the school year may be a little more of a challenge for the children, but it will be a safer choice. This also applies to the children's tournaments or recitals. The abuser will be less on guard to your leaving if he knows important events are planned. However, if you do choose to leave before these events, it would be dangerous to then subsequently attend them, as the abuser may be there waiting for you.

You can use the same line of reasoning for your events. Planning to leave during a time when it would be inconvenient for you is more likely to catch the abuser unaware.

Weather

If possible, wait until the worst of the cold weather is past. Leaving in the spring gives you the longest stretch of time to be settled somewhere else before winter returns. Moving your belongings and finding housing is less of a challenge if you do not have to do it in the cold. The children will also have the majority of their school year completed.

How Do I Go?

Obtaining a driver's license will go a long way towards empowering you. It will greatly increase your safety if you can take a vehicle when you escape the abuser. This will also increase the children's safety. To get your license before you leave, you could spin it to the abuser to emphasize the benefits in order to minimize his resistance to it. If you want to hide this from your abuser, you have to choose your method of learning carefully. Asking friends or relatives to teach you could increase the chance of the abuser finding out. Using a professional organization, such as AAA, is another option.

You could also encourage your children to get their driver's or learner's license.

You should have a valid passport and your children's passports and proof that you are their parent.

If the vehicle registration is in just his name he can report it as stolen if you use it to escape. Alternatively, you can rent a vehicle, but you need to remember that the rental company will know the drop-off location and could tell the abuser. Airports are a great place to rent vehicles.

You could box up your belongings and have them shipped if you decide to fly or

> *If the vehicle registration is in just his name he can report it as stolen if you use it to escape.*

take the train or bus, but consider where to ship them. Shipping will create a record that your abuser could use to find you.

You could rent a U-Haul and take everything yourself, but again watch the paper trail, as the drop-off destination will be in the system. Trucks are not that difficult to drive, and neither is it difficult to pull a trailer, but you need a hitch and ball and proper wiring for the signal lights. We always assume that driving anything bigger than a car is too much of a challenge for a woman, but they are very similar to a car.

Hedge of Protection

A hedge of protection is very important when you leave. Just before and just after you leave are statistically the most dangerous times for you. Even if the abuser does not have a history of violence, his desperation may give him justification to cross that line. The cleanest break you can make is the safest break. Having no contact with him diminishes any opportunity for him to entice you back or abuse you for leaving.

To protect yourself, you should consider changing your name, your job, your city, maybe changing your vehicle, your computer, your cell phone and number, and also your e-mail, your hobbies, your school, your doctor and your dentist.

To keep the abuse out, eliminate contact with the abuser. If he does confront you, you keep things calm and impersonal, and you leave. You don't answer questions and you don't explain, because you know, in his eyes, nothing you say or do will justify your leaving.

He will try to reconnect, to reestablish the hook, hold, or bond he had in order to regain control, to reclaim his power, to repair his status, to renew his indulgence.

He will try to lure you back with promises of treasures, a new life, a changed man. But you are not deceived by the illusion of the honeymoon. He will try to shame you back with guilt over all he's done for you, over the children needing their father, over his not being able to survive without you. But know the guilt is built on his craving to control. He will try to bring you back by mesmerizing you with confusion, blaming your leaving on mental breakdown, on being led astray, on believing lies. But you know the confusion is to knock you off balance so you will seek his support. He will try to terrorize you into returning by threatening your resources, by threatening your loved ones, by threatening you. But you know you are safer away from him than with him.

He will try to gather information—having information is his power, his right and your vulnerability. He will try to get it by deception or force, through family or friends, or through you. But you are no longer his business, no matter what he believes.

When he calls, he'll hear "This number is no longer in service"; when he e-mails they'll turn to "junk"; when he writes he'll see "Return to sender."

> *The safest path is to negotiate only through your lawyer, and since lawyers are expensive, negotiations should be kept to a minimum.*

The safest path is to negotiate only through your lawyer, and since lawyers are expensive, negotiations should be kept to a minimum.

For the first few months (or years if warranted), you do not disclose details of your new life to family and friends. You can call them instead of them calling you and arrange to meet them somewhere instead of going to their home or them coming to yours. You can use public transit to meet them. You should stay off social media—it is scary how it uses endless avenues on the Internet to supply information about you.

A LOT TO THINK ABOUT

We have considered many details as we covered the Who, What, Why, When, Where and How of leaving the abuser. And yet we could never cover every scenario. Each situation is unique, and your plan has to be adjusted to fit your particular circumstances. Always keep safety in mind when considering a course of action. And always keep your vision in your heart.

I'm on My Way from Misery to Happiness

REPIDATION INCREASED MY SPEED. MY VISION WAS DRAWN repeatedly to the side mirror of the SUV as I watched for Ed's familiar work truck. I had the inside of the vehicle so packed full of containers I could not use the rearview mirror. If he returned home from work early and found me gone, he might try to catch me.

There were several highway routes I could take. I took the one Ed was least likely to choose if he followed me. I had my new cell phone beside me. The RCMP knew my plans, and they also knew the make, model and license plate number of Ed's truck, so if Ed caused trouble, it would be easier for them to help me.

Packing the containers in the morning took longer than I expected. I was moving fast, but I was so nervous. I kept running to the upstairs window where I could see down the road, anxious about Ed coming home unexpectedly. The RCMP had offered to oversee my leaving, but I remembered Ed's comment about not calling the police when we watched the news of the four RCMP who were shot. I also did not think I was important enough to take up their time. I told them I would phone if I needed help.

I backed the truck into the garage with the end gate down and the door to the house propped open so that I could walk straight from the house onto the truck with the containers. When I finally finished, I took a quick walk through the house. I was filled with a mixture of emotions: sadness at leaving behind my pets, fear of the unknown and exhilaration of a new life.

I scanned the unsigned typed note that I was leaving on the counter for Ed. It explained my eating disorder and how life-threatening it was. I also told him that all his talk of killing me was terrifying. I knew I had to leave an explanation or Ed would jump to the worst possible conclusion, that I ran away with someone. Nothing could be further from the truth. Although I hoped most men were good, I never wanted another personal relationship.

It was time to leave. I jumped in the driver's seat of the truck, opened the garage door and drove away.

In town, I parked close to the car rental place. Inside the dealership, I felt so vulnerable with all the glass windows. I struggled to remain calm as I requested the vehicle I had reserved in my late father's name. I sensed my father smiling down on me. So often, I longed for him to come and rescue me from my dungeon. I felt we were co-conspirators in my escape.

Finally, I was driving off the lot, with another step safely completed. I transferred my belongings from our truck to the rental vehicle and parked our truck on the street. In the note I left, I told Ed where I was leaving our truck.

Then as I raced down the highway, my heart got lighter with every mile as I felt the shackles falling off me. Free at last. As the scenery flew by, I was filled with a strange peace that comes when you've stepped beyond the fear.

It was a three-hour drive to Albertville, where I was going to exchange my rental vehicle. It was only halfway to my destination, but if I transferred vehicles midway, at the airport, it would be more difficult for Ed to trace my destination. He knew a lot of people in town, and he probably knew the person I rented the vehicle from.

Another three hours after switching vehicles, I finally reached Clarion. I stopped and checked my maps again (yes, I brought some maps), searching for the best route to the address I was given for the women's emergency shelter. The adrenaline had started to subside, and my nerves were raw.

'What if something goes wrong and they don't have room for me?' I worried with a trace of desperation.

Fear seeped in as I realized I was alone. It was dark out.

'What have I done?' My heart was pounding.

Maybe I made a mistake. I struggled to keep the panic suppressed.

Then I remembered the years of anguish I left behind. I folded up the map and focused on my destination.

A few minutes later, I stood on the stairs, in the glow from the light above the door of the shelter. I glanced behind me, straining to see into the dark. I felt so exposed and vulnerable.

I pushed the button, and a lady's voice said, "Yes?"

"Please let me in. I need help." I heard the tremble in my voice.

As they buzzed me through the double security doors and I stepped inside, I finally felt safe. But I also felt like a refugee seeking asylum. I was in danger and homeless.

I had entered a strange new world, and I was tempted to be fearful, but then I remember Helen Keller's quote "Life is either a wonderful adventure or it is nothing."

I told myself I was on an adventure, free to explore and discover.

Inside, the shelter seemed clean and cared for. A kind, gentle lady took me into a cozy room with nice decor, and we sat in comfy chairs as she asked about me. By then, I was numb and responded on autopilot.

After we finished, she said, "Since you are working on university courses, I'm going to put you in one of the temporary intake rooms for families. It is larger than the rooms for single women, and you will have it to yourself so you have quiet to work." She added, "If a family comes in and needs it, we can always move you."

"Thank you so much," I said, very grateful for the privacy.

Soon I was settled into my room and into my bed. I pulled the blue quilt with daisies on it up under my chin and said a prayer of thanks before I fell into an exhausted sleep.

The next day, I called family that I knew would be concerned about me, to let them know I had left Ed. Ed had already called most of them, looking for me. I was so thankful that no one knew where I was.

When I talked to my sister, she told me Ed had called, trying to convince her that I was mentally unstable and didn't know what I was doing, that he needed to know where I was so that he could help me.

She said, "We all love our sister, and you stole her away from us. I wouldn't tell you where she was even if I knew."

I found out later that he drove a couple of hundred miles to the office of my university to try to find out my address. I had called them after I left and explained that my life could depend on them not disclosing my whereabouts to anyone, especially Ed. They were very understanding and helpful and said they would flag my file with a warning. So Ed received nothing from them.

He tried to get my doctor to tell him where I was. She told him that doctor-patient confidentiality prevented that, but she suggested that maybe Ed should go for some counseling.

Ashley and Connor were the ones he called relentlessly. He tried many different tactics to try to draw out information. He said I was sick, that I didn't know what I was doing, and that I needed his help. He said I must have run off with someone and was under his influence because I would never have done something like this on my own. Then, he was convinced that I had done something so terrible that I could not face him.

Ed would tell the kids I was the love of his life and that he couldn't live without me. Then he would turn around and tell them I was the lowest form of life for putting him through all the pain and embarrassment. He demanded to know how I had left and where I was. He said I could not have done it alone and that he was going to find out who had helped me and make them pay.

He constantly asked them to tell me to call him.

I stood firm through all of this and refused to talk to him or answer his questions. I knew, from years of living with him, that his questions never stopped and that no answer was acceptable to him unless it was the one he wanted to hear.

I also knew he was hurting bad, and it hurt me to know that it was because of me. Talking to him would be very hard on both of us and would only make matters worse.

I tried to focus instead on my future. I spent time each day on my schoolwork, my resume and my chores.

It was wonderful doing chores with the other women who had sought refuge in the shelter. We helped the chef to prepare meals, we cleaned the kitchen and the dining room, and we cleaned our own rooms and linens.

I could stay for three weeks, and in that time I needed to find a home and a job. After touching up the resume I started before I left, I began the job application process.

A week after I arrived at the shelter, Julie, the shelter manager, called me to her office. "Have you looked into a place to stay yet?" she asked.

"I have been looking at condominiums. I have enough money for a down payment on a small one, but I need to find a job first to make sure I can cover the payments," I replied.

She sensed the worry in my voice and explained, "You could start with a rental place and look into purchasing a home after you find a job."

"But if I spend the money on rent, it will be gone, and I'll lose my chance to buy my own home. I want my payments to build my assets instead of being lost in rent," I said with a bit of desperation in my voice.

"Well, you still have a couple of weeks left that you can stay here, but you should start looking into rental places as well, just in case," she said.

Finding a job was more difficult than I had anticipated. I had no office work experience. My only references were from the library, where I occasionally volunteered. I only needed a couple more courses to finish my business degree, but I was finding companies were reluctant to hire me for entry-level positions because, with my education, they questioned if I would stay. Yet I did not have the experience for higher level positions.

Another week went by without a job, so I started looking through the rental listings Julie gave me. I looked for the least expensive place in the area of the city where I lived as a child, an area that would feel like home.

SCENIC VIEW—F/M, N/S, no pets.
Shared townhouse. $450 inclusive.

I checked my transit map. The location was a little far from the light rail train, but the location and the price were good, so I called.

The next day I climbed the stairs of the veranda and rang the doorbell as I wondered what the lady would be like. The door opened, and as I saw her smile and felt her warmth, the grip on my heart released. She was quite young, about my daughter's age, with blond hair and a confident charm. Past her, I saw a staircase that led to the upper level and an inviting living room to my right.

She invited me in, and I sat on the edge of the sofa and tried to still my fidgeting hands. I loved the decor: her walls were taupe, her furniture was a camel color and the carpet was beige. The plants, candles and pictures spoke of her personality. Through the entrance to the kitchen, I saw a computer desk and stone-looking flooring.

"I am interested in renting your room, but I feel I should tell you a bit about myself first. I have just left an abusive marriage, and I am currently staying at the women's shelter. My husband is very angry and wants to find me, so it could be dangerous for you. However, he lives in a city seven hours away, and I have been very careful to conceal my destination." I thought I was rambling, but I continued talking.

"I have enough funds for several months' rent. I have an accounting education and am currently looking for employment," I said, hoping my circumstances had not discouraged her from accepting me.

She nodded her head and said, "I used to work at the other women's shelter, and I currently work for the YWCA, helping youths in troubled families, so I am quite familiar with situations like yours. The safety issue doesn't concern me, and if you are willing, the room is yours." The reassurance in her voice and her background erased my concerns about living with a stranger.

Relief and happiness filled my heart as I realized I had a home. I also looked forward to getting to know this interesting woman.

The next weekend, it didn't take me long to move my things. After leaving behind so many possessions, I loved the light, free feeling of not having the responsibility that comes with owning things.

This marked a transition, out of the confusion and chaos of escaping, into a period of holding my breath as I waited. Resting and waiting. I rested after deliverance from the dungeon, and I waited for the seeds of my new life to sprout.

Monday morning, I stepped off the commuter train into warm golden sunshine. As I walked up the hill to a counselor's office, green shoots of spring lined the edge of the walk and a soft breeze played in my hair.

A church had offered to pay for some counseling for me. I sat in a chair in the waiting room feeling amazed and delighted at their generosity.

As I followed my counselor, Teri, down the hall, her dress flowed freely, setting the pastel flowers in motion. The sandals on her feet seemed a bit optimistic for the spring weather, but I found that her clothes reflected her spirit. I liked my counselor.

"Can you tell me a bit about yourself?" she asked.

After telling her my story I finished with "I'm going to wait for Ed to decide to sell our house, and hopefully he will give me my share."

She looked up from her notepad and asked, "Do you want him to maintain that control over you?"

I pondered her question and slowly realized that as long as I was waiting for Ed to divide our assets he still controlled my life, and he would want to keep it that way.

As I rode the train home, watching the city scenes slide by, I argued back and forth in my mind about whether or not to pursue the separation-of-assets option Teri suggested. I didn't know if I had the courage to confront Ed on this. I had not had, and never intended to have, direct contact with him, so it would all have to be through a lawyer. The shelter had recommended a lawyer. Maybe I should call her.

Partly to please my counselor and partly out of curiosity, I went to talk to the lawyer. She was a very intelligent, forthright woman.

"He's going to believe everything belongs to him, and if he decides to give you anything, he will believe it is out of the goodness of his heart because you don't deserve anything," she stated.

"That's probably what he will think. How did you know?" I asked in surprise.

"I have had a lot of experience with abusers," she replied.

At the end of our talk, I could see that Ed would never offer to give me my share of our assets, because he would never want to accept that I was not going back to him. If I wanted my share, I would need to start the process, and I would need a lawyer.

I recognized that this lawyer was not like me at all; she was a fighter. I thought I needed someone like her, and I felt safe in her care. I asked her to take my case, and I wrote a check for her retainer.

This reemphasized my commitment to live as frugally as possible. A lawyer's work was like pay-as-you-use; I paid up front, and when that money was used, I paid another retainer. I would never know each month how much would be needed, so I saved as much as possible. I bought nothing that could be postponed. I restricted my diet to cheap protein and vegetables.

It was a liberating and frightening feeling to know that the process of severing the last thread to my agonized past had started. I began the long wait for that process to finish.

The next time I saw Teri, she was encouraged by my progress and gave me another invaluable piece of information. She told me about second stage crisis housing and a place called Sunrise. They provided an apartment and counseling to women who had left abusive relationships. I was so excited about this opportunity, I called them as soon as I was back home, safe in my room.

Kim answered the phone and walked me through a series of questions. Then she told me I could go on their wait list, but there were only two apartments for single women. The rest were reserved for single moms. It would be several months before an apartment was available for me, since their program was a year long.

This was both encouraging and discouraging. I was encouraged that Sunrise was willing to consider me for their program, but I was discouraged that it was going to be such a long wait. I liked the place that I was renting and I liked Alison, the lady who owned it, but I had a tendency to hide in my room. I enjoyed solitude, and it would be wonderful to have my own apartment.

So I was now on Sunrise's waiting list and soon to go on another. However, during this time of waiting, I experienced some unexpected pleasures of discovery and adventure with loved ones.

My daughter, Ashley, and I were going to the mountains. She was staying in a resort condominium for a week and had invited me to join her. I had my little travel suitcase packed, and I hopped on a city bus to meet her at a shopping plaza. She didn't come to my place, because we were still cautious about a private investigator following her to find me.

We headed west, and it was so wonderful to be out in the country again and to see the majestic mountains rise higher the closer we got. I love the mountains. We pulled up in front of the resort, which was a lovely blend of rustic elegance.

The next morning was sunny and warm, a beautiful day for a hike. We drove to the parking lot at the base of the mountain. I got out and stretched. Happy anticipation filled me as I reached for my backpack filled with lunch and jackets.

There were a few other cars in the parking lot of other hikers whom we might pass on the trail. The map of the trail showed us the various lookout points and the time it would take to get to our destination. In a little over an hour, we would be at the lake where the main trail ended.

We were at a lookout point watching rock climbers when my cell phone rang. I had registered at several staffing agencies who were trying to find me a job. Maybe it was one of them.

"Hello," I said, trying to sound professional and not desperate.

"Hello, this is Jonathan with the eating disorder program. I was wondering if I could ask you some questions to see if you are a fit for our program?" he asked politely.

It was not a job interview request, but it was still a very welcome call. I had called and requested to take part in their program several weeks before.

He asked me questions on the history of my disorder and what current challenges I was having. Then he let me know that I did qualify for the program. My heart leapt with excitement. I very much wanted to be well in all aspects of my new life.

"However, we do not have any space at the present, so we will put you on our waiting list and call you when we have an opening," he said.

"I'm so excited for you. Your eating disorder was with you for so long, it will be wonderful to deal with it and heal from any damage it caused, especially psychologically." Ashley beamed after I told her my good news.

I wanted to keep healing and growing and learning who it was that I was meant to be. Therefore I was grateful that they had accepted me in the program, but more waiting added to my restlessness.

It had been a couple of months since I left. The last bulimic episode was before my wisdom teeth were removed, but I had been struggling to convince myself to eat enough. This was a concern. My counseling with Karen was cut short when I left, and I had been in limbo, knowing I had only just begun the work I needed to do.

Ashley and I continued our ascent. Words from the past that Rita used to end our session with came to mind: "Onward and upward."

When I started counseling with Rita, my ascent had been the climb out of the pit, out of the dungeon. Now my climb had started the ascent up the mountain, into the clear blue sky with beautiful vistas that brought awe into my soul. Our hike that day was symbolic of that climb.

As Ashley and I climbed from one blue-black rugged stone to the next, we held the pine trees for support. Someone had built a rough bridge over a beautiful little stream. We turned and watched it tumble down the mountainside, sparkling like diamonds in the sunlight.

We continued on the path around a rocky outcrop and stood transfixed and spellbound at the magical sight before us. There was a tiny lake nestled among the fir trees.

Nothing had prepared us for the unbelievable color. It was turquoise blending to a teal blue in the center. Streams flowed into and out of the lake, danced over rocks, and created pools here and there. Little rugged bridges linked the trail that continued around the lake and over the streams and pools.

We took pictures of the lake and each other then found a rock to sit on in the sun and eat the lunch we brought. We were happy being together in such a beautiful place.

Over the next few days, we visited the little shops in town and went on other hikes. The last day of our stay at the resort arrived. We were going back to the city to see a jazz dance performance.

I was so excited. I had loved dance since I was a little girl but was too shy then to dance, and later, even though Ed and I met at a dance, there was no dancing allowed once I entered the dungeon. He had no interest in cultural pursuits, so this was a new facet to my adventure. We dressed to the nines and headed to the big city in excited anticipation.

The dance troupe's performance was exhilarating and inspirational. I wanted to go out right then and sign up for dance lessons. I was surprised by the audience involvement. They clapped and whistled and hooted in appreciation. I could not believe I was sitting in the audience of a cultural performance, freely able to express my joy in the experience.

When the performance finally finished, we were all up on our feet in a thunderous roar of applause. The wave of applause seemed endless, and we all shouted "Encore!"

Finally, we were blessed with one more dance. We left the theater with a touch of sadness mixed with our joy, because we did not want it to end.

That was one unexpected adventure, and I was about to go on another one. My cousin Laura needed to drive to Rockpoint to bring back a new car. She and her husband had booked flights, but he was unable to go, so Laura talked me into using his ticket and going with her. She took me to see friends and sights while we were there. As we were going through a quaint shop on Peter's Wharf, I received a very welcome phone call.

My interlude of resting and waiting was coming to an end, and it was time to step into action. One of my seeds had emerged into the sunshine to grow.

It was then early June, and I had been looking for work for almost three months. Before Laura and I left, I had just had the second interview for a very promising position. This call was the accountant for the company calling to ask if I would like to accept the accounting assistant position I had applied for with them. I tried to contain my happiness and speak professionally as I accepted her offer. My cousin and I hugged in joy as I told her my good news.

Back in Clarion, I got a call from Connor.

"Hi, Mom. The job up north finished, and it will be a couple of weeks till the next one. Melody and I are heading to Albertville to shop and visit Melody's family. Would you be able to meet us there? With my work and your new job starting soon, it may be a long time before we'll have another chance to see you."

I was filled with happy excitement and said, "Yes. That would be wonderful. I can take a bus if you would be able to pick me up."

"For sure. Give us a call and let us know what time. Well, bye for now. Love you, Mom."

I heard the click as he hung up, and I laughed out loud with delight that I would see him and Melody soon. Since they lived a long ways away, I hadn't seen them since the Christmas before I left. Albertville was halfway between their home and mine.

I was very proud of the man Connor had grown into in spite of the example of his father. He could have followed his father down the path of abuse, but he chose instead to follow a path of integrity.

He had a depth of compassion and knowing that was unusual in a man, and yet he was very assertive, confident and competent. His courageousness often brought me fear. His job was dangerous, and if there was ever a risk to be taken, he was the one who stepped up. I loved him dearly, and I was so happy that he had Melody in his life.

They had been high school sweethearts. The first time he met her was in the first aid room at a ski hill. Melody had fallen on her face, and her nose was bloody and swollen. But it spoke of her spunk, and Connor was impressed.

She was a match for his intelligence and assertiveness, and their love had endured quite a few hardships. Because of the hardships, their love had grown stronger.

After returning from my visit with the kids in Albertville, I was excited and nervous about starting work. The day before I started, I took a practice run to verify the timing of the public transit schedule. Since I had a monthly public transit pass, it was like having a chauffeur no matter where I was in the city.

As I rode the bus my first day of work, I occasionally looked up as passengers came and went. Then I returned to my notebook to synthesize my theory for the fall of the Roman Empire. Since I was taking my university degree through distance education, I had no classes, only assignments and exams. I used the two and a half hour commute to work to do my coursework. Not owning a vehicle worked well for me. I saved the expense of owning a car, and someone else did the driving.

From the bus, I had a ten-minute walk to where I worked. I walked past private schools with girls in plaid uniforms and through parks perfumed with the fragrance of lilac.

I loved everything about my new job. I enjoyed the work I did and the people I worked with, and I especially loved where I worked. Our office was a stately two-story vintage home, and the rooms had been transformed into our offices. A cotoneaster hedge enclosed the yard, and flowerbeds full of peonies, pansies and roses bordered the lawn. There was a gazebo in the backyard as well as a patio, with furniture and a barbecue, which we occasionally used for lunch meetings.

My job wait was over, and my next seedling to sprout was the eating disorder program. After being on the waiting list for many months, I got the news that they finally had room for me.

I sat in the waiting room trying to figure out how to disappear. I felt vulnerable when I was in a place where I could attract attention. I felt people would wonder what eating disorder I had and why I had it, just as I was wondering about everyone else who walked in.

I reached in my backpack and pulled out my security shield, my homework. Maybe if people saw me doing homework they would see me as a productive good person and not judge me critically. Maybe they would pay attention to my books instead of me. Maybe I would look boring and they would ignore me.

Soon I was called into the psychiatrist's office. The psychiatrist was a man, which made me somewhat uncomfortable. I would rather have had a lady doctor. After we talked about the abuse I left and my present situation, he asked, "How do you feel about your current weight?"

"I was happy with the weight I lost around the time I left, but the seven pounds I have gained back is a little frightening. I have not had a bulimic episode since I left, but I don't know how to handle weight gain anymore and I don't like weighing 117 pounds," I tried to explain.

What he answered had a profound impact on me. He said, "I would never let a number control my life."

I knew having that self-determination and strength was true and noble and admirable, but I also believed it was something I would never be able to attain. It was so powerful it frightened me, because I felt it was a standard I had to achieve and I was going to fail.

By the close of the interview, I understood that even though bulimia was no longer an overpowering presence for me, controlling food was. I was definitely restricting food, which was the basis of an eating disorder. My disordered beliefs led to disordered eating. Through the program, I would expose and challenge the disordered beliefs while the staff closely monitored my physical and mental states.

There were several modules, and each explored different aspects of eating disorders in a group setting. Everyone in the modules was either a teenager or a young woman. I was always the oldest by far. Even though there were no restrictions, no males were part of the program. It broke my heart to see these young women on the verge of dying because of their lack of self-confidence and self-worth. Most of us felt we needed to fit everyone else's image of what a woman should look like.

The first module, psych-education, dealt with demystifying the beast of the eating disorder and discovering our own self-worth. Other modules built on this.

I learned that a major contributing factor for eating disorders is someone else controlling our lives. Unconsciously, we chose to control our eating in an attempt to maintain our own identity.

A dietician, an occupational therapist, a recreational therapist and a psychologist made up the team of experts who enlightened, coached and encouraged us through the various modules. They covered every aspect of our lives, because eating disorders damaged every area of our lives and every system in our bodies. We also had a nurse, a doctor, a case psychologist and a psychiatrist who worked with each of us one on one.

Although we in the program did not want to admit it and never spoke about it, we all knew that our disorders were deadly.

Maybe it was because I was older, but I found I could not help but share the lessons I learned in my dungeon experience. I was no longer afraid of group counseling; rather, it was an amazing way to share myself, to help others, as well as to see the kaleidoscope of insights and perceptions other people had that could help me grow.

As I processed what I learned of the disorder and practiced what they suggested, I learned that food was not "good" or "bad." It was the rules I made up around it and the myths I believed about it that were controlling me. Disordered eating is an addiction, but unlike alcohol or drugs, we cannot just quit. We need food to survive, and so the challenge was to work on creating a good relationship with our food and our body. I needed to stop abusing myself in the way I talked to myself and in the way I treated myself. I would never tell someone else they were fat; I would never force someone else to live on what I ate.

I finally understood that my body was not the enemy; it was my friend. It was trying to keep me alive the best way it could. Just as eating disorders damage every system in our bodies, eating healthy strengthens every system in our bodies. I needed to care for it in order for it to care for me. Even though it was a huge mountain to climb, with every small step forward I ascended.

Partway through the eating disorder program, I was off Sunrise's waiting list. They finally had an apartment for me. They were so gracious—they dropped the key off at work for me since their office would be closed by the time I finished.

Sunrise had two apartment buildings side by side that altogether had nine apartments, a playroom and two offices. They were old buildings, but well cared for, in a trendy part of the city.

I knew my apartment wouldn't be anything fancy, but I would have solitude. I would have a whole apartment to myself, and, most importantly, I could work on my healing and growth. It was almost a year since I had left the abuse. Spring would be here soon.

The next day, a friend would help me move, but I couldn't wait to see the apartment. I rushed over from work, filled with joy as I mounted the stairs. I jiggled the key to unlock the door, and as the door opened and I stepped inside, I saw on the floor a basket, some boxes and bags, all full of stuff. I looked inside them and almost cried as I realized what they meant. They were full of new dishes, linens and groceries.

I looked around the living room. It was freshly painted with new carpet. The apartment was completely furnished, and there was a bouquet of flowers on the coffee table. There were pictures down the hall and more pictures in the kitchen. The bathroom had new towels, lotions and soaps. I loved the earthy color palette of the whole apartment. The ambiance was whimsical and warm.

I was told they had a program called "Adopt an Apartment" where different organizations redecorated each apartment for each new lady, and we could keep everything in the apartment to use when we completed the program. So everything was not just for me to use, it was for me. I felt like a destitute orphan who was miraculously taken in by a loving family.

The following week, after I was settled in, the counseling part of the program began.

Lana, my counselor, said, "We need to first do an assessment of where you are at now so we can decide which area to start work on."

She showed me the matrix. "I'll ask you the questions in each part, and you let me know how you feel. Okay?"

"Okay." I have always tried to be a good student, and I knew this would have an important effect on my future.

We assessed the strengths and weaknesses of my life skills and decided which area of improvement to start on first.

In my mind I thought, *This is great. As I work on something, we will be able to monitor and measure my progress. I will be able to see and understand instead of always swirling in confusion, wondering where I am at and which direction to go.*

Lana asked questions regarding such things as financial management, stress management, communication, organization, self-esteem and relationships. In each area, she asked specific questions, and I answered on a scale of one to ten. It came as no surprise that my self-esteem was where I scored the lowest. It was connected to my lack of self-confidence. I felt I didn't have a self to be confident in; my identity was lost or buried.

This was where we would begin next week. Lana gave me a wonderful hug when we finished the session.

The next part of the program started Wednesday night. We were meeting in June's apartment for our group counseling session. There was no meeting room at Sunrise, so ladies volunteered to host the group session in their apartments. I was both excited and worried about this. Group counseling at the eating disorder program was so impactful and transformative that I had hopes that this would be as well. But I was self-conscious about joining a group where everyone else knew each other and I was the new person. I was afraid of attracting attention. I was afraid of being judged.

I arrived a little early—one of my security tactics. I could be helpful, maybe gain an ally, and I could choose the safest place to sit. June answered her door, and after I introduced myself, I helped her set out the cookies and drinks. I chose a chair in the corner close to the door so I could see people as they came in without them first noticing me. I was close to the door so I could leave first and not have to engage in the small talk of goodbye.

Lana told me the group sessions covered various modules that also helped us develop our life skills. I was delighted when I discovered that the module we were on was dealing with boundaries, based on the book by Cloud and Townsend that I read and loved. What I had read was very enlightening, and since I was familiar with the subject, I found myself sharing my understanding and insight with these ladies. As I listened to their questions and comments, my heart went out to them. I looked around the room and sensed that each one of them had been battered in spirit, as well as in body.

My personal counseling was more demanding, because I was accountable for my growth. The homework lessons challenged my limiting perceptions, and the exercises I needed to practice in everyday life were reinforcing my changing beliefs. I had made progress in all the areas, but I was still struggling with my self-confidence. In my mind, my self-esteem was better, but emotionally I was still bound by fear.

Either I hid or I was like a chameleon and adapted my identity to my surroundings. Lana gave me various exercises to practice in order to strengthen this, such as creating a list of what I thought my positive attributes were and why, and to try, at least once a day, to share my opinion with someone.

These were so hard. My instinct was to tell myself there was something wrong with all my attributes, but if I wanted to get better, I needed to work on this, so I tried. The thought of actually voicing my opinion was terrifying. It would leave me vulnerable to the humiliation and rejection I always feared, and I really wanted to skip this part.

I had been working on this for over a month, and I was still struggling with it when we went on an adventure as a group to the mountains. All of us ladies and children were going to a YMCA special camp just for us. It was late spring, so it was too early in the season for anyone else to be there. They had activities planned for the children, someone to look after them, and activities planned for the ladies. We would be staying over the weekend.

Outside Sunrise, I helped a young mom carry her bags as she juggled her baby in her arms. We heard the rumble of the bus first. Then we saw it come into view as it rounded the corner. The children were bright eyed and laughed with excitement as they asked endless questions of their moms.

When we were underway, Shanna, the children's counselor, put in a Walt Disney DVD for the kids to watch on the hour-long trip into the mountains. The lady in front of me had never been in the mountains. As I heard her talk of their majestic, rugged beauty, it was delightful for me to see them through fresh eyes.

We arrived at the camp, and as I stepped off the bus, the wonderful smell of a pine forest greeted my senses and brought back memories of childhood camping trips with my family.

The YMCA counselors took our luggage for us and led the way to our cabins. After we explored and had supper, we ladies met by the fireplace in a small adjoining lodge. As the evening progressed, I was impressed with Annie, the YMCA lady in charge of us. She exuded self-confidence, and I wondered what its source was.

Maybe she is secure in her marriage and in her finances, I speculated.

Then I thought, *No, that is not where our self-confidence comes from. Even children have self-confidence. Why is it so easy for some people and so elusive for me?*

The next morning was gray and chilly. All the snow had gone from the foothills where the YMCA camp was, but I could still see snow on the mountains. Since it was spring, the weather could switch from summer to winter in a day, so we all had warm clothes with us. We were all bundled up as we trekked through the pines to the "high ropes."

This was the planned activity that had filled me with happy excitement since I had read of it on the information sheet. They had cables stretched between poles two stories off the ground, and they had made aerial obstacle courses with them. There was also a zip-line and the pole. The pole was three stories high and freestanding with no cables. That's what I wanted to try.

Roo, one of the camp volunteers, showed us the ropes. He handed each of us a harness and a helmet to put on and then gave us a quick talk on safety and belaying. We would be attached to safety ropes, like wall climbers, the whole time we were off the ground.

The cable courses were challenging and fun. We all laughed as Julie struggled for balance on the swaying boardwalk high over our heads. When the boards slipped out from under her feet, we all held our breath, but her harness and the safety ropes held her safely as she dangled in the air and was slowly lowered to the ground.

Okay! We were safe if we fell. We all became a little more daring.

"Are you ladies ready to try the pole?" shouted Suzanne.

There were a few yeses, including mine, as I headed for the pole.

When it was my turn, I scrambled up the spikes in the side of the pole with ease because of my love of tree climbing when I was young.

As I reached the last spike, I thought, *Now for the tRoby part, to get both feet on the top of the pole and stand up.*

The top was about the size of a dinner plate, so there was no room to kneel first and then push myself up. I had to put one foot on top first and then the other. The first foot wasn't too hard, because I could still use my hands, but the second foot was harder. I put my weight on the foot on the top, let go with my hands, and stepped up on top with my second foot.

Wow! I have done it. I am standing on top of the pole! I thought to myself in exhilaration.

I couldn't use my safety rope to steady myself since it was out to the side. I just had to balance. I lifted my eyes and looked out over the amazing vista. I could see the main lodge and the cabins surrounding it. I could see over the top of the pines to the little lake. I could see where the foothill, dark with evergreen trees, met the bottom of the mountains. I could see for miles.

Then I remembered I was on top of a pole three stories high, and my knees began to shake. The shaking got worse and started making the pole shake. Then the shaking of the pole turned into a wobble. Roo was telling me to imagine a golden thread running from the top of my head down to the center of the earth in an effort to steady my legs. I tried to imagine it, but it was not helping. My legs were starting to get tired, and they were telling me I had to make the shaking stop before I could jump off.

I tried harder to stop shaking, and I couldn't. Then I remembered that I had angels protecting me. I held my arms out and imagined them holding me up. My legs stopped shaking, and I jumped out into the air, confident that my harness would catch me. I was laughing with joy as they lowered me to the ground. That was so much fun!

But once again at campfire that night, as I listened and watch Annie, I struggled to discover the key that would unlock the secret of her self-confidence. I believed once I discovered it, I could recreate it in myself.

Yet, as my thoughts struggled with this dilemma, I failed to see the irony of my courage in standing on top of the pole and my belief that I had no self-confidence.

Even after I returned to Sunrise, my mind kept working on this concept of self-confidence, and I kept practicing. Nevertheless, I could not feel confidence, no matter how hard I tried. All I felt was the fear.

Soon, I had another opportunity to escape the city. Springtime was the best time of the year for skiing, and Ashley convinced me to go skiing with her. Every winter since I was first married, we went on ski vacations. Ashley started skiing when she was four years old. After all those years of skiing, I was a fairly competent skier as well. However, my skiing was much better, and more fun, in the days when I could have a good stiff drink before hitting the slopes.

It was wonderful to be with Ashley at a ski resort again, and as we headed down the hill, the familiar tension and fear inhibited my skiing.

By the middle of the afternoon, I still hadn't had a good run. Then a voice inside me said, *If you could do this when you were drunk, you can do this when you're sober. You still possess the skills.*

All of a sudden, as I switched from fear to trust, my tensions vanished, and I could feel myself flowing on a perfect line through the moguls, not resisting the speed, and trusting my skills. It was exhilarating. I had discovered the key to self-confidence. I just changed the channel from fear to trust! I could not hold both fear and trust within me at the same time.

Often since that time, whenever fear started creeping in, I would tell myself to switch the channel to trust.

From This Moment On

"Freedom is what you do with what's been done to you."
Jean-Paul Sartre

S TATISTICS
The average prison sentence of men who kill their women partners is two to six years. Women who kill their partners are, on average, sentenced to fifteen years.[1]

SOMETHING TO KEEP IN MIND

We are better together. Just as a braid is stronger than a single strand, we are stronger and safer when we receive and give support than when we try to do everything in our own strength. When we are stronger, we can pick up the thread of the life of another woman in need and weave it into our life until she is stronger. *"Though one may be overpowered, two can defend themselves. A cord of three strands is not quickly broken"* (Ecclesiastes 4:12).

Illuminate the Illusion

Don't ever forget how the lies and illusions shriveled your dreams. Your time to embrace your dreams is now. Don't ever let the world steal your faith in a woman's worth. Our gift to the world is our worth. Don't ever believe we are too small to answer the call. Our endurance has magnified our strength.

Our light shines on the path for other women to follow us into the light. We have gained clarity, through our adversity and through our liberty. We see the veil that is covering the eyes of the world. As we who are victorious over the adversity sing with one voice, we can create a wind to blow away the mist enshrouding the oppression of women. This is our time to infuse the spirit of the world with a longing for justice, compassion and liberty for all. The world is waiting for our sunrise.

A HEDGE TO HEAL

How do we dance on the injustice of the abuse?

We dance on the injustice by transforming what was meant to harm us into our strength, into our gift.

Character cannot be developed in ease and quiet. Only through experiences of trial and suffering can the soul be strengthened, vision cleared, ambition inspired and success achieved.
Helen Keller

Although abuse has the potential to destroy us, if it does not destroy us we cannot help but emerge stronger, wiser and more compassionate. However, when we first emerge, we need a time to heal and a hedge of protection around us to allow for the healing.

We want to keep abuse and destruction out and wellness and wholeness in. To do this we must determine our boundaries. Eliminating contact with the abuser eliminates contact with his toxins. Where can we draw the line in all our other areas?

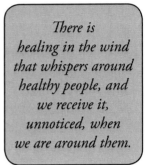

There is healing in the wind that whispers around healthy people, and we receive it, unnoticed, when we are around them.

Part of our protective hedge is people. If we purposely surround ourselves with caring, wise, healthy people who are strong and uplifting, we will receive protection, support and encouragement.

The fastest road to healing is in community. We must shut out the lies that whisper we are a burden, we are undeserving.

There is healing in the wind that whispers around healthy people, and we receive it, unnoticed, when we are around them, especially people who are healthy in their souls. A grateful, generous spirit will bring happiness, friends and abundance into our lives.

Places also provide protection to heal. Places that are safe, serene and beautiful bring the peace we have longed for. The places where we live and learn, work and play, contemplate and participate must nurture our souls.

SELF-NURTURING SUPPLANTS SELF-DESTRUCTION

How do we dance on this injustice?

A powerful way to dance on the injustice of the paradox—the protective destruction—is to replace the self-destruction with self-nurturing to permit the gift of our true self to blossom.

Even though our self-destructive coping served a protective purpose in the midst of the violence, it is still destructive. Also, as long as we still believe in our unworthiness and the entitlement of others, we are vulnerable to attracting another abuser. We must stop abusing ourselves.

It is only when we are healthy that we are attracted to, and attractive to, healthy people.

We must begin the healing with self-nurturing.

Our addictions and disorders are psychological, emotional and biological, and so they require an orchestrated solution. Others like us have succeeded; they can lead the way. Counselors have the calling and schooling; they can guide our journey. Resources leverage our efforts. A plan gives us a path, an organization gives us support, and family and friends give us love.

As you remove the self-destruction, keep in mind that when your house is "swept clean" it is easy for new troubles to fill the void. So your "sweeping" process must introduce aspects of your vision to displace the destruction you are discarding.

The more good things you bring into your life, the less room there is for the unhealthy things. But keep it simple at first to ensure small successes on which to build your faith and self-esteem. As your courage builds, your progress abounds.

The first good thing to try to bring into your life is a support community (real or virtual) who can encourage, comfort and coach you so that you can draw from their strength and wisdom.

A plan to prepare the path and help you with your motivation is another good thing. Your plan should evaluate each area of your life: physical, emotional, spiritual, intellectual, social and financial. Then decide what it would look like if it was exactly how you would love it to be. Write these down and use as many senses as possible to imagine them. From this, you can take either a small step for each area or a few steps for one area.

For example, a physical step may be to create a clean attractive room or improve your personal hygiene. An intellectual step may be to read an autobiography of someone you aspire to be like or research to educate yourself on changes you would like to make. A spiritual step may be to journal your meditative thoughts or attend a worship service.

The self-destructive coping mechanism that is the most detrimental to your future is the first one to focus most of your energy on transforming. However, it will not be a process of first addressing one challenging area and then moving on to the next challenge. Your coping mechanisms are intertwined. As you make progress in one area, it will have a positive effect in another area, and it will be helpful to take steps towards any solution as you gain insight and

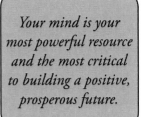

Your mind is your most powerful resource and the most critical to building a positive, prosperous future.

strength or as opportunities arise regarding each of your challenges.

Your mind is your most powerful resource and the most critical to building a positive, prosperous future. Therefore regaining your mental health is your highest priority. You need to look at your disorders and addictions to see where you are willing to start.

The addictions are the biggest thieves. They steal the capacity of your brain to function, they rob you of your funds, they cheat you out of your time, they deprive you of relationship, they devastate your health, and they destroy your looks. You will gain the most advantage by making progress conquering your addictions.

Overcoming addiction, whether it is alcohol, drugs, food or behaviors, is a huge challenge, and so you need to be gentle and encouraging with yourself in order to promote perseverance. With every attempt, you gain insight and strength, so you must not worry if you fall back occasionally. You are still further ahead. It may be helpful to understand a bit of the physiology of an addiction in order to avoid self-recrimination and discouragement.

The mid-brain is your center for gratification, and your prefrontal cortex is where you reason. The mid brain is five times as powerful as the prefrontal cortex. A pathway connects these two parts of the brain so that your logic can help you choose wisely. However, addictions erode the pathway. Your addictions damage brain cells and the brain chemical balance, disrupting your reasoning, your emotions, your sense of pleasure and meaning, and your identity.

When you stop alcohol and drugs, the brain cells will often crave sugar and flour to fill the void. Replacing these with complex carbohydrates and protein will dissipate the cravings.

Healing your brain from addiction will take some time, but it will give you a powerful ally for overcoming your other self-destructive issues. A proven key to success in anything is repetition. You can use this key to achieve success in transforming your life. With every repetition of the good things, the neural path in your mind gets stronger, and every time you resist what you do not want, that path becomes weaker. With every step you take you grow; with every choice you make you grow. Patience is the friend that strengthens you. This is where you can use the swing analogy.

RECLAIM YOUR MIND, REGAIN YOUR SOUL

How do you dance on the injustice?

You can dance on the injustice of your stolen identity by embracing the truth of your power, wisdom and worth.

A Return to Love
by Marianne Williamson
"Our deepest fear is not that we are inadequate.
Our deepest fear is that we are powerful beyond measure.
It is our light, not our darkness, that most frightens us.
We ask ourselves, Who am I to be brilliant, gorgeous, talented,
fabulous?
Actually, who are you *not* to be?
You are a child of God.
Your playing small does not serve the world.
There's nothing enlightened about shrinking so that other
people won't feel insecure around you.
We are all meant to shine, as children do.
We were born to make manifest the glory of God that is
within us.
It's not just in some of us; it's in everyone. And as we let
our own light shine, we unconsciously give other people
permission to do the same.
As we're liberated from our own fear, our presence
automatically liberates others."[2]

Because you have been a victim, you may be tempted to remain in the mindset that others control your future. You may wait for others to solve your problems. However, in order to survive and thrive, you must take the reins of your future in your own hands. Your life is your responsibility, no matter how inept you believe you are.

We are all familiar with the learning process, and that is what we use to learn how to become good managers of our lives. With each step we learn; with each step we become stronger and wiser.

Our identity was trampled and destroyed, but now we must refute the importance of what others think of us in order to discover what is true about ourselves. We give our power away when others determine who we are. They always control us; we are never free to choose, because a word from someone else robs our power from us.

If we stay "until death do us part," we deny the purpose for our existence. There is a purpose for our lives, and we cannot fulfill our purpose unless our minds are free to discover and pursue it. We cannot embrace a victim mentality; we must embrace a victor's mentality to show others that they too can have victory.

We must release the emergency brake. We must be bold enough to come out of hiding.

The United States' Statue of Liberty is symbolic of us. Her torch held high lights the way to liberty, freedom of choice and movement. The tablet she holds declares her independence; we have gained our independence, our liberation. She wears a crown—she is royal—and the seven spikes of her crown portray the world—the seven seas and the seven continents—as her domain, as our domain. This monumental woman bears around her ankle the shackle of tyranny that she has escaped, that we have escaped.

We have escaped to embrace abundant life. Our enlightenment enables us to bear the torch to light the way for those that follow.

Reclaiming Our Lives

By using the keys we hold to release our treasures and unlock our future, we dance on the injustice of our lives being stolen.

Above us, there is an enchanted castle with chambers full of treasures. We are the ones who now hold the keys; we unlocked the

> *If we embark on discovery, eventually the truth will set us free.*

dungeon; we banished the tyrant; the castle is ours; the kingdom is ours. We mount the stairs with the keys to the chambers jingling in one hand and our light in the other.

If we embark on discovery, eventually the truth will set us free. Still, it will take courage and perseverance to start up the steps out of the darkness of our familiar dungeon.

Exploring the various places in our castle also takes courage and perseverance. We may be afraid to open the doors, unsure of what is on the other side. Each room has different treasures and different risks.

There is a relationship room. Loving, nurturing relationships are vital to our well-being. We long for these. We believe the ones we once had are lost. We have no hope of new ones in the future. However, when we are free to open the door to that room, we will discover the treasure of family and friends on the other side. Old ones have not abandoned us, and new ones are waiting. The door we open may be to someone's home, a volunteer organization, a spiritual organization, a hobby or sports organization or an educational institution. We will unlock the treasures of companionship, laughter, support and love on the other side of the door when we take the chance and open it.

There is a self-esteem room. As we gain an understanding of our value, we will gain the courage to explore the room of self-esteem. When the truths move from our heads into our hearts, light enters the room of faith, and as our experience supports the truths, our self-esteem grows.

We gain faith in ourselves and our fear dissipates as we come through each new experience strengthened and empowered to some degree.

There is a room that holds our purpose. Our dreams and desires, our skills and talents are locked inside. In addition to the noticeable skills that we may be currently using, we have sharpened other skills as well. We have learned flexibility as we struggled to accommodate his moods. We have learned to anticipate scenarios and their potential problems, to evaluate options, to analyze the possible consequences, and to mitigate negative effects. We are resourceful. We have learned to tackle problems others would not consider.

There is a finance room. Create good financial habits, and time along with diligence will create financial strength. Through small changes, or life altering changes if necessary, we can find a way for our money to grow and strengthen along with us.

There is a pleasure room, our rest and recreation. Here we experience friends and family, culture and travel, sports and reading, peace and joy.

After we go through our season of healing and creating a new life, there will come a time when we will be strong enough to contribute to the well-being of others, to offer others a helping hand or heart by using our gifts and talents. We can redeem the time stolen from us.

As we enter these rooms, open the curtains to let the light in and remove the dust, we will discover our value and strength, light and life.

Dancers Who Dance on Injustice

The illusions we believed in created injustice. We dance on the injustice when we rise out of the ashes, give wing to justice, and unshackle others.

The enlightenment that emerges out of the mist brings joy, hope and courage. We dance on the injustice when we affirm our skills, our strength and our perseverance. We dance on the injustice when we pursue our passions, our visions and our dreams.

We can reclaim and transform our identity. Now, we are free to discover who we are. Now, we are free to determine what our values are and how we will uphold them. Now, we are free to decide where our boundaries should be and how to maintain them.

We must never forget we have a right to decide instead of hide. We have a choice; we have a voice. We are born to participate in life, and we must celebrate our lives. We must live the truth of our worth and leave a legacy of justice for our children. We have come through the battle, and now it is time to dance as the princess at the ball.

AT LAST

IT WAS LATE SEPTEMBER, ONE AND A HALF YEARS AFTER STARTING MY new life, when I received a registered letter from my lawyer. I could barely breathe as I opened it. Was it what I thought it was, or had the divorce process taken a turn for the worse? As I read the letter, the tension in my heart expanded into exhilaration.

At last. It was finished. The cord that bound me to the abusive past was finally severed. I could fly. Soon, I would have the funds for a home. I also dreamed of how I could participate more fully in life if I did not have to be home by dark. With a car, I could do so much more in less time.

Everyone at Sunrise was happy for me, and Lana was so impressed with my healing, growth and development over the past nine months that she felt comfortable that I was ready to leave the program, even though I had not completed the full year of counseling and group modules.

Within a few months of moving into my home, my sanctuary, my oasis, I reached another milestone. I passed my last university course. At last, after seventeen years, I was a university graduate. It was hard for me to comprehend that I had earned my degree!

All seemed to be going well in my life. I was blissfully happy with my freedom, with the places and ideas I explored, with a career that provided for me. I was amazed and encouraged by my emotional, mental and spiritual growth. I had wonderful relationships with family and friends, and I used my blessings to bless others. I was happy, happy, happy.

But there was one area of my life where I was still wounded. Wonderful women surrounded me, but I avoided and blocked any unnecessary contact with men. When I left my past behind, I knew I never wanted to have another relationship, I never wanted to marry again, and I kept that door shut tight. I wouldn't even open it a crack to ask God what he thought. As long as I didn't ask him the question, I could assume what I wanted.

However, early the following spring as I drove down the long hill by my home, the vista of the mountains filled the horizon beyond the city and I felt God asking me, "Who convinced you to never have another relationship?"

Then something Ed had gotten me to agree to when we first married came into my mind. He told me that if he died before I did he wanted me to never marry again. He would not let it go until he was sure he had convinced me beyond a doubt.

As I drove, the light dawned on me that Ed had wanted to control and own me even from the grave, and it was that agreement I made so long ago that was controlling me now.

Did I trust God with my destiny? Sadness filled me as I surrendered control and opened the door to a possibility I did not want to contemplate. However, I soon put the thought out of my mind as I focused on the wonderful life I had been given.

Later that spring as I was reading on the sofa in front of the fire, I heard the melody of my cell phone ringing.

"Hello?"

Sarah's enthusiastic voice said, "Hi, Aunt Jacquie. We're back from our honeymoon."

I was happy it was Sarah. We had grown very close since I had come to Clarion. Our long conversations about relationships, dreams and spirituality meant a lot to us.

"Sarah! How was Jamaica?" I asked.

"It was amazing. I can't wait to tell you about it," she said. "Dave and I are moving down to his parents' place in Pennsylvania soon, and I really want to see you before we go. Could we get together and do something?" she asked.

"I'd love to. I'm really going to miss you, but I am so happy for you. You've found an amazing guy," I said. I had met Dave before their wedding a couple of weeks before, and, of course, Sarah told me all about him even before that.

"The weather has been so nice for this time of year; do you want to go hike Pederson's Canyon?" I asked.

Sarah said, "Sure, that sounds great. I love Pederson's Canyon, and then Dave can feel what it's like to be in our majestic mountains."

"Okay, I'll call you to see when to pick you both up."

I was so excited. I couldn't wait to see Sarah again and hear all about Jamaica.

A few days later, the weather turned cold. It was still spring, and although it had been sunny and hot a few days before, now everyone was bundled in heavy coats again. Pederson's Canyon was definitely out. It was too cold. But we could go to Ashton.

Ashton is diverse and distinctive, with lots of character and charm. I loved meandering in and out of the unique little shops that featured local artisans. It is in the mountains, so Dave could still experience them.

Saturday morning I awoke to the sound of howling wind and the hiss of snow hitting the window. As I peeked through the curtains, I saw snowdrifts forming around the shrubs, and driving snow blurred the outlines of the homes across the street.

My heart sank. Our plan to drive to the mountains was too dangerous in this weather. I didn't want to give up the opportunity to see Sarah, even though a blizzard like this usually kept most people home.

I threw on my housecoat and turned to the Internet to search for something in the city that Sarah would enjoy. *Maybe Beauty and the Beast,* I thought. It had been playing on a stage downtown for a few weeks. I looked for tickets online—all sold out.

There must be somewhere interesting to go in the city. As I scrolled down the city's website of things to do, I saw a castle.

A castle? How can there be a castle in Clarion and I did not know about it? I thought. I love castles.

I read the description beside it. It was close to downtown and was open for lunch and tours. I was so excited, I hoped Sarah and Dave liked the idea.

I called her up, and she was delighted when I told her about it.

Yes! I was going to see a castle.

I printed the page with the picture, address and phone number. I rummaged through my maps until I found a small one of the downtown and uptown. Stewart's Mansion was uptown. I marked an X on the map at the address.

The hours passed slowly. I kept busy with household tasks until it was time to go. I always liked being early, but I gave myself even more time than usual in case the weather caused me problems.

I thought about Sarah and Dave, and I was happy for them. When I first came to Clarion, before Sarah met Dave, she was in a very stifling relationship with another fellow and was miserable. As I went through my various counseling programs, I shared my insights and discoveries with her. We discussed how the concepts applied to her relationship and who she believed she was as a woman. We also talked about the direction and purpose of her life.

Sarah loved the outdoors, had a talent for writing, and she also wanted to be a mother more than anything in the world. The fellow she was with wanted nothing to do with any of these and discouraged Sarah's dreams.

Even though I shared with Sarah what I was learning about relationships, I knew I never wanted another one. I was only discussing the ideas with her in hopes that it would raise questions in her mind about what a loving, nurturing relationship should look like.

I was very happy when my sister told me Sarah had broken off that relationship and was going on a mission trip to help at an orphanage in Africa. That was where she found her love. Dave was working at the orphanage as well. From what Sarah told me, I thought they were a perfect match.

After driving at half the speed limit through the drifting streets, I was finally close to the address of Stewart Mansion. I was watching with excited anticipation for the mansion to appear before me.

I was there. I was at the address. But where was the castle?

There were large buildings on each of the four corners, but none of them remotely resembled a castle. I checked the address on the paper. I checked the address on the street signs. Yes, I was at the right address.

Well, instead of driving around I decided to phone. I touched the numbers into my cell phone and listened to it ring.

"Stewart Mansion" a deep voice answered.

"Where are you?" I asked.

"I'm here; where are you?" he said, matching the lilting curiosity in my voice.

I laughed, and then he asked where I was and what buildings I could see. I had missed the castle by a block. Since it was set back in the middle of its four acres of grounds, you couldn't see it until you were right beside it.

I smiled as the stately sandstone turrets came into view. I loved it. It was not as large as an actual castle, but it was lovely, mysterious and romantic.

After parking, I huddled against the wind and snow as I hurried up the walkway and up the stairs to the door. As I entered, I was spellbound. The ornately carved woodwork warmed the vestibule and the front foyer. Colored light streamed through stained-glass windows of beautiful birds and flowers. Period paintings and ornaments adorned the walls and mantelpiece.

I was early. A lady dressed in an era costume, a floor-length navy blue dress, made me feel welcome and suggested I have a look at their gift shop downstairs while I waited.

I loved the feel of the old wood balustrade under my hand as I descended the stairs to the lower level. There was a gentleman at a computer behind the desk. I wondered if he was the man who gave me directions. He looked up and smiled warmly.

"Can I help you?" he asked.

"Do you answer the phone?" I asked.

He looked a little confused.

"Are you the one who gave me directions?" I asked.

"Oh. Yes, that was me. I'm happy you found us okay," he replied.

"Thank you so much for your help. It would not be fun to be lost on a day like today. I am Jacquie," I said as I held out my hand.

"I'm Thomas. I'm pleased to meet you," he said as he reached his long arm across the counter and shook my hand.

He seemed gentle and nice.

After browsing the shop a bit, I said, "Well, it's almost one o'clock. I'd better go up to the dining room. I'm meeting people for lunch. Thank you again for the directions."

He looked up from the computer, smiled and said, "Enjoy your lunch."

I ascended the staircase into the main foyer. Sarah and Dave were there, smiling and happy as we shared hugs and hellos. The lady in the long vintage dress approached and asked if we were ready to dine.

As she escorted us through the main dining room, we gazed around in wonder at the china cabinets displaying antique china and silver, the ornate woodwork, the art and the dramatic domed skylight. She took us through into the sunroom full of windows framed in celery green drapes. The windows displayed the swirling snow and the grounds covered with billows of white. But the room was warm and inviting with its gold filigree ceiling, walls patterned with yellow flowers, wood wainscoting, and crisp white linens on the tables.

After we were seated, we were so excited to share our stories that we tumbled over each other's conversations. Eventually, we settled into a happy stream, and I heard all about their adventures in Jamaica. Their tans from the trip looked out of place against the snowy background.

We gave up the option of dessert, as we knew we were running out of time for the tour of the mansion. When we reported at the tour desk, the lady looked a little anxious.

"We are only allowed ten per tour group, and the last group for the afternoon already has ten," she said a bit apologetically. She thought a bit, then said, "Wait, I will call down to the supervisor and see if he is free to give you a tour."

After a brief conversation on the phone, she smiled and said, "He is on his way up. You are lucky. You get a personal tour by the most knowledgeable person on staff."

A few minutes later, Thomas came up the stairs two at a time. He carried his tall frame with ease. He was well dressed in gray slacks and white shirt, which gave him an air of distinction.

"Good afternoon. I'm Thomas. I hope you enjoyed your lunch," Thomas introduced himself to Sarah and Dave. He turned to me and said, "I guided you here; now I can guide you through Stewart House."

"So do you want the long version of the tour or the short version?" he continued with a lively smile.

Sarah and Dave had to go soon, so we opted for the short version.

"All right, let's start upstairs. This way, ladies and gentleman." He held out his hand with a flourish, indicating the staircase that led to the upper floor. Sarah and Dave went first, and Thomas followed me.

As we reached the top, we stopped by an antique chair and storyboard. I turned to Thomas behind me as he started the story of the Stewarts. Past his shoulder, a majestic stag stood in the center of a beautiful large, ornate stained glass window. Light shone through on Thomas. He was still on the stairs, with one foot up on the landing, and yet he was still taller than I was standing on the landing.

Thomas was giving the history of the couple who built the mansion. I was intrigued with the couple's story. They wanted to bring culture to the Wild West, and they built the mansion to display and live in their vision. Senator Stewart was a prominent businessman and politician, but Thomas had as many stories about Lady Stewart as he did about Senator Stewart.

Thomas then took us down the hallway to a cutaway in the wall that revealed the wiring within the wall as well as the wood of the wall, the plaster and the hand-painted filigree wallpaper. It was covered with glass to form a display. I was amazed that they had had electricity in the mansion. It seemed so ancient. And as I considered all the walls covered with the beautiful wallpaper and the time it must have taken to hand-paint the intricate pattern, my mind could not fathom it.

I peeked in the door of the room beside me as Thomas led the others back down the hall. I stepped in the doorway of the room, and I heard Thomas scooting back to me.

He said, "Wait, wait, you need to come this way."

"I'm sorry," I said. "I didn't know I wasn't supposed to go in the room."

"No, no," he said. "It's okay. It's just that my story sounds better if we go this way first," he explained lightheartedly as he guided me back down the hall.

We started with Senator Stewart's bedroom and sitting room, then a joint room shared by Senator and Lady Stewart, and on into Lady Stewart's sitting room. Then we came to the room that I had tried to enter, Lady Stewart's bedroom. I could see now that Thomas's tour started with what we thought would be the most prominent room, Senator Stewart's bedroom, but instead it was just to escalate the impact of Lady Stewart's bedroom. Hers was larger and by far the most opulent. As Thomas described it, I could sense the respect and admiration in his voice.

We continued through the house, hearing fascinating stories of the times, the house and the people. But intermingled in the stories were comments about Lady Stewart being the catalyst for developing various cultural events in the city, for which she received little or no recognition since, as a woman, she was not considered a person.

"Funny how a non-person could be the mother of several little persons. I wonder how that happens," Thomas said with irony in his voice.

He was very informative and charming throughout the tour, which made the house and its former residents come to life for us. The best story Thomas told was of Lady Stewart's love of driving, and of course it was illegal, since non-persons were not allowed to drive. The chauffeur was her accomplice. One day, with the chauffer beside her, she drove several hours—the cars were very slow in those days—to visit a nearby mountain town. When she reached the town, she telegraphed home to see when her husband would be back from his trip to parliament. To her shock, it was that afternoon. So her chauffeur arranged for them and the car to go back to the city by train. As the train pulled into the platform in the city, Senator Stewart disembarked from one end of the train while, unbeknownst to him, his chauffeur and Lady Stewart drove the car off the train at the other end of the platform, just in time to pick him up.

Thomas's tour ended in the ballroom near the entrance where we started. The fireplace in this room had an unusual feature, and I asked Thomas, "What is the significance of the scene on the inside of the fireplace?"

It was a black raised motif of a tree with a snake coiled around a branch, and a bird sat on the branch with the snake in its talons. I believed it might mean something like the triumph of virtue over villainy.

"That's a very good question," said Thomas. "I have worked in this house for five years, and I thought I knew all there was to know about the mansion. No one has asked me that before," he said with surprise in his voice. "Would you like to leave your e-mail address? I could contact the restorative architect and e-mail you the answer."

I hesitated for a moment, since I had been very selective about who I gave my e-mail address to in order to prevent it from making its way back to Ed. But there seemed no chance of that, so I wrote a thank you and my e-mail address in a note and left it with Thomas.

It was time to leave, and Sarah, Dave and I gathered our coats. Thomas helped me on with mine, and we thanked him for the wonderful tour as we said goodbye.

Monday came, and it was back to work. I didn't give much thought to the question I left with Thomas as I moved back into my regular routine, but a few days later there was an e-mail from him:

> Jacquie,
> Finally heard from Lorne Simmons on Saturday—seems the insert in the fireplace is not all that impressive—he advised it's made of cast iron—
> The bird is probably an eagle and of course the snake is a symbol of evil/bad being beaten by the good eagle—he does not think (as I did) it has anything to do with St. George slaying the dragon.
> So there you go—nothing exciting or stimulating—much—
> I enjoyed the search—Lorne's a wonderful person and very helpful.
> Hope to hear from you again some time.
> Regs
> Thomas.

I knew at this point if I asked one more question it could lead to a friendship, and I struggled back and forth as I tried to understand my fear. Ashley and her friends had been saying it was okay to have a guy as a friend and I could stop it whenever I wanted. So I e-mailed Thomas back and asked him about the books on the desk in the library that he said were his.

I was surprised to learn he had retired from working many years at an airline and wanted to return to college because he had always loved architecture. He was studying for his final exams.

We continued our e-mails for a few weeks until I received one that would change my world:

> Jacquie, hello again—
> Your e-mail was amazing—yes you certainly made up for the short ones—and then some—where to start in response???

It's wonderful you are writing a book—what a great and inspiring skill—the ability to write—I envy people who have the magic skill required to put words together into a meaningful series of thoughts—I enjoy reading. To write with the aim of helping others is doubly significant. I would be honored to read a draft or book if you wish to share it with me.

You mentioned "abusive relationship" " freedom" and "after I left my past"—these tell me it was not a past, in part, filled with joy. For this I'm truly sorry—why would I be sorry when I'm not involved??? Because it saddens and angers me to know there are men out there who abuse people (verbally, physically or mentally)—women, children or other weaker men, whatever—doesn't matter—I know they're out there. As a man who finds this appalling I feel in part responsible for these atrocities each time I hear or read about it—on behalf of those who feel as I do, and they are the majority, I apologize with feelings.

A CGA—wow—I'll hire you to help me set up my company when I finally raise the money to do it—I've seen the billboards with the suit wearing woman kicking the soccer ball saying—"I understand your business"—I can believe it—a business degree is no small thing either—I took a 4-year international business course while I worked, but it wouldn't be relevant in this day and age.

You mentioned you would have been at Beauty and the Beast instead of Stewart Mansion had you been able to get tickets—it may be selfish on my part but thank goodness for sellouts—I'm glad—otherwise I would not be writing this particular e-mail—I also don't believe in coincidence in a sequence of events—everything happens for a reason.

I'm amazed by the things you mentioned you enjoy—Pederson's Canyon—my favorite walk to the upper falls with a light lunch, cool drink on a warm day—another is a walk down Bobbin Creek or a cross-country ski in the winter with lunch again of course—I haven't been into Pederson's Canyon in the past 2–3 years because each time I went the bear activity

was intense and the trail was closed—it's time to go again—
——Jazz Danceworks I love—I've been in the past to several
shows—they had two shows this year I wanted to see, one with
dancing to live jazz, but as you say school interfered—I attended
a flamenco dance presentation at the U of L this spring, and a
Gypsy dance performance last fall—I love dance—unfortunately
I have never learned how to do it properly—never seemed to be
time, nor did I have a partner who liked to dance—I was about
to take lessons at my college this spring term (it's at the top of
my list of things I want to do properly along with horseback
riding) but was unable due to course load—I've already checked
and it's offered this fall again and alumni are welcome—THIS I
HAD PROMISED MYSELF I WILL DO——

I find music is something that comes to me as I feel—
sometimes it's jazz (Stan Getz, Herb Alpert, Redman, Ella
Fitzgerald, Louis Armstrong, Al Green, Sonny Terry, Brownie
McGhee) sometimes it's blues (Blues Brothers, Janice Joplin,
Jimmy Boskill, Ray Charles—never heard the Safire but would
like to). I'm a member of C-Jazz, which is Clarion's jazz club, and
plan to attend the jazz festival in June—I was hoping to go to the
Montreal Jazz festival (July) but the musicians I want to hear are
playing the weekend we run our fundraiser for a children's charity
so I'm going to have to pass on that opportunity. Al Green was
playing and he's in his 70s—it could be the last chance to hear
him, but so be it, the cause is worth it.

Other music includes everything from modern through the
Beatles, the Man in Black, the Nylons, Roy Orbison and Elvis
to classical (excluding rave and heavy metal).

I plan to attend Beethoven June 7 and Pops June 4th—
would You be interested in going???? (sorry if this comment is
inappropriate but I'd have to get added tickets soon).

Golf!!!!!—what can I say about this sport—if you need
a caddy I'm your man—the walk is great—I do enjoy the
driving range, but there are no little holes and I can handle this
omission—

I've written so much already I should stop yet I have questions/comments——daughter—how old?? with you?? what does she do?? is she in school still??—

When do your studies start again???—how is your friend—recovering I hope?? I also have a friend in pain—a woman I work with in her 50s, a co-worker, was told after 17 years marriage her husband wants her to move out—she's a meek insecure yet wonderful person and this was devastating for her—myself and several friends plus her family have been helping her through this crisis.

You are a wonderful person to give up a personal desire to help a friend. She/he is blessed.

Spiritual Journey—another fascinating topic, perhaps at some time you might want to talk about yours? mine? Are you working (other than writing) right now??

Travel—another topic for hours—I have a list a mile long of places I want to experience—I want to sleep on the great wall of China—I want to walk down the narrow pass to the temple of Petra in Lebanon, I want to again sit in the Coliseum now I have studied it, see the Royal circle in Bath, England, Stone Hedge, again climb the Cologne cathedral tower steps, visit Notre Dame, Pantheon, Parthenon, and this is just the tip of the iceberg—where do you want to go???

This is way too long already, I'm sorry—I'll sign off for now—I didn't mention Bon Jovi and Rod Stewart—both great—lucky you—I also like The Doors—heard them in a bar in Niagara Falls, New York, before they were making records when I was in university back east.

All the best—by the way Happy Mother's Day—may it be a special day for you, regards Thomas

I felt a mixture of fear, delight and confusion as I read this. Too many things were too close to my desires and dreams.

I went down to the living room, seeking some grounding.

Ashley was at her computer.

"Can I pull up an e-mail Thomas wrote and see what you think of it?" I asked her.

"Sure."

I went on her computer, signed into my e-mail account and opened Thomas's latest e-mail. Then I stood back and waited.

The minutes went by as she read. I watched her expression as I tried to figure out what she thought of it, but her face remained impassive.

When she was finished, she turned to me with a wry smile on her face. "You're in trouble, Mom," she said facetiously.

Well, that answered my question.

In the next e-mail Thomas asked if we could meet for lunch or supper. I sought guidance from Ashley. She informed me that if you went for coffee or tea it was not counted as a date and you could maintain the "just friends" status; however, if you went out for a meal it was considered a date and that you had more serious intentions. So I agreed to tea on Sunday afternoon.

Friday came, and it was the hottest day yet that year. Thomas had a four-day long weekend—he started a full-time job after graduating "With Great Distinction"—and I was always off work at 3:00 in the afternoon. He asked if I would like to go for a walk by the river. I accepted, not knowing what the dating rule was for a walk.

We walked and talked. We were quite nervous at the start, but soon we gained a measure of ease since we had been e-mailing for a while. We walked for hours; we went to dinner, and when I got home, seven hours later, Ashley met me at the door.

"Where have you been? I thought you were going to keep it as just friends for a while. Seven hours is a date, not just friends getting together," she informed me.

I almost laughed at the role reversal. "I called you to let you know we were going for supper," I explained like a schoolgirl.

On our official date on Sunday, I met Thomas at Stewart Mansion, and I suggested we take his hurting friend to tea with us. I helped her understand the dynamics of the abusive relationship she was in, and we explored what support she had from family and friends. By the time we said bye to her, her anguish had lifted and she was feeling optimistic.

As Thomas walked me to my car, he stopped for a moment at his. When he turned around, he had a lovely little bouquet of pink roses in a vase.

"These are for you," he said in a soft voice.

Flowers were so dear to my heart, and I had been missing my flower gardens that I left behind. A lump formed in my throat, and I buried my face in the blossoms to hide my emotion.

"Thank you," I said as I looked up into his gentle eyes. I couldn't decide if his eyes were gray or blue or green. They suited his mysterious good looks.

A couple of weeks later, my cousin Laura and I headed north to the small town where the campus for my university was located. She was coming to convocation with me. I was receiving my degree!

She was lovely company, and the graduation ceremony was one of the highlights of my life, but I missed Thomas.

Laura and I stayed overnight and drove back the next morning. As I drove up my driveway, I saw three large moss-green ceramic planters by my front door. They contained gorgeous arrangements of begonias and feather grass. I knew who put them there. Maybe they were my graduation present from Thomas.

When Thomas found out I was home early, he couldn't wait to come and pick me up. We drove to a beautiful park overlooking the river. When he stopped the car, he turned to me and pulled out of his jacket pocket a long flat box wrapped in silver paper with a navy blue silk ribbon.

He drew me into his arms and said, "There are three things in there. One is for the question you asked about the fireplace that connected us, one is for our first walk, and one is for your graduation."

I slowly opened the beautiful gift. Inside was a necklace with three pearls on it. How lovely; how charming; how thoughtful. I couldn't believe this man. As we embraced and I melted into his kiss, I faintly heard bagpipe music. I thought it was my imagination, but it grew louder.

We got out of the car, and Thomas took my hand as we followed the sound and discovered bagpipers practicing under a canopy of trees. It was the perfect touch to such a tender moment.

Almost daily a new wonder came to me about this man. So many little things that had brought me pain in the past he transformed into new moments of beauty; treasured moments from my past he claimed back for me. Yet Thomas was oblivious to the cherished gifts he was giving to me.

Time went by, and the treasure chest in my heart was overflowing. Then one evening Thomas arrived to take me to the symphony. We were so excited! As a new way of marketing, an orchestra played popular music at unusual venues to attract new clientele. For this event, they were going to play at a historical theme park.

We had looked forward to this evening for a long time. After he parked the car, he gently pulled me into his arms and kissed me deeply. I loved his kisses, I loved the smell of his cologne, I loved the way his arms wrapped all the way around me. But, most of all, I loved how he caressed me with his endearing words of love.

His words were flowing sweetly. Then he hesitated and waited. Then I heard words that penetrated deep into my heart, into the deepest part of my soul, and my spirit soared.

"Will you marry me?" he asked.

I was filled with joy and amazement, with overwhelming love, as I realized Thomas had just proposed to me. This warm, wonderful, compassionate, intelligent, insightful, spiritual, generous, passionate, magnificent man loved me and was asking me to marry him.

I became aware that it was a question—Thomas was waiting for my answer. My whole being filled with "yes." And I said, "Yes," through his kisses.

He stopped and lifted my chin, and I saw his eyes sparkle with moisture.

"My darling, my angel," he said as he gently brushed my hair from my cheek. He drew me close and just held me.

Then, filled with emotion, he whispered, "I can't believe you've agreed to be my wife. I'm the luckiest man in the whole world. No, I'm the most blessed."

Throughout the evening, all the way to the finale and the encore, I felt the orchestra was playing their beautiful pieces just for us in celebration of our betrothal. Afterwards, as the final strains drifted away on the breeze, Thomas walked with me to the hilltop overlooking the lake. The evening was beautiful. The sun was setting behind the foothills, the sky was deep purple, and the clouds were trimmed with gold. It was so serene and quiet.

Thomas enfolded me in his arms and whispered, "Thank you, God, for giving me this love in my heart and someone to share it with."

At last, I felt the joy in my heart. I had found my true love, my soul mate, my friend for eternity.

Still holding me in his arms, Thomas looked down at me and said, "I know where I would like to take you on our honeymoon: to Europe to show you your castle."

Appendix A

PRECAUTIONS **W**HILE **S**TILL WITH THE **A**BUSER
You will have already instinctively implemented some safety measures, such as keeping your distance or keeping knives in a drawer rather than in a knife-block on the counter. However, the lists that follow will give you some additional safety measures.

Your Children's Safety
- Plan and rehearse an escape route with your children.
- If it is safe, teach them a code word to call 911 and how to use a public telephone.
- Let a neighbor know what is happening and make arrangements for your children to go there in an emergency.
- Keep dangerous items out of their room.
- Remove draw strings from their curtains.
- Keep a flashlight in their room or a nightlight.

Safety at Home
Go through each room and, as much as possible, improve its safety, keeping in mind that the abuser will become suspicious if you change too much too quickly.

- Put dangerous objects away, such as knives, glass objects, heavy blunt objects, cords, fireplace tools, work tools, sports equipment.
- Leave windows ajar.
- Have phones in as many rooms as possible (911 can trace your house phone and some cell phones) and know how to use them, especially speaker phone and speed dial (practice).
- Leave curtains open and lights on.
- Leave doors unlocked while awake when the abuser is home.
- Stay in rooms with two exits when interacting with the abuser.
- Preplan exit paths to use if you have to run and position large items that you could knock over to block his path.
- Have vehicle keys with remote horn option on you and activate horn if you are in trouble.
- Have cell phone on you (some take movies and pictures; however, when you are in highly stressful situations you lose some of your fine motor skills and may find it difficult to press the right buttons).
- Set up Skype for free Internet phone calling (with video if your computer has a camera).
- If other people can hear you and you need help, yell "Fire" instead of "Help," as people are more willing to respond to it.

- Set up a code word with a friend or relative for them to call the police.
- Purchase bear spray from a camping store and hide it where it is easily accessible.
- Wear shoes or slippers when indoors.
- Have shoes, coats and keys easy to grab if you need to run.
- Remove bolts or hide the trigger keys for any guns.
- Make a list of the caliber, serial number and model of any guns the abuser has and leave it with someone in case something happens to you.
- Avoid dangerous rooms such as kitchens and garages.
- Stay in rooms with more than one exit and locks on the doors.
- Stay on the ground floor (practice getting out a window).
- Keep something large between you and the abuser.

> *If a vehicle is registered in the abuser's name (the pink slip kept in the vehicle with the insurance), he can report the car stolen to the police. However, if your safety is at stake, it may be better to take it to protect yourself and your children. After you leave, you can call the police to explain.*

Keep in mind that phones keep a history and tell a story. Do not assume that he will never get access to your cell phone. Some crisis centers have phones, available free of charge, that can only call 911. You could obtain and hide one for an emergency.

The Internet is another safety issue. As you use the Internet, it keeps track of the sites you've been looking at. To remove the evidence from your personal computer, you have to clear the cache, history, cookies and registry. But if the abuser is monitoring your Internet activity he will know that there is missing information. It is also possible for him to have invisible monitoring software running in the background undetectable to you. The safest way to find information on the Internet would be at a library, Internet cafe, a trusted friend's house, or possibly at work.

Safety at Work

- Tell your employer and co-workers about your situation (before doing this, evaluate possible consequences, as you may lose your job if an unsympathetic employer or co-worker has safety concerns).
- Learn where all the exits are and how they operate.
- Keep spare keys, clothes and personal items at work for contingencies.
- Know how to contact security personnel.

Health

Physical fitness is an important aspect of your physical safety. The lives of you and your children may depend on it. You need your strength; you use it to defend or to flee. You can start with the basics, which include diet, sleep, exercise and regular physical and dental checkups. Many people take their right to these for granted; however, even these basics can be a challenge when living with an abuser. Fitness options beyond this may be difficult to achieve, depending on the level and type of control the abuser uses.

Other options could include a personal safety course, which usually has a psychological as well as physical components, martial arts classes, swimming lessons or strength training.

Another aspect of fitness is a healthy weight. A reasonable weight reduces health problems, increases your ability to protect yourself and will also eliminate a common justification abusers use for mistreating you. However, if you face challenges with eating disorders, be careful to not judge yourself if weight is an issue. Body size may be a protection for you in the current situation.

It is quite likely that you are suffering from some form of mental stress. Before seeking professional help, you should weigh in the balance the benefits and the costs of such help. A diagnosis of a mental disorder may be used against you in the future, possibly by the abuser in custody battles for the children. You should however utilize the best means you can to achieve and maintain mental health, as it is so vital in dealing with the abuser.

Emergency Bag

While you ponder your very real challenges, even if you're *"sure"* that you won't leave, you may have accepted the fact that you're *not in a safe,* let alone nurturing, environment. Therefore, you should prepare for the possibility that you may have to leave without warning to ensure your safety. If you have to leave the home during a turbulent incident and your abuser thinks you've left him, you may never see the things you left behind. There have been stories of abusers putting all the partner's belongings in the front yard and burning them or else giving them all to charity. So ask yourself, "If something happened, what would I absolutely need to have?" It will not only be more difficult to retrieve what you need if you leave it behind, but it will also require contact with him to get it.

In case you have to leave in a hurry with no chance to take what you need, buy a set of luggage with cash so it does not show up on credit card or bank statements and leave it with a trusted friend or relative. If that is not an option, you can leave it at work, your church, the gym, an organization or club you are a member of, at school or in storage.

Because of your isolation, this may be difficult, but be creative. You can divide and store it in different places, but keep accessibility in mind. Some items might take time to gather, especially when you have to do it in secret, so do not wait until you have everything together. Start by getting what you can and what's important to a safe location, and keep adding to it as the opportunity arises. Ideally, the bag should contain

- small toys for the children
- night clothes
- driver's license (copy)
- children's birth certificates
- your birth certificate
- marriage license
- copies of any custody papers from previous relationships
- government identification card
- government program documents
- medical insurance cards
- copies of necessary telephone numbers

> *Extra house and car keys should be cut and hidden outside (he may lock you out) as well as in your emergency bag. Other keys to consider are postal keys, safe-deposit box keys, storage key and business keys.*
> *If possible, take his keys to the vehicle as well as yours when leaving so that he cannot unlock the door.*

> *If you earned low or no income on your tax return, you can use this as proof of eligibility for special programs that are based on a sliding income scale, such as second stage crisis housing and YMCA memberships.*

- banking information
- investment information
- liability information
- the abuser's and your last three years of tax returns
- money
- credit card—preferably one that is not jointly controlled by the abuser
- bank cards and checkbook
- savings books
- lease, rental agreement, or deed to house and properties
- house insurance documents
- car registration and insurance papers
- health and life insurance papers
- medical and shot records for you and your children
- school records
- work permits, green card or visa
- passport
- divorce papers
- custody papers
- extra set of keys to house, car, and safety deposit boxes
- medications for you and your children
- small objects to sell
- jewelry
- address book
- phone card
- pictures of you, the children, and your abuser
- toiletries and diapers
- clothing—at least one change of clothing for each person and something suitable for a job interview

Appendix B

PRECAUTIONS **A**FTER **L**EAVING THE **A**BUSER
Proactively perceive possibilities.
Protecting the Children
- Let school personnel know to whom children can be released.
- Ask the school to notify you immediately if your children are not in school if you've not informed them that they are absent with reason.

- Give school personnel a photo of the abuser.
- Warn school personnel *not* to divulge your address and phone number.
- Give copies of the order of protection to schools, daycare, and babysitters.

Other Safety Steps

- Seek legal advice as soon as possible.
- Obtain an order of protection (called a restraining order in some places).
- Change locks on *all* doors and windows immediately.
- Insert a peephole in the door and *always* look through it before you open the door.
- Change telephone number, screen calls, and block sending caller ID.
- Install or increase outside lighting or get motion detector lights that ring an alarm inside the house.
- Consider getting a dog (retired police dogs can often be obtained).
- Inform landlord or neighbor of situation and ask that the police be called if the abuser is seen around the house.
- Have friends check in on you on a regular basis.
- If you have a security system, change the passwords immediately.
- Change any shared passwords for ATM cards, computer or e-mail access, or any other thing that is password protected.
- Once you have obtained an order of protection or restraining order, make copies and keep them with you at all times.
- Change vehicle, house, life and health insurance information.
- Change vehicle registration information.
- Open a personal bank account.
- Update personal information for all agencies connected with your banking, especially for deposits.
- Give security at work a photo of the abuser and a copy of the order of protection.

- Screen your calls at work.
- Have an escort to your car or bus.
- Vary your routes.
- Consider a cell phone.
- Carry a noisemaker, bear spray or personal alarm.

Data Safety

Computer

- If your abuser knows the IP address of your computer, your abuser can locate you using a process called pinging (Internet providers use IP addresses to pinpoint the location of the computer).
- Forms you fill out online with your personal information may be searchable (through Google, etc.) if the site is not security protected.

Cellular/Landline Phones

- Your phone number can be searched on the Internet then through reverse lookup sites to sell others your information.
- If someone has your cell phone number it is possible for the phone to be located as long as it has a battery in it, regardless of whether the phone is on or off.
- If you independently purchase a cell phone and use pay as you go instead of signing up for a plan with a carrier, neither the phone nor the call can be traced by the police or the carrier.
- Use *67 to block calls and *69 to find the number of the last person who called if someone calls and hangs up.
- Avoid a landline in your name.

Public Records and Registries

- birth, death and marriage certificates
- driver's license
- personal property registry (will show major purchases such as real estate, vehicles)
- Keep your name and address off as much administration as possible.

- Use a pay as you go credit card to prevent it from showing up on a credit check.
- Census bureau—Avoid having your name appear on a voters' list by applying to the Chief Electoral Office.

Physical Safety
- If followed by a vehicle
  — Look for distinct things in the vehicle like things hanging from the mirror or on the dashboard.
  — Pull over to the side and document the first four vehicles that pass you (anyone following has to pass).
  — Come to full stop at a stop sign to get a good look at who's behind.
  — Pull into someone's drive or go to a police station.
  — Document and remember vehicles that usually park on your street so you notice if there is an unusual one.
  — Call police if someone is sitting in a vehicle for any length of time
- Surveillance
  — The abuser can monitor you or your children through home, work, school, medical care, recreation.
  — He can hire a private investigator.
- Live in a condominium or an apartment where there is access security.
- Vary your daily routine; drive to work, where you shop, bank, etc.
- If people call asking for information, saying they have a parcel to deliver, for example, take their number and call back to verify. Do not give out information unless you initiate the call.
- Access through the children
  — GPS devices used to locate stolen property such as laptops can be put in your children's belongings during visitation, then the abuser can track them to you when they come home. Meet children in a public place and search their belongings before returning home.
  — Check children's books, backpacks, etc., for address or phone

number or other identifying information and clear cell phone and e-mail history.

— He'll chat the kids up when he has visitation, not only to try and win them to his side (or they may already be there), but to find out information such as friends' names, school or after school activities.

— Don't give your children your cell number. Relay messages through a friend or relative.

— Restrict the abuser's access to the children's medical, dental and educational records.

Stalking and physical attacks on you, your children or your property are what you are protecting yourself against by vigilantly protecting your location and information. You may feel at times that you are being irrational, but remember that your complacency may ruin or end your life.

Legal
Proof of Abuse

Collect and safeguard any proof of his abusive behavior (physical, mental, emotional, verbal, financial, social, photographs of your cuts and bruises from the abuse etc.). This includes such things as doctors' reports, police reports and statements from witnesses of incidents. These will be useful for a restraining order, child visitation and custody and possibly suing for damages. You should also write out a history of the abuse.

Leave this information with your lawyer, friend, relative or in a safe-deposit box. You could also scan and e-mail it to yourself, preferably not from your home computer or to your usual e-mail address. Keep in mind that originals are the most valuable, as copies may not be admissible.

Cases are starting to arise concerning workplace bullying and the damage it causes. When people sue for damages, elevated cortisol levels are used as evidence. Chapter 6 discussed the abuse and cortisol level relationship. Obtaining a cortisol test could prove beneficial in the future, but you need to have it done while in the abusive relationship. You may never use it, but at least you will have it if you choose a course of action in the future that requires it.

You could consider hiring a private investigator if you need proof of his abuse to strengthen court or custody cases.

Documents

Documents will be very important for starting a new life. If you have to leave suddenly, having your essential documents in a safe place, unknown to your abuser, will make your life easier. It will also help your sense of security until you leave. Several of these are listed previously under What You Should Take.

When you file for a separation of assets or a divorce, the documents will give information to your abuser that could put you in jeopardy. The address of your lawyer will be on documents, giving your abuser a clue to where you live.

For this process, the court needs to establish your abuser's and your net worth as well as each of your income and expenses. You are entitled to half of the net worth accumulated while you were together (married or not) as well as half of the net income earnings. Even if you stayed in the home, you gave up a career and contributed to his ability to earn income since you took on the role of maintaining the home and raising the children instead of him. If he had stayed home, you could have pursued a career.

To prove your income, expenses and net worth, the courts and the abuser's lawyer will want your recent bank and credit card statements. These will contain the places of your purchases, so using cash will help safeguard your location. They will also want your pay stubs, which will show your place of employment. You can choose to blank out any revealing information and explain it to the court if required.

You will need several past income tax returns to verify past income. You can use land titles and property tax assessment to establish dower rights to the house, even if it is not registered in your name, for separation of assets. Make and safeguard copies of his and your retirement savings plans, pension plans (you will need your marriage license to divide these) and other investments. Collect proof of child support payment obligations as well as assets, such as land titles, proof of purchases for major items like vehicles (make, model and year can be used to verify value), collectibles, savings, loans, lines of credit and mortgage.

Last Will and Testament
The three types of wills are also something that you should consider. The three types include the familiar last will and testament, the living will and the enduring power of attorney. The regular will makes sure your possessions go to the people or institutions you want. A living will allows you to state what type of medical treatment you do or do not wish to receive should you be too ill or injured to communicate your wishes. An enduring power of attorney names someone to handle all aspects of your life if you are incapacitated, including the authority to sign anything that you would normally sign, determine where and how you live and ensure that you receive the care you need.

Preparing these will safeguard your wishes if you are gone and will safeguard you and your assets if you are mentally incapable. The last thing you want is to be at the mercy of your abuser.

Child Custody
This is a complicated area of law, but there are many organizations that will help you with this. Make sure you take the children with you when you leave to avoid any potential charges of abandonment. To avoid kidnapping accusations have the children's birth certificates available and inform the police that you have left with the children and why. Document the time of the call and the officer's name and ID number (record it if possible).

When you leave be prepared to call the abuser's bluff regarding honeymoon tactics and realize that you are not responsible for his choices.

ENDNOTES

INTRODUCTION
1. "Domestic Violence and Abuse," HelpGuide.org, helpguide.org/ mental/domestic_violence_abuse_types_signs_causes_effects.htm.

CHAPTER 2
1. L. L. Heise, M. Ellsberg, M. Gottemoeller, "Violence by Intimate Partners," chap. 4, table 4.1, in *Ending Violence Against Women,*

Population Reports, series L, no. 11, Baltimore, MD: Johns Hopkins University of Public Health, 1999, *http://www.who.int/violence_injury_prevention/violence/global_campaign/en/chap4.pdf.*

2. Patricia Tjaden and Nancy Thoennes, "Extent, Nature and Consequences of Intimate Partner Violence: Findings from the National Violence Against Women Survey" (National Institute of Justice and the Centers of Disease Control and Prevention, 2000).

3. Henry Cloud and John Townsend, *Boundaries in Marriage* (Grand Rapids, Michigan: Zondervan, 1999), 97-98.

4. Nathaniel Hawthorne, in John Eldredge, *Wild at Heart* (Nashville, Tennessee: Thomas Nelson, 2001), 97.

5. Lundy Bancroft, *Why Does He Do That?: Inside the Minds of Angry and Controlling Men* (New York: The Penguin Group, 2003), 111.

6. *English-Word Information,* s.v. "obsession," http://wordinfo.info/unit/1928/page:2.

7. *Wikipedia,* s.v. "oppression," http://en.wikipedia.org/wiki/Oppression.

8. First Corinthians 13:4–7.

Chapter 4

1. *National Crime Victimization Survey,* 2007, United States Department of Justice, Bureau of Justice Statistics.

2. Sara Beattie and Adam Cotter, "Homicide in Canada, 2009," *Juristat* 30, no. 3 (2010): 14.

3. United Nations, General Assembly, 23 February 1994, Forty-eighth session, agenda item 111, Resolution Adopted by the General Assembly, Declaration on the Elimination of Violence against Women.

4. Dolf Zillmann, "Mental Control of Angry Aggression," in Daniel Goleman, *Emotional Intelligence: Why It Can Matter More Than IQ* (New York: Bantam Dell, 1995), 60.

5. Larry I. Meadows, *Adrenaline Notes* (1995), http://www.adrenalineaddicts.org/docs/1.pdf.

6. Bancroft, *Why Does He Do That?*

CHAPTER 6

1. J. M. Golding, "Intimate Partner Violence as a Risk Factor for Mental Disorders: A Meta-Analysis," *Journal of Family Violence* 14 (1999): 99-132.

2. Joseph M. Carver, "Love and Stockholm Syndrome: The Mystery of Loving an Abuser, Page 1," Counselling Resource, http://counsellingresource.com/lib/therapy/self-help/stockholm/.

3. Judith Herman, *Trauma and Recovery* (New York: Basic Books, 1992), 120.

4. Ibid.

5. Martin Seligman, *Helplessness: On Depression Development and Death* (San Francisco: W. H. Freeman, 1975), 22.

6. Harlan Lebo, "UCLA Researchers Identify Key Biobehavioral Pattern Used by Women to Manage Stress," *UCLA News*, May 17, 2000, http://newsroom.ucla.edu/portal/ucla/healthscience.aspx.

7. Teresa McBean, *Physiology of Addiction*, Special Interest Videos, Recovery: It's a God Thing, http://www.northstarcommunity.com/special.

8. *Anxiety Disorders: An Information Guide,* Centre for Addiction and Mental Health, 2005, http://www.camh.net/About_Addiction_Mental_Health/Mental_Health_Information/Anxiety_Disorders/causes_anxiety.html.

9. Stephanie S. Covington, Cynthia Burke, Sandy Keaton and Candice Norcott, "Evaluation of a Trauma-Informed and Gender-Responsive Intervention for Women in Drug Treatment," http://www.centerforgenderandjustice.org/pdf/Covington-evalSARC5.pdf. "Among women with PTSD, 28% also met criteria for an alcohol use disorder and 27% for a drug use disorder, nearly three times the prevalence rate of substance use disorders among women without PTSD." R. C. Kessler, A. Sonnega, E. Bromet, M. Hughes and C. B. Nelson, "Posttraumatic Stress Disorder in the National Comorbidity Survey," Archives of *General Psychiatry*, 52, 1048–1060, quoted in Margaret Gatz, Vivian Brown, Karen Hennigan, Elke Rechberger, Maura O'Keefe, Tara Rose and Paula Bjelac, "Effectiveness of an Integrated, Trauma-Informed Approach to Treating Women with

Co-Occurring Disorders and Histories of Trauma: The Los Angeles Site Experience."

Chapter 7

1. Paul Brandt, "Leavin'."

Chapter 8

1. *The Cost of Violence in the United States,* Centers for Disease Control and Prevention, National Centers for Injury Prevention and Control, Atlanta, GA, 2007.
2. "Free Your Mind," En Vogue.
3. Joseph M. Carver, "Love and Stockholm Syndrome: The Mystery of Loving an Abuser, Page 3" Counselling Resource, http://counsellingresource.com/lib/therapy/self-help/stockholm/.
4. "Domestic Violence," YWCA Omaha, http://www.ywca.org/site/pp.asp?c=6nJCLONmGiF&b=225511.
5. Bancroft, *Why Does He Do That?*
6. Helen Keller. Brainy Quote, Helen Keller Quotes, p 2, http://www.brainyquote.com/quotes/authors/h/helen_keller_2.html

Chapter 10

1. Carolyn Rebecca Block, "How Can Practitioners Help an Abused Woman Lower Her Risk of Death?" *NIJ Journal* 250 (2003), 4–7, https://www.ncjrs.gov/pdffiles1/jr000250c.pdf.

Chapter 12

1. Jacquelyn C. Campbell, Daniel Webster, Jane Koziol-McLain, Carolyn Rebecca Block, Doris Campbell, Mary Ann Curry, Faye Gary, Judith McFarlane, Carolyn Sachs, Phyllis Sharps, Yvonne Ulrich, and Susan A. Wilt, "Assessing Risk Factors for Intimate Partner Homicide," in "Intimate Partner Homicide," *NIJ Journal* 250, 2003, 14-19.
2. Marianne Williamson, *A Return to Love: Reflections on the Principles of a Course in Miracles* (New York: Harper Collins, 1992), 190-191.

ADDITIONAL RESOURCES

Jill Cory and Karen McAndless-Davis, *When Love Hurts: A Woman's Guide to Understanding Abuse in Relationships* (BC: WomanKind Press, 2000).

Jack Canfield, Jennifer Read Hawthorne, and Marci Shimhoff, *Chicken Soup for the Woman's Soul* (Deerfield Beach, Florida: Health Communications, 1996).

Henry Cloud and John Townsend, *Boundaries in Marriage* (Grand Rapids, Michigan: Zondervan, 1999).

Lundy Bancroft, *Why Does He Do That?: Inside the Minds of Angry and Controlling Men* (New York: The Penguin Group, 2003).

Nicholas Sparks, *Safe Haven* (New York, NY: Grand Central, 2010).

Daniel Goleman, *Emotional Intelligence: Why It Can Matter More Than IQ* (New York, NY: Bantam Dell, 1995).

Jack Canfield, *The Success Principles: How to Get from Where You Are to Where You Want to Be* (New York, NY: HarperCollins, 2005).

Please visit my website at www.jacquiebrown.com *for helpful information, resources and links.*

INDEX

A

Abandonment ... 22
abuse ... 50, 55
abuse cycle ...54
addictions ... 96, 98
adrenaline ... 54, 95, 97
alcohol ... 84, 99, 117
anger ...20, 53, 136

anorexia ...100
antidepressants ...112
antisocial personality disorder ...101
anxiety disorders ... 101
arrogance ...23, 136
assaults ...18, 64
avoidant personality disorder ...102

B

banking ... 63, 165, 236, 238
biochemical ... 95
borderline personality disorder ... 102
boundaries ... 28, 52, 198, 205
brain ... 95, 101, 207
budget ... 164
bulimia ... 36, 100, 120

C

captive ... 31, 50
child care ... 174
children ... 57, 63, 88, 126, 129, 176
codependents ... 23
coercion ... 50, 58,
cognitive dissonance ... 125,
community ... 123, 156, 205
complex post traumatic stress disorder
(C-PTSD) ... 93
Compliance ... 25, 55, 65, 88
Confrontation ... 41, 51
Conscious ... 22, 87,
Control ... 20, 51, 55, 101, 154
Coping ... 205
Cortisol ... 95, 241
Cravings ... 55, 99, 207
Custody ...63, 158, 234, 235, 241, 243

D

Debt ... 21, 56, 167,
Defense ... 11, 171,
Demeaning ... 24, 58
Depression ... 86, 96, 103
Desensitized ... 52

Devalue ... 24, 58
Disempowering ... 24
Dismissive ... 25, 61, 64
Disorders ... 95, 100, 234
Dominates ... 21, 60,
Dopamine ... 95, 96,
Dysfunction ...23, 63

E

eating disorders ... 100, 194
economic ... 56, 121, 127
education ... 32, 56, 129, 170, 174
employment ... 91, 170,
empower ... 31, 134
endorphins ... 54, 101,
enforcement ... 23, 50, 65
expectation ... 24, 157

F

fight-or-flight ... 97, 102
finances ... 21, 56, 164

H

healing ... 205
health ... 172, 207, 234
honeymoon phase ... 50, 55, 88, 126
hook ... 21,178
housing ... 165, 171
human rights ... 55, 128,
humiliates ... 58
hypervigilant ... 97

I

ideology ... 23, 50, 65, 125
illusions ... 22, 100, 126, 204
immune system ... 98
incompetent ... 25, 125
inferiority ... 24
inhibits ... 19, 56
injustice ... 17, 34,
insufficiency ... 26, 125,

insurance ... 165, 173
intimidation ... 58,
intuition ... 67
investments ... 168, 242,
isolation ... 62, 88

J

jealousy ... 62
justified ... 19, 50, 55

L

learned helplessness syndrome ... 96,
legal ... 63, 93, 241
liberty ... 50, 154, 204, 209
love ... 29, 34, 51

M

manipulate ... 24, 61
mindset ... 31, 209
minimizing ... 55, 60
mobility ... 88, 172
money ... 21, 56, 161, 211

N

neurotransmitters ... 95
norepinephrine ... 95, 102

O

objectification ... 58,
opportunities ... 129, 155, 175
oppression ... 34, 51, 55, 204
overachiever ... 22

P

panic ... 102
patriarchal ... 24, 62
pattern ... 20,23, 87, 128
peptides ... 53
perception ... 22, 31, 124, 130
phobias ... 96, 101
pituitary ... 53

police ... 18, 58, 63, 92, 160, 174, 241
protect ... 32, 66, 97, 178
psychological ... 56, 87, 93, 206

R

rape ... 59
red flags ... 18
rejection ... 22, 88,
respected ... 18,
responsibility ... 28, 60, 128, 209
restraining order ... 63, 129,
rules ... 23, 50, 60

S

safety ... 33, 129, 154, 231, 234, 238
self-destructive ... 100, 205
self-confidence ... 31, 96, 201
selfishness ... 21,
self-preservation ... 22, 31, 65
serotonin ... 95, 101
sexual ... 59, 98,
silence ... 60
spiritual ... 63, 206
stalking ... 61, 241
Stockholm syndrome ... 87, 97
stress hormones ... 93
submissive ... 53, 91
subservient ... 25
suicide ... 96, 103
SWOT ... 155

T

Tactic ... 51
Taxes ... 174
tend-and-befriend ... 95, 97
trapped ... 90, 125,
trauma ... 93, 100

U

unconscious ... 28, 87
unworthiness ... 22, 67, 205